COLLEGE FOR STUDENTS WITH LEARNING DISABILITIES

College for Students with Learning Disabilities is the high school counselor's best resource for preparing college-bound students with learning disabilities and related disorders.

Through a comprehensive lens, the book provides an overview of learning disabilities and related issues as they apply to the role of the high school counselor. The 6- to 8-week program outlined in the book provides a step-by-step guide for high school counselors to create and implement the program in their own schools. Each area of the program is explored in detail, covering topics such as college readiness, study skills, self-advocacy, and picking the right school.

Drawing on the lived experience of students with learning disabilities, current research, case studies and more, *College for Students with Learning Disabilities* advises counselors in a positive way and aims to change the lives of students with learning disabilities by preparing them for college in an effective, concrete way.

Mati Sicherer, EdD, is a high school counselor in special education with a focus on learning disabilities. She has worked in education for more than 20 years.

COLLEGE FOR STUDENTS WITH LEARNING DISABILITIES

A School Counselor's Guide to Fostering Success

Mati Sicherer

NEW YORK AND LONDON

First published 2020
by Routledge
52 Vanderbilt Avenue, New York, NY 10017

and by Routledge
2 Park Square, Milton Park, Abingdon, Oxon, OX14 4RN

Routledge is an imprint of the Taylor & Francis Group, an informa business

© 2020 Taylor & Francis

The right of Mati Sicherer to be identified as author of this work has been asserted by her in accordance with sections 77 and 78 of the Copyright, Designs and Patents Act 1988.

All rights reserved. The purchase of this copyright material confers the right on the purchasing institution to photocopy pages which bear the photocopy icon and copyright line at the bottom of the page. No other parts of this book may be reprinted or reproduced or utilised in any form or by any electronic, mechanical, or other means, now known or hereafter invented, including photocopying and recording, or in any information storage or retrieval system, without permission in writing from the publishers.

Trademark notice: Product or corporate names may be trademarks or registered trademarks, and are used only for identification and explanation without intent to infringe.

Library of Congress Cataloging-in-Publication Data
A catalog record for this book has been requested

ISBN: 978-0-367-14116-5 (hbk)
ISBN: 978-0-367-14117-2 (pbk)
ISBN: 978-0-429-03027-7 (ebk)

Typeset in Minion
by Apex CoVantage, LLC

Visit the eResources: https://www.routledge.com/9780367141172

This book is dedicated to all students with learning disabilities and to all of the people who care about them. It is a result of my own experiences, both as a parent and as a school counselor. It is the result of trying to find a path for students with learning disabilities and discovering that although it existed, it was far more complicated and far less understood than I would have imagined. It is my hope that my experiences and all of the things that I have learned along the way will help people to understand, support and guide all of these incredibly special children.

Of course, there are so many people without whom this book would never have been written. I have been extraordinarily fortunate in my career to have always been surrounded by remarkable people who have dedicated their lives to helping others. These people deserve more thanks than I could ever give them, but I will say it anyway; Thank you to my counseling colleagues (old and new) and all of the staff at Wayne Hills and Wayne Valley High Schools, my old friends at Ryerson School and all of the teachers, administrators, supervisors, directors, staff, parents and students who make the Wayne School District the magical learning environment that it is. My pilot group, which was the impetus for this book, would not have existed without the support of all of these wonderful people. A special thanks to Dana Clark, Lauren Zaccone Carney and Nancy Kowalski for reading and reviewing my initial proposal—so grateful for that! A very special thanks to the many special young people who agreed to be interviewed. Cass, Syd, Josh, Amber, Kyle, Emilee and Bianca, you are amazing and special, and I thank you for allowing me to hear your stories. I promise that I will use what you have taught me to keep helping other students.

Thank you to my sisters (you know who you are) for understanding that I needed to hide for a little while so I could write this book. Thank you to my whole extended family—all of you who I love and who always support me and love me back. And finally, my biggest and most noisy thank you to my family. Thank you to my husband Scott, who inspires me every day and always believes that I can do things even when I am not as sure as he is. Thank you to my three older children, Andrew, Zach and Maya, who, as the impressive adults that they are now, encourage me to be as amazing as they are. Through this journey we have taken as a family, they have learned to respect, advocate, accept and understand all kinds of differences, and that is more than any parent could ever ask for. Finally, thank you to Cass and Sydnee. From the minute the impossibly tiny twins that they had been entered our lives, they changed everything. They taught us patience and kindness and acceptance and hope, and they took what I thought I knew about learning and replaced it with more and more and more. Thank you all for everything.

CONTENTS

List of Tables	*ix*

PART 1
The Background Work — **1**

1 **Why This Book?** — **3**

2 **What Are Learning Disabilities?** — **11**

PART 2
Most Common Learning Disabilities — **15**

3 **Dyslexia** — **17**

4 **Dyscalculia** — **22**

5 **Dysgraphia** — **27**

6 **Processing Disorders (Visual and Auditory)** — **33**

7 **Nonverbal Learning Disorder** — **39**

PART 3
Related Disorders — **47**

8 **ADHD (Attention Deficit Disorder/Attention Deficit-Hyperactivity Disorder)** — **49**

viii Contents

9	**Dyspraxia**	**57**
10	**Executive Function Disorder**	**62**
11	**Memory Issues**	**67**

PART 4
Our Role as Counselors — **77**

12	**Our Role**	**79**
13	**What Counselors Need to Know About Working With the Child Study Team**	**82**
14	**What Counselors Need to Know About College Readiness**	**93**
15	**What Counselors Need to Know About IEPs**	**108**
16	**What Counselors Need to Know About Self-Advocacy**	**116**
17	**What Counselors Need to Know About Study Skills**	**137**
18	**What Counselors Need to Know About Choosing Colleges and Universities**	**156**

PART 5
The Comprehensive Program — **173**

19	**Building the Program**	**175**
20	**The Program**	**180**
	Part 1: College Readiness	180
	Part 2: Understanding Strengths and Challenges	192
	Part 3: Self-Advocacy	203
	Part 4: Study Skills	219
	Part 5: Picking the Right School	227

Index — *236*

TABLES

15.1	IQ Chart	113
15.2	Deficit Chart	114
16.1	Types of Assistive Technology	123
17.1	General Study Tips	153
18.1	Levels of Support	160
18.2	Specialized Programs	163
19.1	Pretest	179
20.1	College Readiness Skills	186
20.2	Executive Function Skill Self-Assessment	187
20.3	Accommodation/Modification Chart	188
20.4	Accommodation/Modification Worksheet	189
20.5	What Are You Good At? Part 1	200
20.6	Assistive Technology Part 1	201
20.7	Assistive Technology Part 2	202
20.8	Negative/Positive Reframing	208
20.9	What Are You Good At? Part 2	213
20.10	Reframing the Label	214
20.11	Time Flies Part 1	224
20.12	Time Flies Part 2	224
20.13	Time Flies Part 3	224
20.14	Studying Tips	225
20.15	Levels of Programs	231
20.16	Posttest	235

PART 1
The Background Work

1

WHY THIS BOOK?

In the winter of 1998, I was 7 months pregnant with my twin daughters. At the time, two of my three other children were already in full-time school and my youngest was a toddler. My two oldest children had both learned to read very early and very easily. My toddler was sounding out letters and showing signs of early literacy. Books were everywhere in my house, and my children knew that if they had a question about something, they could find the answer by reading. The library was our second home, and my children, allowed to check out as many books as they could carry, liked to bring home as much of it as possible. Each night, after everyone had their baths and had put on pajamas, we snuggled together on the couch, my toddler on my lap and each older child on either side of me, while I read aloud whatever book we had chosen for the night. To this day, so many years later, they still remember so many of the books we read as we sat nestled together on those nights. I was so proud of them for learning so quickly and so pleased that we all shared the same passion for books. I was, of course, convinced that their passion, aptitude and skill for reading came directly from me. I was convinced that my own love for reading and books was so great that it was only natural that they should pick up on it. I was also convinced that my own skill as a teacher and a counselor was certainly the catalyst that propelled them toward being the shining star readers that they were becoming. I could not help but take full credit for it. After all, I was an educator. I was a school counselor, and I certainly understood children. I was also secretly convinced that children whose parents read to them regularly became avid readers. I may even have harbored some judgment against parents of children who struggled to learn to read, thinking that those parents were just not doing their jobs. I never thought for a moment that everything that I thought I knew

4 The Background Work

about teaching, learning and counseling was about to get completely turned upside down.

Cass and Sydnee were born a full nine weeks before their due date. When we held them, they were so skinny and tiny that all we felt were their little bones. Their prematurity required that they spend a full month in the neonatal intensive care unit, and, in the beginning, every day was touch and go. When they came home, still fragile and tiny, each one of them sported a Velcro strap around their little bellies, attached to electronic boxes that monitored their breathing. Despite these inauspicious beginnings, the "plugins" (as Cass and Syd were affectionately nicknamed) soon began to grow stronger, and by the time they reached preschool, there was little physical difference between them and any other toddler. What there was, however, was what seemed to be a giant gap when it came to the preliteracy skills that are necessary for learning to read and write. No matter how much I read to them or what they did in school, they mostly could not make any sense of letters. It seemed that no matter what I did, the alphabet just seemed to be a bunch of squiggles to them. Some days, though, something would seem to click, and they would suddenly know the name or sound of a particular letter. On those days, I would breathe a sigh of relief and convince myself that, just like my other children had, they were learning to read. Invariably, though, the next day would come, and anything that they seemed to have learned the day before would be gone as if it had never happened at all. Not only were they struggling with the alphabet, but they also could not remember the days of the week, their address, their phone numbers and sometimes even their middle and last names. I knew about the relationship between prematurity and learning disabilities, but I realized, as we moved forward, that I had no idea what learning disabilities really were or how I was supposed to help them. I read to them every night, but it was no longer the same idyllic evening calm that reading brought to my other children. These girls would not let me read to them! They struggled to get free from my lap and ran as far away from the book as they could. They did love it when I told them stories from memory, but as soon as a book was involved, they could not disappear quickly enough. I was devastated. By kindergarten, it became clear that there was a problem, and when the child study team at their school evaluated them and gave them a diagnosis of "specific learning disability" (which we later learned was dyslexia) and a 60% placement in the school's resource room (a pull-out program for reading and math), we were not surprised.

Everything that I knew about learning and teaching was different for Cass and Syd. School was a nightmare for them. No matter how smart I believed they were, the only measure of success in school is success in school, and they were not finding it. They could not read; they could not compute numbers and they could not remember things that the other children seemed to find effortless. School was a continuous struggle. I found that if I pushed

Why This Book? **5**

too much, they would shut down, but if I pushed too little, they were happy to stay where they were. I knew that they needed the resource room for the extra time and attention that they needed in order to learn, but I also knew that there would come a time when they would have to leave that safety and comfort in order to reach their full potential. As a counselor, I knew what the risks related to learning disabilities were: failure, dropping out, higher risk of drug and alcohol abuse and higher risk of incarceration, among so many other things. Already I could see worrisome signs. They were having trouble making friends, stomachaches were a normal part of our morning routine, and homework, especially from their general education classes, was a lurid, tear-filled and nightly event. For most students, homework is meant to solidify the learning that has occurred during the day. For my daughters and other students with learning disabilities, when learning does not necessarily happen during the day, homework can be a nightly reminder of their deficits. For these kids, homework, no matter how "easy" (a word I have learned to hate), becomes a nightmare. For us, it was a nightly battle and the core of regular shouting matches and tears in our home.

I learned quickly that if I wanted these girls to learn, I had to help them find a middle ground. I had to figure out when their frustration about something like homework was getting in their way of learning and when it was necessary to push them past that frustration in order to get to the next step. There was a "sweet spot" somewhere in there that I viewed as the middle ground, and it was my job as their mother to help them find it. That middle ground lived somewhere where they would continue to feel successful without complacency, where they would keep working hard without shutting down, where they would keep trying even though it was hard and where they would stay interested in school while still feeling smart and capable no matter how frequently their reading levels, grades, peers or even teachers made them feel otherwise. I made it my mission to learn as much as I could about dyslexia and learning disabilities in general so that I could help them achieve the potential I knew they had. Every day was a discussion of how to best compensate for their challenges. Every day was a practice in self-advocacy for themselves and patience toward those (including some teachers) who did not understand that their disabilities did not define their intelligence. While most students work hard and study in school, my daughters had the added job of constantly assessing their needs and finding ways to address them in order to succeed. By the end of third grade, they were proficient, if not advanced, readers. By the end of middle school, resource room was just a memory. By the middle of high school, both girls were in advanced-placement and honors classes and getting high grades. By junior year, both girls were admitted into the National Honor Society. They had proven to everyone that they could do it, but as easy as they made it look, it never was. They were smart and hardworking and diligent, but they had

6 The Background Work

a learning disability that would always have an impact on them. They had to work harder and differently and more to achieve what their equally capable peers could do in so much less time. Their disabilities would never go away, because that is not how disabilities work. They will always have to work harder, differently and more in order to achieve the same as other people. Most of the time, they don't feel sorry for themselves, but when they do, it is fleeting. They have such an intensive understanding of their challenges and strengths that there is very little room left for self-pity. Those brief moments are usually followed by thoughts of their accomplishments, both in spite of and because of their disabilities. When the time came to start looking at colleges, those same strengths and challenges were the crux of what we used for the search. We wanted to be absolutely sure that we found the best programs to fit all of their needs, both disability related and not. They each had different interests, different challenges and different strengths, and we played to all of that in the search. In the end, both girls won nearly full scholarships and admittance to honors programs at their respective universities. More importantly, both girls found their niche and paths toward fulfilling careers that play continuously to their strengths.

My girls were lucky. They had me, my husband and our whole family as constant advocates for their success. As I learned more and more about learning disabilities, eventually getting a doctorate with a focus on the study of dyslexia, I was able to even more effectively help my daughters. Because I learned how important it was for them to understand their disabilities, we insisted that they learn to understand their disabilities. Because I learned how important self-advocacy was going to be for them, we insisted that they practice it continuously. Because I learned that different colleges offered different kinds of services to address their needs, we were able to find the best and most appropriate fit for them academically, emotionally and socially. What became astounding during this process was that it seemed that we were in it alone. Despite good intentions, very few people at their school could partner in helping us. It became clear that the school counseling office in their high school believed that the child study team would be able to help guide us and that, at the same time, the child study team seemed to see the school counselors as the obvious choice for guidance about college. Each office seemed to work independently of the other, and the overlap that occurred had more to do with course selection on a yearly basis than working together to help students like my daughters. But again, we were lucky. I was a school counselor, and I knew about learning disabilities. By the end of high school, it seemed clear that my daughters were among the very small minority of their old resource room class to make it to college, let alone into honors programs. I could not help being proud. My daughters had worked hard and fought and did all the right things, but as I sat in the bleachers at graduation and spoke with parent after parent of the students who had been in that resource room with my daughters, the obvious advantage of my knowledge base became clear. There was nothing that different between my daughters and all of their old classmates outside of the knowledge that I was able to bring into play to their advantage. Yes, they worked hard, and they deserved all the great things that were happening to them, and I was so very proud, but what about everyone else? Didn't those children work hard too? Hadn't those children been just as smart as my daughters? Didn't they deserve those advantages too? These thoughts colored my practice as a school counselor and changed the way I approached students with learning disabilities. As a school counselor, I realized that I had the opportunity to make sure that the same advantages that I was able to give my daughters would be shared with others as well.

As school counselors, it is our responsibility to reach every single student. It is on us to understand exactly what we are looking at when we see a student with a learning disability sitting in front of us. In 2015–2016, special education students comprised 13% of all students enrolled in public schools. Of these, 34% were diagnosed as having specific learning disabilities (National Center for Education Statistics, 2018). As high school counselors, we are required to meet the needs of students with disabilities as well as the needs of general education students, even if their needs are different. According to the American School Counselor Association (ASCA, 2017):

> *High school counselors are educators uniquely trained in child and adolescent development, learning strategies, self-management and social skills who understand and promote success for today's diverse students. They implement a comprehensive school counseling program to support students through this important developmental period. The program provides education, prevention and intervention activities, which are integrated into all aspects of students' lives. The program teaches knowledge, attitudes and skills students need to acquire in academic, career and social/emotional development, which serve as the foundation for future success. High school counselors do not work in isolation; rather they are integral to the total educational program. They provide a proactive program that engages students and includes leadership, advocacy and collaboration with school staff, administration and community/family members in the delivery of programs and activities to help students achieve success.*

Young adults with learning disabilities attend 4-year colleges at half the rate of the general population. These students have lowered aspirations regarding postsecondary education and less confidence in achieving goals, are more likely to have some involvement with the criminal justice system and most markedly, are *less likely to have received support or guidance from teachers and school counselors about how to prepare for college* (Cortiella & Horowitz, 2014). In addition, the 4-year college completion rate for young

8 The Background Work

adults with learning disabilities is 34%, compared to 52% in the general population. One in two young adults with learning disabilities reported having some type of involvement with the criminal justice system within 8 years of leaving high school, and one in three have been arrested. These students are more likely to have co-morbid social issues, tic disorders, ADD, depression, emotional regulating issues and anxiety (Cortiella & Horowitz, 2014).

For those of us who work with children in poverty, the statistics are even more dire. The prevalence of reported learning disabilities is much higher among those living in poverty. Among all students over the age of 5, the rate of learning disabilities is 2.6% versus 1.5% for those living above poverty (Gartland & Strosnider, 2011). In general, students living in poverty attend college at much lower rates than their peers who do not live in poverty (Lacour & Tissington, 2011). For this population, the addition of a learning disability makes the possibility of college attendance even more miniscule.

School counselors are frequently the quiet voices in the background that teach, encourage and create opportunities where none exist. We are infrequently acknowledged, rarely thanked and occasionally misunderstood in terms of our roles. The beauty of it is that we don't care. All we care about is the fact that we have the honor and opportunity to help children, and it is this unique and quiet position in these children's lives that allows us to "work our magic." Our encouragement and belief have the power to convince a student that they are, indeed, intelligent and worthwhile. Our encouragement and belief have the power to let them feel as if they have finally been seen as the capable beings that they are. Many of us have been privileged enough to have seen firsthand the transformative power that encouragement and love can have on a child, but where do we begin when we lack knowledge about the very thing at the center of the struggles and challenges? When we don't understand what a learning disability is or the many ways it can impact a child, not only can we not help them, but we might even be hurting them instead. We cannot cast aside students with learning disabilities and decide they are someone else's problem or, worse yet, discount the needs of these students just because we don't understand them. When we do this, we have made a decision not to help them at all. As school counselors, our job is to be there for all children, not just the ones whose issues we understand and are familiar with. This book exists because I saw firsthand what could happen when children are encouraged, empowered and educated about who they really are. This book exists because we must, as educational professionals, make it our mission to become educated about what we do not yet know about this sizeable percentage of students. Through my own personal experiences with my daughters, it was clear to me that I needed to bring what I knew about high school students with learning disabilities into my practice as a high school counselor, and I was glad that my experiences could help so many of my students. As time went on, however, it also became clear to me that this knowledge base that I had was somewhat unique. Most school counselors do not take coursework in special education topics. This means that many school counselors might not have an understanding of how to help students with learning disabilities prepare or have appropriate information about postsecondary programs and options for them. It became clear that I needed to share this information with my professional peers and work toward making the practice of school counseling even more powerful than it already is.

The book is divided into five distinct parts. The first four portions of the book present the information that will be the backbone of everything needed for working with students with learning disabilities. These chapters discuss the background of the book, common learning disabilities and related disorders and our role as counselors within the spectrum of working with students with learning disabilities. These parts of the book align with the program itself and give counselors specific and helpful information about topics such as college readiness, self-advocacy, strengths and challenges and choosing the right school. Within these topics, counselors will find information about working with their child study teams, learning how to read IEPs, specialized programs for students with learning disabilities and more. In addition, these chapters also present transcripts from actual interviews with young people with learning disabilities. The experiences of the young people in these interviews can help us understand the experience of students with learning disabilities and inform our practice as high school counselors in an impactful way.

Counselor preparation programs frequently do not present or require that counselors become familiar with learning disabilities or how they manifest. This book fills that gap. Given the high likelihood that we as counselors will have multiple students per grade and year with learning disabilities on our caseloads, this information is presented as both a resource for counselors about learning disabilities and also a springboard toward creating the effective groups for the program presented in the second portion of the book. The fifth portion of the book presents the program itself. While it is possible to implement the program without reading the first four portions of the book, it is best to read through the whole book for the program to give its maximum impact.

The final portion of the book presents the comprehensive program itself. This program was developed over many years of working with students with learning disabilities. The skills taught in the program are based on best practices and empirical research about what best helps these students find postsecondary success. Although the program is skills based, it does not exclude more in-depth discussion. It is meant to be implemented in small groups (8–10 students) over a period of between 6 and 10 weeks. Each portion is clearly marked and easily replicated, but as with all counseling-based groups,

10 The Background Work

the idea is to work with your group as they grow rather than to follow explicit directions. It is meant more as a guide than as a step-by-step manual.

As we begin this journey together, it is important to remember that what we do, what we say and how we behave have an impact. As school counselors, we have the awe-inspiring honor and ability to be a part of changing young people's lives. If we consider this daily, we see that we have the ability to be a part of changing the world.

References

ASCA. (2017). *Why high school counselors?* American School Counselor Association. Retrieved from www.schoolcounselor.org/asca/media/asca/Careers-Roles/WhyHighSchool.pdf

Cortiella, C., & Horowitz, S. H. (2014). *The state of learning disabilities: Facts, trends and emerging issues.* New York: National Center for Learning Disabilities.

Gartland, D., & Strosnider, R. (2011). Comprehensive assessment and evaluation of students with learning disabilities: A paper prepared by the national joint committee on learning disabilities. *Learning Disability Quarterly, 34*(1), 3–16. https://doi.org/10.1177/073194871103400101

Lacour, M., & Tissington, L. D. (2011). The effects of poverty on academic achievement. *Educational Research and Reviews, 6*(7), 522–527.

National Center for Education Statistics. (2018). *The condition of education.* Washington, DC. Retrieved from https://nces.ed.gov/pubs2018/2018144.pdf

2

WHAT ARE LEARNING DISABILITIES?

David was a freshman with a passion for history. He loved anything about history and had a particular passion for early American history. He could recite the Declaration of Independence from memory and had even convinced his parents to spend their upcoming family vacation in Boston so that he could walk the streets of his heroes. When I first met him in September of his freshman year, he was brimming with excitement. He was eager to talk to me, and even though he was only a freshman, he was already asking questions about college and planning his career as a history teacher. His excitement was infectious, and it was obvious that he was a bright and articulate young man. It was with some shock, then, when 2 months later, as I was checking grades, I saw that, although all of his other grades were in the A–B range, his math grade was an F. I called him down immediately. As soon as he stepped into my office, I saw a very different David. He seemed sad and withdrawn and very nervous to talk to me. It felt as if every bit of excitement that he had started with in the beginning of the year had been completely drained from him. "I know you saw my math grade," he said. "I did," I replied, "but I also saw your other grades, and you are doing really great in those classes." For David, as for most students I see, the one bad grade overshadowed all the other good grades. "It doesn't matter if I get an A in history if I'm going to fail math. I just don't know what's wrong with me," he said. "I try and try, and I just don't get it." As we spoke more, he admitted that although he had always managed to get good grades, math had always been a struggle. In my district, the transition from middle school to high school is typically very difficult, so a drop in grades is never very much of a surprise. A drop all the way down to a failure, however, is definitely a cause for concern. We spent the rest of our time together discussing studying strategies

12 The Background Work

and ways to get extra tutoring and even devised some mnemonic devices to help him remember formulas. I assured him that he was not in this alone. We would figure out where the breakdown was, and then we could move to fix it from there. I told him that I would be reaching out to his teachers for input and strategies, and as soon as I had more information, we would meet again. It was hard to imagine that this bright and motivated young man was doing anything but trying his hardest, and I resolved to do my best to figure out what was going on. I immediately reached out to all his teachers and, as expected, his English and history teachers had no concerns at all. He was a bright and hardworking student, and they were impressed with his abilities and work ethic. His science teacher echoed the same sentiments. His math teacher, however, showed up at my door the very next period. "I'm so glad you reached out to me," he said. "I was going to come see you about him by the end of the week if I didn't see any improvement." Mr. Grogan, the math teacher, told me that he had never seen anything like it. David was bright and hardworking, but he could not seem to understand the material at all. Mr. Grogan also told me that David came to him both before and after school for extra help and that they had even worked together to make study sheets, but even with the extra help, nothing seemed to be sticking. He shared that David was well-behaved, took notes during class and really seemed to be listening. We decided to implement a few more strategies including moving his seat to the front and even checking his notes before a test, and to see if the next two weeks showed any improvement at all. When the two weeks were over and there was still no improvement, we felt that it was in David's best interest to move to a lower math level. Even there, David did not find success. David was smart and David was trying, but something was keeping his success at bay. After more unsuccessful interventions, we sent him for a child study evaluation. The evaluation showed that there were significant gaps between his intelligence and his math abilities. He was given a special education classification, placed in specialized math classes and given the extra time he needed. His GPA jumped to a 3.5, and for the first time in his entire life, he got an A in his next math class. When I counseled him about his career and college, we discussed his disability at length and used it as a springboard to bring him to a place where he could showcase his strengths. Today, David is a successful college junior in a BA program in education. The knowledge that I had about his disability led me to be able to help him find a program that gave him alternatives to a typical math curriculum and was also test optional.

There are too many other "Davids" who have already given up. "She's lazy." "He needs to try harder." "She does nothing in class at all." These are all the marking of our students who have already given up, and we are frequently too willing to believe these mantras. How many of our students really do want to fail? How many of them really don't care? Certainly, not all troubled students have learning disabilities, but if we don't even consider it as a possibility, then

What Are Learning Disabilities? **13**

we are not doing our due diligence as counselors. But how can we consider the possibility of a learning disability, or, once it is diagnosed, how do we help these students at all if we do not have an understanding of what a learning disability actually is.

As counselors, we have been taught to understand and respect differences. We have been taught the importance of cultural and even socioeconomic competencies. We are trained to have empathy and inclusion at the core of our practice, but when it comes to students with learning disabilities, our lack of knowledge about these challenges leaves us at a disadvantage. How can we establish empathy, inclusion and understanding if we do not understand the basic challenges that students with learning disabilities face? At its core, our profession is about delving more deeply and asking "why?" "Why is this student, who is otherwise capable, failing this one particular subject?" "Why is this student misbehaving in so many classes?" "Why does this student always seem so sad?" When we start to look for answers to these questions, we begin the process of getting our students the help that they need, and because this help may come in many different forms, we need to have that knowledge base. As professionals in an educational setting, we need to be able to understand learning disabilities, recognize how they manifest and have a core knowledge of how to best guide these students through high school and beyond.

At the most straightforward level, learning disabilities can be defined as substantial struggles with reading, writing, spelling and/or math, despite average or above-average intelligence. These disorders are real. They have been recognized by the medical community for over a hundred years (Hagw & Silver, 1990) and, when they are diagnosed, are managed in public schools through a continuum model that can range from allowing extra time to complete tests and/or assignments all the way to full-time placement in schools specially designed to address learning disabilities.

Reference

Hagw, R. A., & Silver, A. A. (1990). *Disorders of learning in childhood.* New York: John Wiley & Sons.

PART 2
Most Common Learning Disabilities

3

DYSLEXIA

In this part:

- What is dyslexia?
- What is it like to have dyslexia?
- What are some symptoms of dyslexia?
- What might help someone with dyslexia?

What Is Dyslexia?

Dyslexia is a language-based learning disability that is characterized by difficulties with reading, spelling, writing, and processing at any level of intelligence and affects the ability to read (Tanaka et al., 2011). In an IEP it is frequently part of the "Specific learning disability" category. A common myth about dyslexia is that it is a visual problem and that people with dyslexia see letters backwards. Dyslexia is actually a neurologically based language processing disorder which, although it does not cause people to see letters backwards, does cause difficulty processing and interpreting letters and words. Students with dyslexia have had difficulty learning to attach sounds to letters. For a student without dyslexia, learning that the letter "A" is attached to the first sound in the word "apple" happens almost organically. For students with dyslexia, that connection is at the center of a struggle to learn to read. Students with dyslexia have described looking at a reading passage as trying to decipher a foreign language. For these students, it is hard to reconcile their intelligence with their difficulty learning how to read. Watching other students learn so seamlessly while they may continue to struggle with the basics can bring up feelings of frustration, lowered self-esteem, depression and anxiety (Cortiella & Horowitz, 2014). Without proper intervention, students with dyslexia can get stuck in a cycle of frustration that can lead to continued academic, social and emotional issues and, eventually, potential disengagement in school.

Although it seems unclear what the direct cause of dyslexia is, there are many things we do know for certain. When dyslexia is present, it frequently occurs in tandem with other neurological disorders such as dyscalculia, attention deficit disorder and dysgraphia (Wilson et al., 2015). Another thing we know is that it does not discriminate based on gender, socioeconomic status or intellectual ability (Macdonald & Deacon, 2019). Interestingly as well, people with dyslexia can be extremely gifted in areas such as art, music and drama, although whether the reason for this is because of an intrinsic connection or as a reaction to having these academic difficulties, it is hard to tell (Chakravarty, 2009).

Approximately 15% to 20% of the population have symptoms of dyslexia, but not all of them will be identified for special education interventions. Many students with dyslexia do a good job of covering up their struggles and eventually just resign themselves to believing that they are just not smart or academically oriented. Other students, although they may have the disorder, are still not eligible for special education. Of the students with dyslexia who are classified, many of them are classified under the umbrella of "specific learning disability." These students with dyslexia comprise about 85% of all students who are classified under the category of "specific learning disability," and these students make up about 13% to 14% of all public-school students who qualify for special education (International Dyslexia Organization, 2015).

What Is It Like to Have Dyslexia?

Name: Casey
Age: 20
Age at diagnosis: 6
Career: College student. Planning to go to law school

It's hard to explain or to describe what it's like to have dyslexia because I have never not had dyslexia. When I was younger, when I couldn't read, it felt like I knew certain letters but when they got put together, they didn't mean anything. They were just images. I guess that I've compensated for my disability but it's more like I'm still dealing with the facts of being in the public educational system and having dyslexia. I think that one important thing that happened early on was the feeling of being different. I know that the resource room helped me to learn but I don't think it always helps when it comes to feeling like you are a part of a larger community. Having been in the resource room, away from all the other kids, it makes you feel like you're not a part of a community. So then, when you get older, you still don't feel like you belong. It's weird now for me to be a dyslexic person in the Honor's College at my university. In my brain, I'm still kind of programmed to think that I shouldn't be there because of constantly being invalidated academically early on. I was never actually told that I was not an intelligent or even an intellectual being. No one ever said that, not my school or even my classmates but it's always just been a fact that you've been in the resource room and everyone knows you are there because you need extra help. Even when I transitioned out of the resource room, people always knew that I had been a student there and it wasn't until college that I could reinvent myself and not be known as someone who had a disability. Having a learning disability does not mean that you are not intelligent, and I understand that but for myself, there is always that dissonance. I have a 3.9 GPA, I received generous academic scholarships, I'm a student leader in lots of different clubs and activities and I'm currently studying for my LSATs so that I can apply to law school next year, but even with all of that, I still feel like there is something "less than" about me, like I'll always be the little girl with learning problems in the resource room.

What Are Some Symptoms of Dyslexia?

A student with dyslexia may:

- Have difficulty with linking letters with sounds, rhyming, recognizing simple words and hearing individual sounds
- Have issues with articulation
- Have difficulty counting syllables in words
- Have difficulty recognizing rhymes
- Look for ways to avoid reading such as sharpening pencils or asking to go to the bathroom
- Struggle with reading, writing, spelling, decoding and fluent word recognition
- Communicate better orally than in written form
- Be more tired than other students from the extra effort of attending and concentrating
- Have behavioral issues
- Struggle with reading charts and graphs
- Be convinced that they are "stupid" or just not "good at school"
- Have inconsistent learning; they will "know" something on one day but no longer "know" it the next
- Have poor concentration

- Struggle with learning and remembering new terminology
- Forget words
- Have difficulty understanding idioms
- Have difficulty following a sequence of instruction
- Hand in messy papers with many crossed out-words and the same word spelled different ways throughout the paper
- Have trouble completing homework
- Be confused by similar-looking letters (b/d etc.)
- Reverse letters
- Have poor or unusual pencil grip
- Not produce work that seems appropriate to their ability
- Pronounce words in an unusual manner
- Miss or add words when reading out loud
- Have difficulty with supporting an argument or getting to the point
- Not recognize words that should be familiar
- Have low self-esteem
- Have difficulty remembering sequential orders (i.e., days of the week, months of the year etc.)
- Have difficulty learning to tell time
- Be confused by directionality (i.e., right/left, east/west, up/down etc.)
- Be withdrawn or the "class clown"
- Have difficulty remembering dates, phone numbers, birthdays etc.
- Have challenges recalling names of people and/or places
- Struggle with learning a foreign language

(British Dyslexia Association, 2017; Goswami, 2008; International Dyslexia Organization, 2015; Lyon, 1995; NICHD, 2017; Shaywitz, 2003)

(Note: Although many people experience many of these challenges, a student with dyslexia may exhibit several of these challenges simultaneously).

What Helps Someone With Dyslexia?

- Having class syllabus
- Access to recorded lessons
- Having teacher or student notes
- Monitoring of long-term assignments
- Audiobooks
- Access to a laptop
- Study guides
- Extra teacher attention
- Flash cards
- Minimizing distractions

- Breaking up big projects
- Access to outlines
- Access to diagrams
- Reading writing assignments aloud and then editing
- Speech-to-text programs
- Text-to-speech programs

References

British Dyslexia Association. (2017). Screening and assessment. *British Dyslexia Association, 8*(8). Retrieved from www.bdadyslexia.org.uk/educator/screening-and-assessment

Chakravarty, A. (2009). Artistic talent in dyslexia: A hypothesis. *Medical Hypotheses, 73*(4), 569–571. https://doi.org/10.1016/j.mehy.2009.05.034

Cortiella, C., & Horowitz, S. H. (2014). *The state of learning disabilities: Facts, trends and emerging issues.* New York: National Center for Learning Disabilities.

Goswami, U. (2008). Reading, dyslexia and the brain. *Educational Research, 50*(2), 135–148. https://doi.org/10.1080/00131880802082625

International Dyslexia Organization. (2015). *International dyslexia organization fact sheet.* International Dyslexia Organization. Retrieved from http://eida.org/fact-sheets/

Lyon, G. R. (1995). Toward a definition of dyslexia. *Annals of Dyslexia, 45*(1), 1–27. https://doi.org/10.1007/BF02648210

Macdonald, S. J., & Deacon, L. (2019). Twice upon a time: Examining the effect socio-economic status has on the experience of dyslexia in the United Kingdom. *Dyslexia, 25*(1), 3–19. https://doi.org/10.1002/dys.1606

NICHD. (2017). *National reading panel.* Retrieved from www.nichd.nih.gov/research/supported/Pages/nrp.aspx/

Shaywitz, S. (2003). *Overcoming dyslexia: A new and complete science-based program for reading problems at any level.* New York, NY: Vintage Press.

Tanaka, H., Black, J. M., Hulme, C., Stanley, L. M., Kesler, S. R., Whitfield-Gabrieli, S., . . . & Hoeft, F. (2011). The brain basis of the phonological deficit in dyslexia is independent of IQ. *Psychological Science, 22*(11), 1442–1451. https//doi.org 10.1177/0956797611419521

Wilson, A. J., Andrewes, S. G., Struthers, H., Rowe, V. M., Bogdanovic, R., & Waldie, K. E. (2015). Dyscalculia and dyslexia in adults: Cognitive bases of comorbidity. *Learning and Individual Differences, 37*, 118–132. https://doi.org/10.1016/j.lindif.2014.11.017

4

DYSCALCULIA

In this part:

- What is dyscalculia?
- What is it like to have dyscalculia?
- What are some symptoms of dyscalculia?
- What might help someone with dyscalculia?

What Is Dyscalculia?

Dyscalculia is a specific learning disability that affects the normal acquisition of arithmetic skills. It is, like dyslexia, a persistent and neurological disorder, but unlike dyslexia, teaching and environmental factors are also involved in its etiology (Shalev, 2001). It is viewed as difficulty with understanding and representing the number of objects in a set and more specifically with struggles in number processing, memorizing, reasoning and executing calculations (Butterworth, 2018). Dyscalculia has been shown to have similar prevalence as dyslexia (Chideridou-Mandari, Padeliadu, Karamatsouki, Sandravelis, & Karagiannidis, 2016) and seems to affect boys as frequently as it does girls (Shalev, 2001). It affects about 5% to 6% of school-aged children (Shalev, 2001) and, like dyslexia, has also been associated with prematurity and low birthweight (Shalev, 2001). Dyscalculia also frequently occurs in tandem with other neurological disorders such as dyslexia, attention deficit disorder and dysgraphia (Shalev, 2001).

What Is It Like to Have Dyscalculia?

Name: Blanca
Age: 28

Age at diagnosis: 10th grade, 15 years old
Career: Currently not employed

I think it first started affecting me in kindergarten. I remember my teacher wanted us to start learning to count by 2s and 3s and 4s and I didn't understand it all. In first grade it got really bad when we did addition. I couldn't do it. I remember raising my hand for help, but the teacher could never help me enough. I would go home and try to do my math homework and I would scream, and cry and my mom would get mad and then she would cry with me. We would sit on the rug and cry together. Years later I found out that she was also dyscalculic. By 2nd grade, I still hadn't learned anything, and it felt like my teacher didn't like me. They finally put me into a math class for extra help and that was the only place that math felt safe. I remember reading a report from my math teacher at the time and she said that I was learning slowly but was still learning. After 2nd grade, there was no more extra help for me. I don't know why they stopped giving me the extra help and I knew that other kids were getting pulled out, so I was really upset. I was so jealous because they were getting help and I thought I would never learn to do math because no one would help me. In 3rd grade we had our first standardized testing. They told us that that an average score fell into the 66th percentile. I scored 56th percentile for math, which was a score like the kids in special education were getting. In reading comprehension though, I scored in the 96th percentile. I didn't see that high score though. All I saw when I looked at the scores was math and all I thought was, "I am so stupid." All I wanted was to be normal.

In high school, in freshman year, instead of taking algebra like most everyone else, I took a prealgebra class because I was not ready for algebra yet. In sophomore year, I took algebra, but I was doing so badly that, by junior year, we finally had a private evaluation done. They said that my dyscalculia was so great that the only way I would be able to learn math was to have a teacher right near me, teaching me directly. The school gave me an aide and he helped me a lot during my algebra class in sophomore year but the next year, they took him away from me and told me that I could not have any extra help. In my junior year, I took Algebra II but ended up dropping out of it because I was failing. I was not learning anything at all, and I was trying but the teacher told my mom that I wasn't trying at all. The problem was that by then, I was having panic attacks and I couldn't function going into that classroom. Things got so bad that the school told me that the only options I had were to be in that class or have a teacher come to my house. By that time, I had started suffering from serious depression, so we decided that the best option was to have the teacher come to my house. That would have been fine, but the home instructor did not understand my disability. She would try to teach me as if I was just like

24 Most Common Learning Disabilities

everyone else, but I was missing so much that I could not understand what she was trying to teach me. I was so frustrated. I was not learning anything, and she knew I wasn't learning. I ended up dropping out of algebra II for good and only after I had already started my senior year did my counselor tell me that I did not have enough math coursework to attend any state colleges. It felt like no one cared and no one was trying to help me.

My dyscalculia also makes it hard to understand directionality. I still don't know my right from my left. The first college that I went to was crazy because of the whole sense of direction thing and I had to drop out because I could not get to my classes. Then I went to a local community college. My mother had to take a few weeks off work so that she could help me learn how to navigate the campus. If she had not taken the time to do that for me, I would not have been able to find any of my classes.

So, in college, they waived my math classes, but I did have to take 3 science classes and that was hell. I passed by taking only one class per semester. I still made sure to talk to my professors every semester and let them know about my math disability. Even if I was doing well in the class, I felt like it was in my best interest to talk to my professors at the start of the semester. That ended up being a really good thing because the labs for the science classes were impossible. I just didn't understand any of it but, luckily, my professors were really great. I remember once that I was panicking over the class and having a really hard time. The professor, who was really very helpful and accommodating all the time, saw that there was something wrong and he came over to me and asked me if I was okay. He talked to me for a little bit and really helped to calm me down and then he asked if it was okay if he asked another student in the class to come and help me and that made everything so much better. The second science class was a botany class. The way the professor graded it really worked for me because even though I failed every lab, I passed all the tests and did great on the papers, so I passed the class anyway. When I transferred out of the community college and into a 4-year school, I had a little bit of a problem because I knew in order to graduate, they required a computer applications class and I was really worried about it. Although they had waived my math classes, they would not waive the computer class. No matter how much I tried to tell them that I had a math disability and I was scared that I would have a hard time in this class because I assumed that there was some math involved in computer applications class, they would not waive it. As soon as I got into the class, I knew that I was in trouble. The textbook didn't make any sense to me and I was raising my hand every five minutes for help and I was starting to have panic attacks and getting depressed because I just could not do it. I guess we had complained loudly enough because someone finally noticed that there was a math prerequisite for the class, and I had never taken any math classes at all. In the end, the math/ science dean finally waived it for me, and I was allowed to take criminology and psychology instead. I ended up graduating summa cum laude with a BA in sociology.

At this point, I can't drive because I have no sense of direction and don't know left from right. I still have trouble with basic math—even a calculator does not help sometimes because I switch the numbers or symbols while I am trying to do the calculations. I do that with phone numbers too. I switch the numbers around between the time I see them and the time I am punching the numbers into my phone. It's not that I see them backwards. I see them just how they are but when it comes time for my brain to interpret them, I process them all wrong.

I think that if I had gotten the help that I needed early on then things might have been different for me. I think that maybe if I had been pulled into a resource room from the time I was in kindergarten it would have helped to slow the progression or maybe, at least, give me the basic math skills that I just don't have now. If I would have had the time to spend on getting the basics in order, I think I would have been able to add and subtract and do basic calculations. I think it would have been so much better if someone had pulled me out and given me that extra help. Maybe if I'd had a teacher sit with me and just me in middle school or high school, maybe I could have done grade-level math. I don't know. We were fighting to get me help for such a long time but maybe by middle or high school I think it might have been too little and too late.

What Are Some Symptoms of Dyscalculia?

A student with dyscalculia may:

- Have difficulty with word problems
- Be challenged when making change or handling money
- Show difficulty with concepts such as number lines, positive and negative value, place value, quantity and carrying and borrowing
- Exhibit difficulty keeping numbers lined up for calculations such as long division problems
- Have difficulty with sequencing information or events
- Exhibit challenges when using multiple steps in math operations
- Show difficulty with fractions
- Display difficulty recognizing patterns
- Have difficulty understanding time-related concepts such as days, weeks, months etc.

(Shalev, 2001)

What Helps Someone With Dyscalculia?

- Extra time
- Frequent checks for understanding
- Clearly stated steps
- Allowing narration of math problems
- Providing sample problems
- White boards
- Connecting math to meaningful experiences
- Calculator
- Frequent review
- Finding patterns in the work
- Identifying and correcting errors after explanation
- Creating opportunities for success
- Frequent review

References

Butterworth, B. (2018). Dyscalculia: From science to education. *Science*. https://doi.org/10.1126/science.1201536

Chideridou-Mandari, A., Padeliadu, S., Karamatsouki, A., Sandravelis, A., & Karagiannidis, C. (2016). Secondary mathematics teachers: What they know and don't know about dyscalculia. *International Journal of Learning, Teaching and Educational Research, 15*(9), 84–98.

Shalev, R. (2001). Developmental dyscalculia. *Journal of Child Neurology, 19*(10), 765–771. https://doi.org/10.1177/08830738040190100601

5

DYSGRAPHIA

In this part:

- What is dysgraphia?
- What is it like to have dysgraphia?
- What are some symptoms of dysgraphia?
- What might help someone with dysgraphia?

What Is Dysgraphia?

Dysgraphia is a processing disorder that can be explained as an impairment of written expression. Although the disorder is primarily symptomized by the poor handwriting that seems to be its hallmark, it's academic reaches go far beyond just that. The fact that it is a processing disorder means that dysgraphia is not just poor handwriting and can also manifest itself as difficulty putting thoughts on paper (Frith, 1985). There is also evidence that It can interfere with learning how to spell and write, and it has also been associated with dyslexia, ADHD and autism (Naser, Akram, Mandana, Afsoon, & Mehdi, 2016).

Students with dysgraphia may have very messy handwriting that presents with inconsistent spacing, unusual spatial planning, poor spelling and incorrect word choices. They may also have difficulty with choosing appropriate words and using grammar and syntax correctly in their writing. In addition, their writing may have word omissions or redundancies. Typically, these students perform at a much higher level verbally than in written form. For many teachers, receipt of that first written work can be something of a surprise, since the discrepancy between the student's verbal expression and their written work can be so vast.

Students with dysgraphia also often seem to display a tense posture and pencil grip while trying to write (Richards, 1999). This tense posture can exert these students to the point of what might look like unwarranted fatigue. In reality, these students really are exerting great energy in trying to process their thoughts into a written format, and this can and frequently does cause these students to tire very quickly. The fatigue that can be caused by this exertion then creates further challenges with learning to write and can create a cycle of failure that becomes difficult for these students to find their way out of (Richards, 1999).

In addition to the physical act of writing, dysgraphia also refers to difficulty with aspects of written expression in general (Quillen & Gladstone, 2008). It has been suggested that dysgraphia is a dysfunction that creates difficulties with transposing mental language into written language (Naser et al., 2016). This means that aside from the mechanics of the writing itself, students with dysgraphia frequently may have difficulty with organizing their thoughts and expressing them in writing despite an ability to do so verbally. For these students, that act of thinking and writing simultaneously is a great challenge.

Current research about the prevalence of dysgraphia is mixed. Some of the current evidence suggests that dysgraphia affects about 5% to 20% of all students, but this number is not supported across the board. Other researchers suggest that although the prevalence may not be known, it is a disorder that is more than likely under identified (McCloskey & Rapp, 2017).

What Is It Like to Have Dysgraphia?

Name: Sandra
Age: 20
Age at diagnosis: 18
Career: College student

It is hard for me to talk about my dysgraphia in isolation from the dyslexia and ADHD that I also have but if I think about it, I do remember so many things that made everything else even more difficult because of the dysgraphia. It was so hard for me in general because all I wanted was to be able to read and write and count and be like all the other kids.

In kindergarten, I remember that everyone was starting to read and write, and I just could not do either. It was even more frustrating because I was smart, and I loved learning and I just wanted to know everything and be able to do everything on my own and the dyslexia was the wall between me and reading and the dysgraphia was the wall between me and writing but I did not know any of that then. In fact, I didn't realize that it was the dysgraphia that kept me from being able to process my writing until very recently.

I remember the teacher in first grade was always trying to help me with my pencil grip. I gripped it in my fist, like with my whole hand around it, and no matter how much they tried to help, it was impossible for me to hold it any other way. It hurt, my hand cramped up and it felt all wrong. At one point, my mom went and bought a whole bunch of thick triangular pencils that were supposed to help with my grip and my ability to control my letter formation. My letters barely looked like letters. I hated those pencils. I hated how they felt in my hand and I hated how they made me feel like I was different than everyone else in the class. I also hated the slant board that I had to write on. A slant board is a slanted board with a clip at one end. It kind of looks like a thick 3-ring binder. You clip your paper onto the top and it is supposed to help you with handwriting too. I guess I started getting all of that stuff about the time they brought the occupational therapist in to evaluate me. I know that I had been having trouble with writing for a while, so I guess that this was all in about 2nd grade. In any event, I hated all of it because it all drew attention to me in this really awful way.

When I wrote, in elementary school, it sounded so much worse than what I had in my head. I used to think of these great stories or answers to questions but if I tried to write it out myself, it came out like nonsense. I wrote so fast—it wasn't just that it was hard to read my writing, it was also that the ideas in my head came out so much faster than I was able to get it down on paper and I would get really, really frustrated. At one point, my parents bought me a speech-to-text program where I would wear this headphone and speak into it so that I could get my ideas out, but I hated that too. It was all just a reminder that I was different and less than everyone else.

In about 3rd grade, my mom put her foot down and insisted that the only way it seemed that I was going to successful was through the use of a computer. She insisted that the OT focus on teaching me to keyboard rather than only focus on my handwriting, which did not seem like it was ever going to get better. At that point, they gave me a weird laptop thing— an alpha smart, I think? I hated that too. Again, it made me different and I was already different enough. The best thing that happened was that I became really proficient in keyboarding, which was great. In looking back at it, it was a great idea to start me working with the keyboard so young because it took me so long to learn it that by the time I got good at it, I was where everyone else was.

I think it was in middle school where things really fell apart with the writing. Even though they had given me that laptop, I refused to use it. I wasn't good enough at it yet and, like I said, I didn't want to be different. At the same time, my dysgraphia was pretty apparent even though we hadn't known that it was something separate from my other learning

30 Most Common Learning Disabilities

disabilities. We just thought that it was part of the dyslexia. It didn't really matter what we called it, I guess. We had been addressing it consistently regardless. At this point, my parents made sure that, at least for homework assignments., I could dictate to them and they would type it out and then we would edit together. That way, at least, the teachers could see that I knew what I needed to know and that I was smart. It was when I had to do assignments in school that was a real problem. Some teachers understood but most really didn't. I was lucky though, I had a team of really great advocates who kept a rallying cry of, "she is really smart, let her show you in an alternate format" that got me through successfully. Sometimes I would tell the teachers the answers to tests verbally and sometimes I got to take things home and do them with my mom. We kept at it and kept at it and I kept believing that I was smart and capable because no matter how I did the assignments, I was still doing them and doing them well. I can see how kids like me get lost, though. I can see that maybe, without enough people to help and advocate it might be easy to give up and lose faith in yourself. I know that I was truly lucky and by the time I got to junior year, I was in honors and AP classes and using the computer for most everything. By this time, I was truly proficient, and it made everything finally start working for me. Every once in a while, a teacher would decide that kids couldn't use computers in their classroom for writing and then my case manager or my parents would step in and then it would be okay. Each time it happened, my case manager and my parents would step in less and less and give me the space to start learning how to deal with it myself and that was really hard. It was pretty frightening approaching a teacher and telling them that I had this learning issue and I needed a computer. I almost preferred suffering in silence to talking to those teachers but my parents were insistent that I learn to self-advocate and I don't think that I really had a choice about it which I am grateful for. It did take a while for me to learn to do it, but I definitely did.

Now, I'm in college and I always use a laptop. I am in an honors program and there is never a time when a professor wants something handwritten so that doesn't really come up anymore. If they would I would probably ask them to look at my writing and let me know if they might want to change their minds. I joke about how terrible my handwriting is, but I know that it is so much more than that. I think one of the hardest parts of having dysgraphia was that I thought that if I just tried harder, I would be able to do it. I tried. I tried so hard. It was frustrating and almost made me hate writing. What kept me from hating it was based in how my family always took the time to transcribe my thoughts for me and help me edit them. I learned that I was a good writer even if I couldn't physically write and I love to write now. I think if they would have kept forcing it, I would have shut down. Another other hard part was how my writing was an outward expression of my "differentness." Kids would look at my writing and make faces and ask me why I wrote like that. I just wanted to be like everyone else and no matter how hard I tried, I just couldn't do it. If I could go back in time and make sure that I didn't have to suffer with any learning disabilities at all, I would in a heartbeat. It was pretty awful, but I also know that I was so incredibly lucky that I had so many people on my side.

What Are Some Symptoms of Dysgraphia?

- Tight, awkward pencil grip, body or paper position
- Illegible printing and cursive
- Inconsistencies—print and cursive used together, upper- and lowercase interchangeable, irregular-sized, -shaped or -slanted letters
- Unfinished or omitted words or letters
- Inconsistent spacing
- Issues with previsualizing letter formation
- Slow copying or writing
- Unusual spatial planning on paper
- Complaints of hand pain
- Difficulty thinking and writing simultaneously
- Speaking words aloud while writing
- Avoidant behavior toward writing tasks
- Complaints about tiring while writing
- Poor organization of thoughts on paper
- Poor syntax and grammar
- Large gap between written ideas and understanding demonstrated through speech
- Spelling errors
- Very slow or very fast speed of writing
- Obvious frustration and stress associated with writing tasks
- Correlation with ADHD and autism

(Mayes, Breaux, Calhoun, & Frye, 2017)

What Are Some Things That Might Help Someone With Dysgraphia?

- Teach compensatory skills (such as keyboarding) alongside remediation
- Specific and pointed instruction in forming letters
- Graphic organizers
- Occupational therapy
- Speech to text
- Teach proofreading

32 Most Common Learning Disabilities

- Extra time
- Graph paper for math
- Early keyboarding instruction
- Remove neatness as grade
- Copy of notes

References

Frith, U. (1985). Beneath the surface of developmental dyslexia. In K. Patterson, J. Marshall, & M. Coltheart (Eds.), *Surface dyslexia: Neurological and cognitive studies of phonological reading* (pp. 301–330). Hillsdale, NJ: Lawrence Erlbaum.

Mayes, S. D., Breaux, R. P., Calhoun, S. L., & Frye, S. S. (2017). High prevalence of dysgraphia in elementary through high school students with ADHD and autism. *Journal of Attention Disorders.* https://doi.org/10.1177/1087054717720721

McCloskey, M., & Rapp, B. (2017). Developmental dysgraphia: An overview and framework for research. *Cognitive Neuropsychology, 34,* 65–82. https://doi.org/10.1080/02643294.2017.1369016

Naser, H., Akram, A., Mandana, R., Afsoon, H. M., & Mehdi, A. (2016). An overview of developmental dysgraphia. *The Scientific Journal of Rehabilitation Medicine, 5*(1), 224–234.

Quillen, T. F., & Gladstone, K. (2008). About dysgraphia. *Nursing, 38*(5), 26. https://doi.org/10.1097/01.NURSE.0000317668.40925.d8

Richards, R. G. (1999). *The source for dyslexia and dysgraphia.* East Moline, IL: LinguiSystems.

6

PROCESSING DISORDERS (VISUAL AND AUDITORY)

In this part:
- What is a visual or auditory processing disorder?
- What is it like to have a visual or auditory processing disorder?
- What are some symptoms of the visual or auditory processing disorder?
- What might help someone with a visual or auditory processing disorder?

What Is a Visual and Auditory Processing Deficit?

Visual Processing Disorder

A visual processing disorder is a processing problem that can cause difficulty in making sense of information that is taken in visually. Visual processing disorders have nothing to do with eyesight problems. They are, rather, issues that relate more to how information that is taken in through the eyes is interpreted by the brain. This processing issue can affect perception and understanding of concepts, specifically in reading and math concepts (Sigmundsson, 2010).

Research on the etiology of visual processing disorder is mixed. Although there is no consensus across the board, there is some speculation that low birth weight and mild traumatic brain injury (Brousseau-Lachaine, Gagnon, & Faubert, 2008) are related to the development of visual processing disorder. Finally, in terms of gender, there does not seem to be any difference in prevalence of the disorder between boys and girls (Misra & Aikat, 2016; Molloy et al., 2013).

Auditory Processing Disorder

An auditory processing disorder is a processing problem that creates difficulty in making sense of information taken in through the ears. Auditory

34 Most Common Learning Disabilities

processing disorders have nothing to do with hearing problems. They are, rather, issues that relate more to how information taken in through the ears is interpreted by the brain. Since this processing disorder is based on a disconnect between what the student hears and how or how quickly their brain interprets it, the act of sitting in a classroom and listening to a teacher is automatically impacted in a negative way. In addition, this processing issue affects speech and language as well. Since so much of learning relies on being able to listen in a classroom, process the information and create new knowledge, auditory processing disorder has a direct impact on the acquisition of all types of learning (Bamiou, Musiek, & Luxon, 2001).

Auditory processing disorder has a long history of research, and there is quite a bit we know about it. We know that approximately 2% to 7% of children have auditory processing disorder (Bamiou et al., 2001) and that boys are twice as likely as girls to have it (Roeser & Downs, 2004). We also know that auditory processing disorder may be related to prematurity, low birth weight, chronic ear infections and head trauma (Arky, 2018). In addition, there is also some speculation that children with auditory processing disorder are frequently misdiagnosed with ADHD due to what seem to be attentional issues inherent in both. The important difference between the two is found in the cause. Whereas ADHD is a disorder that is characterized by a lack of focus, auditory processing disorder is characterized by difficulty with processing what is being heard. This means that while a student with ADHD may not be paying attention to what is going on, a student with auditory processing disorder actually might be. The student with auditory processing disorder may look as if they are not paying attention but may actually just be processing the information too slowly or incorrectly instead. Even though auditory processing disorder has been researched intensively for many decades, it is important to know that some educators and professionals still express doubts about the diagnosis (Arky, 2018).

What Is It Like to Have a Visual or Auditory Processing Disorder?

Name: Kyle
Age: 20
Age at diagnosis: Middle school
Career: College student. Planning on studying neuroscience

For me, having auditory processing disorder showed itself a lot when I was trying to be involved during conversations. I could hear everything, but it took a minute or two to understand what was actually going on. I could stand in the middle of a group of people and hear everything but still not know what it was that was being said. It was pretty evident in

Processing Disorders (Visual and Auditory)   **35**

the classroom environment too. In elementary school even though I was a bit ahead academically, it was very confusing because I was much slower in processing information. I would have to have things repeated for me all the time because I did not get it the first time. The other kids definitely noticed since I was always asking for things to be repeated in class. I am certain that it must have been hard for the other kids to understand why I needed everything repeated. At the time, since I didn't really know what was wrong, I didn't know how to explain it. All I knew was that I didn't understand things the first time and I didn't want to miss anything, so I kept on asking about it. I think that people must have been confused by me at times. They really didn't know what to make of me. I suppose they thought that I wasn't listening, but I really was. I don't think anyone was really impatient about it. I had a hard time relating to other people and they seemed to have a hard time relating back to me. I was an outcast socially and I guess I remember that I spent a lot of time by myself. I didn't want to be alone. I wanted to have friends, just like everyone else so I would try. I would stand near the other kids while they were talking and jump into the conversation when it seemed like I could. I thought I could make friends by doing that, but it was always very hit or miss and I always ended up seeming like the weird kid when I tried. It felt like no one really understood me.

In high school, it was definitely easier to handle because I actually found out what my challenges and issues were. Knowing what they were made it much easier to tackle them. Another thing that really helped was my mom. She made it a point to teach me to self-advocate and to teach me how to manage my challenges in a positive way. High school also got much better socially because I was finally able to find a circle of friends that I felt comfortable with and I started hanging out with them a lot. I found that if I shared the fact that I had auditory processing problems, my friends would understand. They didn't have to wonder why it took me a little while longer than most people to respond to them. They already knew and they accepted me for myself. It was so much easier to relate to people when they weren't wondering why I was slow to respond to stuff. I suppose that even with knowing what was going on with me, I could still have been a bit better at advocating for myself, but I think that gets easier and easier as I am getting older. I think it also would have been nice to know that there were other kids going through the same or similar things. It might have been kind of empowering knowing that I was not all alone with this. Still it was a pretty positive experience, especially compared to elementary and middle school.

College so far has been kind of like high school. The biggest difference is that I have been away from home. I did have a little bit of trouble adjusting to that in my freshman year. I think I closeted myself a little and that made it hard to adjust easily but freshman year seems hard for a lot of people. The good thing is that I was able to get past it. I forced myself to *join clubs and go out with people. I'd promised myself I would branch out when I got to college, so I really tried to break out of my bubble. It wasn't easy but I did it and again, my mom was a big help and gave me a lot of advice about how to handle different situations. I also always make sure that I am in contact with the office of disabilities at the beginning of each semester. I do that and also talk to my professors personally about my accommodations and my challenges. Those conversations really help, and all of my professors have been really understanding and helpful. I know that the effects are lasting, and this is not something that will go away. But I also know how to compensate, and I am not embarrassed to ask people to repeat themselves if I need to hear something again.*

What Are Some Symptoms of Visual and Auditory Processing Disorders?

Symptoms of Visual Processing Disorder:
- Difficulty with accurately perceiving objects in reference to other objects
- Difficulty perceiving words and numbers as separate units
- Difficulty with directionality
- Visual discrimination problems (color, form, shape, pattern, size and position)
- Difficulty reading charts and graphs
- Object recognition problems
- Difficulty with consistent recognition of numbers and letters
- Difficulty understanding whole/part relationships
- Difficulty with visual motor integration, fine and gross motor skills
- Distractibility when presented with too much visual information
- Difficulty with copying from board
- Letter, number and word reversals
- Difficulty remembering phone numbers
- Frequent complaints of eyestrain
- May skip words or lines when reading
- Weak math skills due to omitted steps and confusion with formulas
- Difficulty with noticing obvious changes in environment (changed signs, displays, etc.)

(Arky, 2018; National Center for Learning Disabilities (NCLD, 2018)

Symptoms of Auditory Processing Disorder
- Difficulty in recognizing phonemes
- Difficulty with following verbal instructions

Processing Disorders (Visual and Auditory)   **37**

- Auditory sequencing issues (i.e. "tevelision" instead of "television")
- Difficulty with discriminating sound (words that are obviously different seem to sound alike
- Inability to focus on important sounds in noisy settings
- Difficulty with reading and spelling
- Oral math issues
- Difficulty following conversations (especially in noisy settings)
- Poor musical ability
- Difficulty learning rhymes or songs
- Difficulty speaking clearly
- Social skills issues
- Comorbidity with dyslexia, ADHD and other related conditions

(Johnson, 2018)

What Are Some Things That Might Help Someone With a Processing Disorder?

Auditory:

- Frequent repeated information
- Preview of information prior to learning in class
- Preferential seating
- Limited distractions
- Chunking of information
- Visual cues
- Clear and concrete directions
- Allowing for processing time
- Frequent checks for understanding
- Teaching note-taking skills

Visual:

- Chunking assignments into smaller steps
- Writing paper with darker lines
- Worksheets that are visually "clean"
- Allowing for alternative methods of checking for understanding
- Matching games
- Limiting copying from board

References

Arky, B. (2018). *Understanding visual processing issues.* Retrieved from www. understood.org/en/learning-attention-issues/child-learning-disabilities/ visual-processing-issues/understanding-visual-processing-issues

Bamiou, D., Musiek, F., & Luxon, L. (2001). Aetiology and clinical presentations of auditory processing disorders—A review. *Archives of Disease in Childhood, 85,* 361–365. https://doi.org/10.1136/adc.85.5.361

Brousseau-Lachaine, O., Gagnon, F., R., & Faubert, J. (2008). Mild traumatic brain injury induces prolonged visual processing deficits in children. *Brain Injury, 22*(9), 657–668. https://doi.org/10.1080/02699050802203353

Johnson, K. (2018). *Understanding auditory processing disorder.* Retrieved from www.understood.org/en/learning-attention-issues/child-learning-disabilities/auditory-processing-disorder/understanding-auditory-processing-disorder

Misra, H., & Aikat, R. (2016). A survey of visual perceptual disorders in typically developing children, and comparison of motor and motor-free visual perceptual training in such children. *Journal of Neurological Disorders, 4*(296). https://doi.org/doi:10.4172/2329-6895.1000296

Molloy, C., Wilson-Ching, M., Anderson, A. Vicki, Gehan, R., Anderson, P. J., & Doyle, L. (2013). Visual processing in adolescents born extremely low birth weight and/or extremely preterm. *Pediatrics, 132*(3), 704–712. https://doi.org/doi:10.1542/peds.2013-0040

National Center for Learning Disabilities (NCLD). (2018). *Visual and auditory processing disorders.* Retrieved from www.ldonline.org/article/6390/

Roeser, R., & Downs, M. (2004). *Auditory disorders in school children: The law, identification, remediation.* New York: Thieme.

Sigmundsson, H., Anholt, S. K., & Talcott, J. B. (2010). Are poor mathematics skills associated with visual deficits in temporal processing? *Neuroscience Letters, 469*(2), 248–250. https://doi.org/ 10.1016/j.neulet.2009.12.005

7

NONVERBAL LEARNING DISORDER

In this part:

- What is a nonverbal learning disorder?
- What is it like to have nonverbal learning disorder?
- What are some symptoms of nonverbal learning disorder?
- What might help someone with nonverbal learning disorder?

What Is a Nonverbal Learning Disorder?

Nonverbal learning disorder is a language- and brain-based disorder that is characterized by challenges with nonverbal cues, spatial and visual organization difficulties and poor motor skills. Many children with nonverbal learning disorder are frequently misdiagnosed with ADHD because the symptoms have overlapping qualities. These children tend to have precocious conversational skills, impressively large vocabularies and average to above-average intelligence, but because of the difficulty with nonverbal cues, they may have trouble making friends and maintaining age-appropriate relationships (Cornoldi, Mammarella, & Goldenring-Fine, 2016).

Nonverbal learning disabilities affect girls as frequently as they affect boys and also tend to run in families. The research is mixed in the prevalence of nonverbal learning disorder. Some numbers put it quite high (25% of students with learning disabilities), and others claim that it is extremely rare (Morris, 2002; Spreen, 2011). Despite the fact that the disorder was first described in 1967 and much research has been done since that point, it has not been considered for classification in the DSM V (Spreen, 2011) and seems to be inherently misunderstood and possibly underdiagnosed as well (Casey, 2016).

What Is It Like to Have Nonverbal Learning Disorder?

Name: Emilee
Age: 22
Age at diagnosis: 10
Career: Politics

In elementary school, I was placed in a gifted and talented program where half of my day was spent in a special gifted class and the other half was in the regular class. I did well in the gifted class at first because I was always bright and could learn things very easily but in 4th grade, something started to change. My teacher from the gifted class noticed that it seemed like my math skills had started to decrease sharply in relation to my peers. My teacher also noticed that I had started to become very quiet in class and that it seemed that I had lost any kind of social ability that I'd had. I remember that I didn't like to hang out with too many people. The gifted class was small and tight-knit and the kids were all friends with each other, but I was just not able to be a part of it. I also started exhibiting extreme anxiety in class. I had been dealing with anxiety for a long time but by the time I got to 4th grade, it got out of control and it made me shut down completely in class. Even when my teacher made sure to ask me questions that I definitely knew the answer to, I would still not answer because I was so scared to be wrong. The fact that I was so bright and having so much trouble really confused everyone but what moved the process along was the fact that I had already been diagnosed with a physical disability and other issues prior to this point. I had already been diagnosed with neurofibromatosis, which is a genetic disorder that can cause tumors to grow. My family had been watching me closely since then and by the age of three, I had also already been diagnosed with depression and anxiety. When my teacher contacted my parents to tell them about the changes in my academics and social skills, because there was already an underlying physical issue, they got really nervous. They thought that if there was something wrong, then there was something REALLY wrong and, at first, they suspected autism. Because there was already an underlying issue, they took me to the doctor pretty immediately. They brought me to Iowa City, which is where the closest medical center to my home is and I had a whole host of testing done. I had a neuropsychologist, and a whole bunch of other specialists examine me. I guess they saw that I had issues with fine motor skills, so they also brought in an occupational therapist to examine me as well. They did a battery of tests and checked my hearing and my sight as well. My neuropsychologist in Iowa City did most of the tests. Between my neuropsychologist and the occupational therapist, they were able to determine that I had nonverbal learning disorder. They said that I was two traits shy of having Asperger's syndrome, which is what they used to

Nonverbal Learning Disorder 41

call a high-functioning kind of autism. They also told us that I was very lucky that we caught it so early because most kids with it get misdiagnosed.

Getting the help I needed was a big stress and anxiety inducer for both me and my mother. It was an uphill battle all the way. When we went back to school to tell them what the neuropsychologist had determined, it was met with some resistance. It was hard because everyone just thought that I was socially awkward and we were just making excuses for it. No one knew anything about nonverbal learning disorder, and they seemed reluctant to accept it. Eventually, after just trying to work with the teachers, we realized that we were going to have to involve the principal, so we started the 504 process. I never had an IEP. In fact, my mom did not know what an IEP was until my freshman year of high school because they never offered it as an option. I'm not sure whether or not my mother would have pushed for it had she known what it was, but I guess, because of that, I was never put into special education classes. It was probably a good thing anyway. My anxiety was so bad already and I know I would have been worried about being singled out, I knew kids in those classes and was glad I wasn't placed in them. It seemed like so many of the people in those classes did not seem to have the same kind of support that I did and they continued to struggle even later on. Even the teachers would just look at them and say "Why are you so weird? Why can't you be normal?" The fact that I was a bright student with family support was a privilege. They tolerated me while the kids on the spectrum were not tolerated as much.

I was pretty lucky that I had a really good team of advocates all along. From the very beginning of my diagnosis, my mom started going to the library and learning everything she could about nonverbal learning disability. She helped me to understand that my disability was just a way to explain how my ability to think was a little different than other people's. I just thought differently and it was okay to think differently. Socially though, I was terrible, I was lucky because I did have one friend. She always understood what was going on and having her be that support for me was really important. Mostly though, until middle school, I was pretty nonverbal. I mostly spent my time just hanging out in my room and internalizing the depression that I felt. One great thing from during that time was the amazing elementary school counselor that I was lucky to have. She taught me so many self-calming skills. I still use what she taught me to this day. I remember that I would get so anxious about everything and she was always there for me, helping me learn the skills that would allow me to calm myself down. She called me "Chicken Little," like in the story. She told me that Chicken Little was always saying that the sky was falling. When I would get stuck in my anxiety, she would say, "Chicken Little, look at the sky. Is the sky falling? The sky is not falling. The sky is still there. Everything is okay." I still use that.

42 Most Common Learning Disabilities

Most teachers did not understand what my disability was and had a hard time helping me. I was just the socially awkward student but in middle school, everything became much more hands on. To his credit, my counselor, who I don't think really understood my disability, was a huge advocate for me all the time. He made sure that all of the teachers knew what it was that I needed to succeed and made sure that everyone was on board. I had a lot of accommodations and they all helped to give me the confidence that I needed to keep growing academically. Since the anxiety was still a huge factor in my life, one of my accommodations was that I got to have advance notice for writing projects. If there was going to be a long-term assignment, I was told about it way in advance so that I would have time to work through my anxiety and get it done. My counselor knew that for me, going to the teachers to ask for help was a really big deal. I had these internal thoughts that if you asked teacher for help, they would think you are stupid and I was terrified of that but he and my mom kept pushing me to do it and I did keep trying. So, one of my accommodations was that if I did go to a teacher to ask for help, they knew that they had to help me as soon as I asked in order to keep me from shutting down in class. So many of my issues came from anxiety but organization was a problem as well so they arranged for me to be able to leave early on Fridays during study and have someone come with me to help me clean and organize my locker. I was also allowed to schedule classes with a friend in my class so that I would have someone familiar to help calm me down. Similarly, if I'd had a teacher who knew me and I was comfortable and familiar with, I was scheduled into classes with them for the next year as well. Another accommodation was about homework. In my school, if you forgot your homework then you would get penalized for it by getting a detention, but I was exempt from that.

I did have a lot of bad experiences up until 6th grade with lots of teachers who did not help me at all. My mother, though, would not let that get in the way. She was always my greatest advocate and when she saw that I wasn't getting what I needed, she made sure to step in. She made sure that even if it started off badly, it always ended well. In 7th grade, I was incredibly lucky and got an amazing math teacher who actually changed so much for me. He worked with me all the time until I understood what I was doing. He never stopped trying to help and I believe that if it was not for him, I would have been too far behind to go to college. He worked with me to find ways to figure out the math even if it was not a conventional way to do it. My main roadblock was telling myself that I couldn't do it. I had anxiety and depression and I was sure I could not do it but when he showed me that I actually could, it was life changing. I was able to overcome that inner dialogue that told me that I could not do it and then realized that if I could overcome that and learn math, I could do everything. At this point, I started to be able to reach out to people more. I started to

Nonverbal Learning Disorder **43**

make more of an effort with my one friend and started being able to spend more time socially with her as well. I was really lucky that despite the fact that I had such a hard time relating to people she stuck around and she stuck with me all through high school.

Even with all the interventions and my amazing advocates, I still struggled until about midway through high school. Even though I had been diagnosed early on and everyone knew that I had nonverbal learning disability, the fact that nonverbal learning disability is an invisible disability makes it very hard to recognize it for what it is. To most people, I was just a socially awkward kid. The fact that I was smart as well made it difficult for them to understand what it was that was really going on. I think that it might be hard for people to put together the idea of a disability that they can't see with the idea of that same person being intelligent. Like I said, they mostly looked at me as a socially awkward kid but, despite what other people thought, my 504 stayed with me all through high school. I know that it must have been a little difficult to keep it in place since I was able to achieve academically but my mom did not back down, so it stayed. Thankfully, also because of my mom, I had a really good sense of what my needs were in order to be successful. By the time I hit high school, I understood what I needed to work to my best level. I had an understanding of the fact that even though I was excelling in English and government classes, I was processing at the speed of an average student. Because I understood my learning needs and my learning style, I knew what I had to do to compensate for that discrepancy and I was able to succeed and do very well. The downside is that the more successful I was, which hinged on my using my compensatory skills and my accommodations, the more difficult it was for people to understand that I did still have a disability. I was taking AP classes and getting A's in all of them and my teachers, I know for sure, did not understand how my disability affected me at all. Maybe it is because, if you are academically successful with an invisible learning disability, by the time you get to high school or even beyond, no one sees the back end of your struggles. They don't see what you have to do at home, or the amount of mental energy it might take to get things done. In the end, it didn't really matter because I was able to navigate regardless but I know that it was hard for people to handle. By the middle of high school, I had progressed so much. By that point, so many of my hurdles were more about anxiety than anything else and with all the support I got I was able to work past so much of it. I had the greatest counselor in high school, and she was able to help me navigate through so much of it, which was really wonderful. She was supportive and encouraging and she was a huge support. Eventually, I was able to become really social and make more friends. Eventually, I even became captain of the cheerleading team. I am still very social, even more so now since I work in politics where being social is the nature of the job.

44 Most Common Learning Disabilities

When I was ready to go to college, my counselor told me that with my grades, I could go anywhere. By that point my learning needs were more about what I did for myself as opposed to accommodations that school was giving me so I didn't really need to look at colleges based on my learning needs. The only thing I needed was for the school to be close to home. I had given birth to a daughter when I was still in high school, so I needed to be near family. I applied to and was accepted to a college near my home and when I registered for my classes for the first time, one of the forms that I had to fill out had all kinds of demographic questions. One of those questions asked if you identified yourself as having a disability so I checked off the box and a short while later, this woman named Joy from the office of disability services reached out to me and she became my savior. It was nice that all I had to do was check off that box in order to be connected with the office of disability services. It was a pretty seamless process, which was nice. So, Joy called me and we made an appointment to meet so she could show me the campus and fill me in on all of the things I would need to know. Even though I had come so far, I still had a lot of anxiety and a big fear of the unknown and I let her know about this. She wanted to make sure that I had enough tools to make my transition to college a positive one so, about two weeks before school started, she literally walked me through my schedule. She walked the campus with me and took me to the buildings where my classes would be. She made sure to show me where everything was. It was important that I knew what my hurdles were because if I couldn't tell her, she wouldn't have been able to help me. I told her what my needs were and what my hurdles were and she was able to help me through this new and unknown situation in a way that completely addressed my needs. I knew walking in that my anxiety was still one of my biggest hurdles. I knew that if I were stuck in my anxiety then it would affect my academic performance. The anxiety would take over and everything else would be pushed to the side. She helped me deal with all of that in such a concrete way. For the most part, everything worked out well in college but there was one time when one of my professors would not adhere to my college 504 and Joy advocated for me. With nonverbal learning disability, if you are writing by hand, it is hard to process as quickly so I do better when I work on a computer. This professor would not let us have computers in the classroom so that was a problem. Then he took my paper from me before my time and a half was over. I went to Joy immediately, and she advocated for me and I was able to fix it. I could go to her for anything. Coming into college, she was my saving grace. I come from a family where mine is the first generation to go to a four-year college so even outside the nonverbal learning disability, I was facing some challenges. Having Joy as a point person was my saving grace on so many different levels.

I have been lucky throughout everything to have people in my life who were willing to look at my issues and be realistic. Being realistic about what my challenges were was what allowed me to find ways around them. If we had ignored them, or not dealt with them head on, I don't know that I would have been able to find success.

From my counselors in elementary school, middle school, high school and my mom, I had a very good sense of my needs. I learned early on what I needed to do to be successful and I was lucky to have a team of advocates always ready to help me.

My counselors had a profound and positive impact on me. They never gave up on me and they were always there even if they did not completely understand nonverbal learning disability. I was so lucky to have this group of people who kept supporting me and believing in me and teaching me things. Like I said before I still use the same self-calming methods that my elementary counselor taught me. I am so grateful that I had so many people making such a positive and profound impact on my life.

What Are Some Symptoms of Nonverbal Learning Disorders?

- Difficulty recognizing nonverbal cues
- Poor reading comprehension despite large vocabulary
- Very early and precocious language acquisition
- Gross and fine motor skills issues
- May appear clumsy and have difficulty using scissors etc.
- Frequent, repetitive questions
- Difficulty understanding idioms or spatial information
- Difficulty understanding sarcasm due to literal interpretations of events
- Difficulty handling change in life or routine
- May seem overly trusting due to inability to understand nonverbal cues
- May have trouble following multistep directions
- May have difficulty extracting generalizations from reading or real-life situations
- May have highly advanced verbal skills
- May have academic challenges in math computation, science, writing and reading comprehension

(Franz, 2000)

What Are Some Things That Might Help People With Nonverbal Learning Disability?

- Explicit and direct instruction
- Creating connections to new learning from previous learning or experiences
- Reduction of visually distracting information on worksheets
- Clear and concise verbal feedback

46 Most Common Learning Disabilities

- Minimized distractions
- Frequent checks for understanding
- Compensatory skills instruction (such as keyboarding) and remediation (such as handwriting skills) simultaneously
- Occupational therapy
- Providing examples for problem-solving questions
- Teaching a variety of problem-solving skills
- Graphic organizers
- Speech-to-text programs
- Allowing narration of math problems
- Graph paper for math problems

References

Casey, J. E. (2016). Nonverbal learning disorder: Past, present, and future. In *Special and gifted education: Concepts, methodologies, tools, and applications* (pp. 130–168). Hershey, PA: IGI Global.

Cornoldi, C., Mammarella, I., & Goldenring-Fine, J. (2016). *Nonverbal learning disabilities*. New York and London: The Guilford Press.

Franz, C. (2000). *Diagnosis and management of nonverbal learning disorders*. Paper presented at the Annual Convention of the National Association of School Psychologists. New Orleans, LA. Retrieved from https://eric.ed.gov/

Morris, S. (2002). Promoting social skills among students with nonverbal learning disabilities. *Teaching Exceptional Children, 34*(3), 66–70. https://doi.org/10.1177/004005990203400309

Spreen, O. (2011). Nonverbal learning disabilities: A critical review. *Child Neuropsychology, 17*(5), 418–443. https://doi.org/10.1080/09297049.2010.546778

PART 3
Related Disorders

8

ADHD (ATTENTION DEFICIT DISORDER/ATTENTION DEFICIT-HYPERACTIVITY DISORDER)

In this part:

- What is ADHD?
- What is it like to have ADHD?
- What are some symptoms of ADHD?
- What might help someone with ADHD?

What Is ADHD?

Attention deficit-hyperactivity disorder (ADHD) is classified as a neurobehavioral disorder (Curatolo, D'Agati, & Moavero, 2010) that can interfere with a person's day to day activities and their ability to stay focused on a task. It affects 3% to 5% of American children and, although we do not know what causes it, there are certain risk factors that seem to play a part in its development. These risk factors include issues such as low birth weight, family history, cigarette use during pregnancy and brain injuries (National Institute of Neurological Disorders and Stroke, 2017).

It is characterized by at least a 6-month period of inattention and/or hyperactivity and/or impulsivity symptoms that adversely affect daily life (Noorbala & Akhondzadeh, 2006). Although the disorder itself is not considered a learning disability, school-aged children who are diagnosed with the disorder may have difficulty attending and/or focusing on information that is being discussed in the classroom, and this difficulty in attending can have a significant and negative impact on learning. Early identification and treatment are pivotal in the prevention of associated later-life risks of social and behavioral issues, depression, anxiety disorder, substance abuse and associated learning disorders (Noorbala & Akhondzadeh, 2006). ADHD is usually diagnosed in childhood and is a lifelong disorder (National Institute of Neurological Disorders, 2018).

Although the disorder is officially known as ADHD, it is actually classified into three distinct subtypes. These subtypes are the hyperactive/impulsive subtype, the inattentive subtype and the combined subtype (Qureshi, Min, Jo, & Lee, 2016).

The student with hyperactivity and impulsivity may be viewed as having a disruptive presence in the classroom. They may be unable to sit for long periods of time and may appear restless. They may shout out answers or say inappropriate things to adults and peers alike without an awareness of consequences. Their loss of focus is frequently obvious and externalizes as hyperactivity and impulsivity (Noorbala & Akhondzadeh, 2006).

The student with a diagnosis of the inattentive subtype of ADHD, while still having difficulty with focus and attention, tends to display behaviors that are less externally obvious. These students may get distracted from a task quickly and easily. They may have difficulty finishing homework assignments or staying organized, they may lose things easily and they may have trouble attending to details (Noorbala & Akhondzadeh, 2006).

Although statistics show that ADHD is more common in boys than it is in girls, recent research has shown that girls tend to present with more inattentive qualities of ADHD and may frequently go undiagnosed. In addition, girls with ADHD also seem to present with more symptoms of anxiety and depression than do boys, and this can also lead to both continued underdiagnosis and misdiagnosis (Quinn & Madhoo, 2014).

ADHD is a highly treatable disorder, and treatment can help reduce symptoms. Treatments such as psychotherapy, medication (stimulant and nonstimulant), training and education about managing the disorder have all been shown to have a significant positive impact on adults and children who have the disorder (Noorbala & Akhondzadeh, 2006).

What Is It Like to Have ADHD?

Name: Cindy

Age: 20

Age at diagnosis: about 8

Career: College student. Planning on graduate school for biomedical engineering

From what I remember teachers would always say, "Cindy does not pay attention," even though I was getting good grades. I guess I spent a lot of time staring out of the window and doodling. It didn't really affect my grades too much because, academically, so much of school was easy for me anyway. Even so, I did have a lot of teachers tell me to stop staring out of the window.

In general, I remember elementary school feeling a lot like a weird daze. I was not always aware of what I was doing, and I wasn't paying attention to stuff—it was kind of a whir. That went on for years and I did fine because, again, the academics were easy for me. I could stare at nothing and have no idea what the teacher had just said but still figure it out in time to answer any questions. Thankfully, I wasn't hyperactive. I think that might have made a lot of things harder but still, being so inattentive did make it easier to miss that I was even having a problem at all. I've heard that is a real problem for a lot of girls with ADHD and I can understand why that would be. I was a quiet little girl and I didn't create disruption but there was certainly an awful lot that I missed. I just wasn't there. Even now, there are blips in my knowledge base that came from not having been completely aware early on. I just have some gaps—like I still don't know Roman numerals and telling time is hard too. I was also super messy. I used to collect rocks at recess that I just piled into my desk until there was no more room for books and once, I left my lunch in my backpack for months. I also remember a shrimp dinner that somehow ended up in my desk at school for a long time. It was awful. I don't know if kids made fun of me but that's kind of the blessing of ADHD because, if they did, at least I didn't notice.

I have a lot of hyper-fixations. When I was really little, I needed to know everything about blood cells, chlorophyll, the brain—whatever was my interest at the time. I think that might be a part of ADHD too but, I'm not sure. I was really lucky though. I had a lot of really good teachers who let me shine in ways that made me feel like I was smart and capable. In middle school, for example, before I went on medication, I had a lot of teachers who saw my interests and actually let me learn using the things I was interested in. I remember that I did a whole presentation about how the 7 deadly sins were related to neurosis. I guess that is a little weird for middle school but I guess I was a little weird. I was in advanced classes for English and history, but math was hard and that was definitely a concentration issue more than an ability issue. I would zone out and it took a lot of energy to do stuff in math but if I thought something was interesting, I would finish it immediately. Some of my teachers used this to my advantage. One math teacher would always make math about things that he knew I would find more interesting. That really helped a lot. He would also grade us on how we took our notes, not just on the grades and that worked for me as well. As soon as I thought something was boring though, it would take me weeks to get it done.

I had a really difficult time with being able to schedule long-term assignments to get them done in time. My backpack was a mess, my binders were filled with garbage and all of it was definitely detrimental. I'm lucky that my fixations have always been academic and educational,

52 Related Disorders

and I like gaining knowledge. If I had not had those kinds of interests, I am sure that I would have done really poorly all through school. If my hyper-fixation was about cars or something, I would have been in trouble.

I think that my teachers started to realize that I was smart somewhere between elementary school and middle school. I think that a student with ADHD who is interested in school and wants to do well needs to have the things that they are interested brought to them. They need to be connected to their classes and have the learning be something relevant; otherwise they are gone into their own worlds. ADHD is not just a lack of focus—it is a huge part of your personality. Having it makes you a little bit of a challenge to teach but It's so important not to lose those kids. I guess that I was pretty lucky. Being smart made learning a lot easier but I learned pretty quickly that I needed to work harder to keep my grades up. No matter how smart you are, if you can't stay focused or organized, life gets really hard.

I think that, for a long time, I thought I was fine. I would get mad when people would constantly reprimand me about my unorganized habits. But at the same time, I knew that the truth was that I was stressed and freaked out when everything was messy. I also knew that when I was organized and on top of things, life was far more efficient. I think that the fact that being organized is not a natural state for me and is hard to do is almost as stressful as being unorganized is. I did learn a lot of good habits that have stuck and those habits make it much less anxiety inducing to be organized. I still lose things. I've lost coats in the winter, keys, shoes, things like that. My closet is just a pile of laundry but I'm getting better.

It was a struggle trying to learn to be organized. In middle school, I could never remember to write my work down. I knew that if I didn't write it down, it wouldn't get done but I still couldn't seem to do it. It's so stressful because you want to be a good student but you don't have the means to get there and no one is actually teaching you how to do it. At least I had my mom who would help me but it was still hard.

I was also still so unfocused. Every paper I handed in was covered in doodles. For some reason, the teachers were okay with it but doodling was definitely a distraction. I guess that they were just happy that at least I was handing in something. In general though, I think I was only present in the class about 35% of the time. I was there physically but my mind was always somewhere else. I'm lucky that I'm smart and I was always able to come back from it but I was really not present in most of my classes until high school.

By the time I got to high school I was able to sustain my attention for a lot longer and I'd stopped doodling on most of my work so that was good. I still struggled though. I'd started getting into the habit of writing things down in my planner but then I would lose my planner. I was on Strattera in high school and that helped but it was too subtle. I started to learn a lot more than I did in middle school and elementary school and I think it was the Strattera that was helping. I still had trouble focusing though. In freshman year I got the first C I'd ever gotten in English and it was because I still had not learned how to focus on my work. I thought I could still get away with not paying attention in class but that didn't work as well in high school the way it had in middle school. I couldn't not pay attention in class and still expect to do well, especially given the fact that I had been placed in a lot of advanced-placement and honors classes. I remember that I was doodling on the first day in math class in freshman year and the teacher ripped the paper out of my hands, yelled at me in front of everyone and threw it away and that reaction startled me so much. It's not like I wanted to be doodling and not paying attention. I was just not there yet.

For college, I was accepted into an honors program in biomedical engineering. That first semester, I was still doodling in my notebooks and then I got my first C in a math class. I had to reteach myself everything about studying and that was when I asked to have my medication changed because I just could not keep up. I needed a level of self-awareness that I did not have in high school and I realized that I still was not focused like my peers were. I was not doing the things I needed to do to be successful. I was not going to the professor for extra help, I was not studying appropriately. With ADD, you don't think like that—you think, I should go for extra help or I should study and then you go bowling instead. In college though, as an engineering major, you can't just float by. I need to study and I take a lot of math classes and there is frequently new material that I might have a hard time getting at first. I realized in my freshman year of college that I had to take the next step and try different medication because things were just not working for me. I realized that there was always something that I was missing out on. I would either miss class, socialization or sleep and I knew that I needed to find balance in order to be successful. There was a lot of figuring out what worked for me and what did not. I still struggle—it is not something that is a one and done. If I don't put the time and energy into the learning curve that is myself then I do poorly, but I have gotten better at it. One thing that helps is that everything in college has been cyclical kind of work and when there is a pattern, things are much easier to remember. I do keep a Word doc with all of my test dates and project dates and I will go through it and delete things that have already happened. I know that if I don't keep track of stuff and write it down, I don't remember that it is going to happen. I have gotten much better with that stuff.

Excluding the anxieties I have had about it, having ADHD has helped me attract certain friends who have become lifelong friends. ADHD doesn't *allow for linear thought—it is like you think in fireworks and millions of thoughts happen at once. I think the zoning out happens when you can't focus or pick one. In college, having ADHD lets me think outside the box when other kids can't. With the medication, it lets me work through those thoughts all the way to the end which is nice. There was a robotics class I took where I was in a group of very linear thinkers and we were stuck and could not get the robot to work. I watched my classmates struggle through the linear code that was just not working and jumped in with no idea other than to play around with it until something happened. I found the problem, which I then followed through and solved. It was great and our robot actually won a prize! With ADHD 6 million different thoughts come into your head all at the same time but it becomes an issue when you just can't stay with one. I think that when you are successful with ADHD, you have the gift of being able to think in these out-of-the-box, creative ways. Success with ADHD is being able to take those thoughts and put them to use. Otherwise, it's just like being lost in your own head.*

What Are Some Symptoms of ADHD?

Although it is normal to have some inattention and impulsivity, people with ADHD experience much more severe, frequent and disabling symptoms. Symptoms for ADHD can appear as early as age 3 and may change over time.

General

- Difficulty with following instructions
- Inability to organize oneself
- Leaving projects unfinished
- Difficulty paying attention to details
- Poor academic performance
- Difficulty with relationships
- Social issues
- Disciplinary issues

Inattentive

- Missed details
- Difficulty with maintaining attention
- Easily sidetracked by other projects
- Frequent incomplete projects
- Difficulty with sequencing
- Poor time management
- Messy classwork or homework
- Messy room, locker and backpack

ADHD **55**

- Difficulty meeting deadlines or being on time
- Avoidance of tasks that require sustained attention
- Losing unexpected things (such as coats in winter, glasses, etc.)
- Easily distracted
- Difficulty remembering to keep appointments
- Anxiety and/or depression

Hyperactivity

- Frequent squirming and fidgeting in seat at school
- Frequent leaving seat unexpectedly
- Restlessness
- Difficulty with playing quietly
- Constant talking
- Shouting out answers
- Interrupting people while they talk
- Difficulty with taking turns
- Lack of inhibition
- Impulsive behavior (can become risk taking in later school)

What Are Some Things That Might Help Someone With ADHD?

- Consistent rules
- Daily routines
- Reduction of distractions for test taking, homework or classwork
- Direct instruction in organizational methods
- Direct monitoring of organization early on to establish routines
- Advance notice to prepare for transitions
- Extended time
- Shortened assignments at first to encourage engagement
- Color-coded notebooks
- Class notes
- Praise and positive reinforcement for positive behavior
- Acknowledgment of frustrations
- Nonverbal signals from teacher to help refocusing (Post-it note on desk, tapping on desk, etc.)
- Clearly written schedules
- Creating specific places to store frequently used items (keys in a box on the table, pens in a bin in kitchen, etc.)
- Homework and notebook organizers/planners
- Direct instruction in the use of calendars, lists and reminder notes
- Breaking down large tasks

References

Curatolo, P., D'Agati, E., & Moavero, R. (2010). The neurobiological basis of ADHD. *Italian Journal of Pediatrics, 36*(1), 79.

National Institute of Neurological Disorders. (2018). *Attention deficit-hyperactivity disorder information page.* Retrieved from www.ninds.nih.gov/Disorders/All-Disorders/Attention-Deficit-Hyperactivity-Disorder-Information-Page

National Institute of Neurological Disorders and Stroke. (2017). *Attention deficit hyperactivity disorder information page.* Retrieved from www.ninds.nih.gov/Disorders/All-Disorders/Attention-Deficit-Hyperactivity-Disorder-Information-Page

Noorbala, A-A., & Akhondzadeh, S. (2006). Attention-deficit/hyperactivity disorder: Etiology and pharmacotherapy. *Archives of Iranian Medicine, 9*(4), 374–380.

Quinn, P. O., & Madhoo, M. (2014). A review of attention-deficit/hyperactivity disorder in women and girls: Uncovering this hidden diagnosis. The primary care companion. *To the Journal of Clinical Psychiatry, 16*(3). https://doi.org/10.4088/PCC.13r01596

Qureshi, M. N. I., Min, B., Jo, H. J., & Lee, B. (2016). Multiclass classification for the differential diagnosis on the ADHD subtypes using recursive feature elimination and hierarchical extreme learning machine: Structural MRI study. *PLoS One, 11*(8), e0160697.

9

DYSPRAXIA

In this part:

- What is dyspraxia?
- What is it like to have dyspraxia?
- What are some symptoms of dyspraxia?
- What might help someone with dyspraxia?

What Is Dyspraxia?

Dyspraxia is a form of developmental coordination disorder (DCD) that can cause difficulty with fine and gross motor skills. It is a disruption in how messages from the brain are communicated to the body, and children with the disorder may have difficulty with coordination and motor skills (Portwood, 2013). Since the disorder occurs across a continuum, its effect varies from person to person and can change over time as the individual takes on different types of tasks and responsibilities. For example, when dyspraxia presents in a young child, that child may have difficulty learning how to tie shoelaces, ride a bike or even play with other children. As that same child grows into adulthood, those challenges may transform into issues such as learning how to drive or learning to make food, but ultimately, no matter how the symptoms present themselves, dyspraxia can impair day-to-day functioning. Problems with time management, memory, processing and organization are common and frequently result in difficulties with reading, reading comprehension and spelling. The disorder frequently occurs alongside other related issues and learning disabilities such as dyscalculia, dyslexia, and ADHD and occurs across all levels of intellectual abilities. In addition, because the disorder can create such a negative impact on daily function and participation in

58 Related Disorders

daily life, people with dyspraxia also frequently experience social and emotional difficulties (Dyspraxia Foundation, 2018).

Dyspraxia seems to occur more frequently in boys then in girls, and there seems to be a hereditary connection, although no specific gene has been found yet (Lingam, Hunt, Golding, Jongmans, & Emond, 2009). While dyspraxia has not been associated with brain damage, it does seem to have a neurological basis and also seems to be related to risk factors including prematurity and low birth weight (Sugden, Kirby, & Dunford, 2008; Zwicker, Missiuna, Harris, & Boyd, 2010). In addition, recent research indicates that there is a 95% correlation between dyspraxia, ADHD, dyslexia and autism spectrum disorder (Richardson & Ross, 2000).

What Is It Like to Have Dyspraxia?

Name: Sarah:
Age: 19
Age at diagnosis: 6
Career: College student. Studying psychology

I was diagnosed with dyspraxia super early. I was lucky because it doesn't seem that dyspraxia is easily recognized in the United States but mine was caught early anyway. I was diagnosed right after kindergarten. I remember that every day was frustrating, and I couldn't sit still. I got into trouble all the time and could not write my name or remember my phone number or address. My speech was difficult to understand. My coloring looked like I was just scratching lines into the paper, I couldn't climb the monkey bars and I was always, always falling down. I tried so hard to make friends but all loud noises made me feel overwhelmed and when I felt overwhelmed, I screamed a lot and no one, not even the teacher understood what was happening. The teachers and the school could not figure out how to help me. My parents could not figure out how to help me. I remember that I just felt out of control and not wanted anywhere. School became a nightmare and I started having stomachaches every morning. Thank god for those stomachaches! When my parents took me to the doctor, she, very astutely, started asking questions about school. I guess she figured out that they were connected. The more questions she asked, the more it became obvious to her that there was something going on and I was officially diagnosed soon after that. From that point on, I started getting all kinds of therapies. I got speech therapy, I got occupational therapy and eventually, I got psychological counseling as well. I remember that my occupational therapist once told my mom and I that people with dyspraxia were 8 times more likely to suffer from anxiety than other people. I don't know if that is true or not but it must have put my mom on alert.

Dyspraxia **59**

The first time I had a panic attack, she immediately made an appointment with a psychologist. Eventually I went on medication and I'm still on it. It's mostly under control most of the time.

The therapies were really helpful and I was lucky that there were plenty of people all around me who understood dyspraxia and were ready to advocate for me whenever they had to. But even with all the help, school was still pretty hard. I was still the "weird kid" for a long time. I was terrible at sports, I was learning super slowly and I was pulled out of the regular classroom for all of the therapies that I was getting so making friends was still difficult. Again, I was lucky because I had all these good people on my side and I was also way above grade level, at least intellectually. The school was great about letting me do the gifted track while still giving me modifications and accommodations. I still felt frustrated but I also felt valued for my intelligence so it kind of evened out.

By middle school, I had already learned to work on a keyboard so I didn't have to worry about my handwriting anymore. I had this one terrible English teacher who would not let me use the computer in class. She made me write everything with a pen and then would give me failing marks because she could not read what I wrote. I was so scared of her that I never told anyone why I was doing so poorly in her class and when my report card came out and my mother saw an F she freaked out. When she came in for a conference and the teacher pulled out my work, in pen, I thought my mom would rip this lady's eyes out with her fingernails. Instead, she looked at the paper, folded it under her arm and said something like, "Sarah, I think we've seen enough of your terrible penmanship," and then looked right at the teacher and said, "You would think that someone as smart as Sarah would know when she was dealing with an imbecile. I guess I have more work cut out for me." I'd never heard my mom say a mean word to anyone and to have the first mean thing she said in front of me be something so cool and so controlled gave me this crazy respect for her from that point forward. She laid into me later though and lectured me about self-advocacy and never letting anyone push me around. She had me read my IEP and tell her what my modifications and accommodations were and then made me promise that I would, if not handle it myself, at least tell her if someone wasn't giving me what I needed to succeed. I guess the whole thing kind of scared me in a way because after that, I never needed her to step in again. Since then I've always been really good at advocating for myself.

I think that was also actually the beginning of me feeling good enough about myself to start making friends too. I ended middle school in a really good place. I'd caught up academically and I was in all kinds of clubs and I even started bringing friends home to hang out with. Sports were, and still are, really hard for me but I learned to be honest about my disability and it became something that my friends and I could joke about.

60 Related Disorders

By high school, I don't think it was even that much of an issue anymore. I got and used my extra time (which I still use and need, in college). I had learned to compensate for so many things and I was so used to explaining my challenges that it felt more like I was doing a public service by teaching people about dyspraxia than anything else. I liked feeling good about myself.

College has been great so far as well. I'm a sophomore now and I'm studying psychology. I want to go to graduate school and become a psychologist and help kids in the same way so many people helped me. Like I said, I've been lucky. What makes me sad about that is that there were so many other kids who might not have been as lucky as me. Maybe they never got diagnosed and maybe they still feel like crap about themselves. There were so many times that people said things that weren't even meant to be mean and they just cut me down, little by little. Like one teacher I had who kept telling me that of course, I could cut in a straight line. Everybody could cut in a straight line. She said it just took practice. She meant well but when I couldn't do it, it made me feel smaller than small. And that kind of stuff happened all the time but my family would always intervene and make it stop and make me feel better. But what happened to those kids who didn't even know that there was anything wrong?

What Are Some Symptoms of Dyspraxia?

- Poor balance or clumsy movements
- Difficulty with motor planning
- Difficulty with coordinating both sides of body at the same time
- Hand–eye coordination issues
- Difficulty with organizing self and belongings
- Sensitivity to touch
- Handwriting issues
- Spelling and reading problems
- Distressed by loud or constant noises (i.e., pencil tapping, clock ticking)
- Difficulty with manipulating objects by hand (i.e., fine motor tasks, puzzles, cutting etc.)
- Social and emotional difficulties
- Issues with time management
- Memory difficulties
- Processing issues
- Speech articulation difficulties
- Sensory issues from clothing (tight, rough, scratchy etc.)
- Difficulty judging speed and/or distance
- Poor spatial awareness
- Poor stamina
- Difficulty adapting to new situations

Dyspraxia **61**

- Literal use of language
- Difficulty remembering or following instructions
- Immature behavior
- Extreme emotions
- Lack of awareness of potential danger

(Learning Disabilities Association, 2018)

What Helps Children With Dyspraxia?

- Reassurance and acceptance
- Specific and honest praise on both effort and performance
- Reasonable and realistic goals based on students' abilities
- Early instruction in keyboarding
- Specific and constructive responses to work
- Extra time to compensate for slow processing of information
- Breaking new tasks and information into smaller chunks
- Allowing for time to practice
- Instruction of specific skills with an eye toward generalizing
- Step–by-step checklists for learning
- Verbalizing one direction at a time
- Minimized visual distractions
- Multiple modalities for teaching

References

Learning Disabilities Association. (2018). *Dyspraxia*. Retrieved from https://lda america.org/types-of-learning-disabilities/dyspraxia/

Lingam, R., Hunt, L. P., Golding, J., Jongmans, M. J., & Emond, A. M. (2009). Prevalence of developmental coordination disorder using the DSM-IV at 7 years of age: A UK population-based study. *Pediatrics, 123*(4), 693–700. https://doi.org/10.1542/peds.2008-1770

Portwood, M. (2013). *Understanding developmental dyspraxia: A textbook for students and professionals.* London: David Fulton Publishers. https://doi.org/10.1111/1475-3588.00046_4

Richardson, A. J., & Ross, A. J. (2000). Fatty acid metabolism in neurodevelopmental disorder: A new perspective on associations between attention-deficit/hyperactivity disorder, dyslexia, dyspraxia and the autistic spectrum. *Prostaglandins Leukotrienes and Essential Fatty Acids, 63*(1), 1–9. https://doi.org/10.1054/plef.2000.0184

Sugden, D., Kirby, A., & Dunford, C. (2008). Issues surrounding children with developmental coordination disorder. *International Journal of Disability, Development and Education, 55*(2), 173–187. https://doi.org/doi:10.1080/10349120802033691

Zwicker, J., Missiuna, C., Harris, S., & Boyd, L. (2010). Brain activation of children with developmental coordination disorder is different than peers. *Pediatrics, 126*(3), 678–686. https://doi.org/doi:10.1542/peds.2010-0059

10

EXECUTIVE FUNCTION DISORDER

In this part:
- What is executive function disorder?
- What is it like to have executive function disorder?
- What are some symptoms of executive function disorder?
- What might help someone with executive function disorder?

What Is Executive Function Disorder?

Executive function disorder is a disorder that affects the ability to plan, organize, pay attention and develop strategies to cope with day-to-day life. People with this disorder show working memory deficits that affect the ability to plan and organize in advance. Children who have executive function disorder benefit from direct instruction and regular feedback about organization and planning. This early intervention is an invaluable aid to later life. In general, people with executive function disorder need help with managing time, space, materials and work. They need to be taught to use things like planners, timers and alarms. Although many people with ADHD have executive function disorder, they are separate disorders and can exist independently of each other (National Center for Learning Disabilities, 2005). A student with ADHD may have executive function disorder, but it is not necessarily always the case, Nor is it always the case that a student with executive function disorder has ADHD (Willcutt, Doyle, Nigg, Faraone, & Pennington, 2005). If the executive function disorder is related to the ADHD, medication therapy might have a real and positive impact. If, however, the executive function disorder is related to a learning disability, medication therapy may not help, since in that case, the issue revolves less around loss of focus and more around a direct learning disability.

Executive Function Disorder **63**

Executive function disorder tends to run in families and affects girls as much as it affects boys (Skogli, Teicher, Andersen, Hovik, & Øie, 2013). Since the disorder is characterized by difficulties with planning and organizing, the disorder does not become obvious until children enter school and the demands of projects, homework and schoolwork begin to be more prevalent.

What Is It Like to Have Executive Function Disorder?

Name: Amber
Age: 25
Age at diagnosis: 8
Career: College student. Studying education

I can clearly remember the first time executive function disorder affected me. I had gone to my dad and was really upset because the other kids in school had all started reading and I just wasn't able to yet. He immediately got me a tutor and I was so excited that I would finally be able to learn to read. Well, that developed into a thing where it seemed like I needed a tutor for everything all the time. The person they hired turned into more of a babysitter than anything else. She was pretty much there just to make sure I was doing all of my work all the time. She didn't really teach me how to get things done on my own, she just made sure that it got done. It was fine for then but it made it much harder later on because I was never able to learn how to do it on my own. I relied on it much too heavily and didn't even realize that I was having trouble until she wasn't helping me anymore. It got easier around sophomore year when I went on medication and then my grades turned around from Ds to As.

I know that my parents were so frustrated with me. I would get the work done but then shove it into my backpack and never hand it in. I would get these bad report cards and my parents would look in my backpack and find all the work that I had not handed in. Then they would get in touch with the teachers and say "she did it and she did it right but she forgot to hand it in." It was pretty frustrating for my parents and for me too. I also knew that this was something that was not happening to everyone around me and that made it even harder because I could not figure out what was wrong with me. At that point, I started to freak out before school on a daily basis and that definitely did not make things any easier.

I tried to stay positive. Every year, before school started, I would get so excited buying school supplies. We bought different-colored notebooks and planners and folders and it was so exciting to think that this was the year that I would organize everything. Every year though, by the time late September rolled around, everything had already fallen apart.

64 Related Disorders

I know that it affected me socially as well. I wanted to be reading the books my friends were talking about but my attentional issues made it difficult to learn to read. All of my friends were in advanced classes and I remember the great resentment I felt toward them. I knew somewhere inside of myself that I was just as smart as they were but this thing was keeping me back and I didn't really know what it was. I felt inferior and even though I did kind of know that I was as smart as my friends were, I really didn't feel very smart or very good about myself. I just never felt like I was quite good enough.

At one point in high school they had set up a meeting with me and all of my teachers where all of them had to sign off and make comments about my work. I remember that one of the teachers said, "she has great ideas and she creates these long papers but they have too many ideas on one paper." I know that was frustrating for all of us. I remember I had multiple meetings with my counselors and they always told me the same thing. They would always say that I really had to get it together. I would try, and I would keep on trying but I could just never seem to get things done right. Not being able to finish things was frustrating and upsetting and it definitely did not make me happy.

I know that I've always had a problem losing things and not being able to keep track of things and staying organized. Keeping on top of stuff is half of what makes you successful in school. I didn't know how to do it on my own and no one ever taught me how to stay organized but still I loved the idea of a fresh start every year. My dad had this massive obsession with buying me planners every year and would find me these giant and wonderful planners but no one ever sat down with me and told me the things that I actually needed to do in order to be organized and use those planners effectively. There was no outreach for specifics.

I had a 504 but all I got was extra time. It made a really big difference with tests but it only made a difference when I could actually remember to study for those tests, which was not very frequently. It got so that I would hide assignments from my dad because I was doing so poorly. At the time, they were posting assignments and grades online and I would lie to my parents about it so that they wouldn't know how badly I was doing. I was always scrambling. The majority of my education was scrambling. If someone would have sat me down and said, "here is how to fix these things" it would probably have helped a lot. If someone would have sat me down and said, "this is how to flesh out your ideas and go beyond an initial thesis," that would probably have helped a lot too. I know that I was overwhelmed. I couldn't tell what was important from what was not so important; everything seemed equally important, which made it hard to figure out what to do first. I still have one of my old history books and when you open it up, you can see that every line is highlighted in some of the chapters. I guess it makes sense to shut down when you feel so overwhelmed.

In college, my first year, even though I was full of anxiety, I did really well. I wanted to prove that I could be successful. Sophomore and junior year, however, fell apart quickly. I wouldn't feel like I could go to class until I completely finished everything and then I would forget to do things and when I couldn't finish it all, I would just avoid class until it became a huge vicious cycle. I also signed up for huge course loads but saving 40 pages of essays to write until the day before is not doable or healthy. I also did not know that I could have taken my 504 with me to college. No one told me that I could have done that but I was so embarrassed about having one I might not have done it anyway. It was a hard thing to live with in high school and no one talked about it so I didn't know anyone else who had one. I probably should have brought the 504 with me into college. I'm sure it would have helped.

Even now, planning things is a scary thing to me. I feel like I need to plan out my whole life but I am back in school now and I have a mentor who helps guide me and keep me on track. I have to answer to her and she gives me guidance and that really helps. I know that it is not completely under control. I still have issues like when we came back from vacation or after we moved, it is really hard to get back into a routine but having someone to report to weekly is really helpful. I have to talk to her and let her know what I have done and she tells me what she expects.

In general, I have a hard time keeping track of things. I can walk into a room and can't remember why I went into it. I've lost my wallet twice this past year and lost 4 hours at the DMV because of it. In high school, I got into a fender bender when I forgot that my foot was on the brake and I just let it slip off. I wasn't on my phone, there was no radio playing. I just forgot. I am sure that this makes the people around me feel like they have to keep track of things for me. I don't want them to take on that responsibility so I am trying to get into the habit of having a specific place for everything and I am trying to keep things in order. I don't want to feel like I am always frustrating the people around me.

What Are Some Symptoms of Executive Function Disorder?

- Difficulty making plans
- Difficulty keeping track of time
- Difficulty keeping track of more than one thing at a time
- Inability to finish work on time
- Difficulty planning long-range projects

66 Related Disorders

- Difficulty communicating details sequentially
- Difficulty with memorizing and retrieval
- Difficulty starting tasks

(Semrud-Clikeman, Pliszka, & Liotti, 2008)

What Helps Someone With Executive Function Disorder?

- Step-by-step instructions
- Routines
- Prior access to contents of lesson
- Frequent checks for understanding
- Clear and concise directions, given one step at a time
- To-do lists/checklists
- Chunking information into smaller bits
- Speech-to-text software
- Breaking large goals into smaller parts
- Timers for planned breaks
- Planners
- Direct instruction in the use of organizational materials
- Rewards
- Mnemonic devices

References

National Center for Learning Disabilities. (2005). Executive function fact sheet. *Retrieved, 8*(15). Retrieved from www.ldonline.org/article/24880/

Semrud-Clikeman, M., Pliszka, S. R., & Liotti, M. (2008). Executive functioning in children with attention-deficit/hyperactivity disorder: Combined type with and without a stimulant medication history. *Neuropsychology (Journal), 22*(3), 329–340. https://doi.org/10.1037/0894-4105.22.3.329

Skogli, E. W., Teicher, M. H., Andersen, P., Hovik, K. T., & Øie, M. (2013). ADHD in girls and boys—gender differences in co-existing symptoms and executive function measures. *BMC Psychiatry, 13*(1), 298–298. https://doi.org/i: 10.1186/1471-244X-13-298

Willcutt, E. G., Doyle, A. E., Nigg, J. T., Faraone, S. V., & Pennington, B. F. (2005). Validity of the executive function theory of attention-deficit/hyperactivity disorder: A meta-analytic review. *Biological Psychiatry, 57*(11), 1336–1346.

11

MEMORY ISSUES

In this part:

- What are working and short-term memory issues?
- What is it like to have working and or short-term memory issues?
- What are some symptoms of working end or short-term memory issues?
- What might help someone with working and short-term memory issues?

Memory is composed of multiple moving parts, and these different kinds of memory are interconnected. The dependence these interconnected parts have on each other is an important component of learning. A breakdown in one aspect can have serious effects on any or all of the others. The ability to keep information readily accessible for new learning (working memory) can affect the ability to integrate new tasks later on (Learning Disabilities Association, 2018). Therefore, memory issues, although not directly viewed as learning disorders, can have serious and detrimental effects on learning at all levels.

Working Memory

What Are Working Memory Issues?

Working memory is the part of memory that holds information briefly in order to learn new things. It is the ability to hold onto little chunks of information until that information is able to turn into a complete concept. The briefly stored memory may eventually become part of long-term memory, but the brief hold of it allows us to engage in daily activities, such as following directions or driving, successfully. Students and adults with working

68 Related Disorders

memory issues have a difficult time following a sequence of directions and following through on tasks (Cowan, 2008; Holmes, Gathercole, & Dunning, 2010; Rosen, 2018). The working memory deficit makes it difficult if not impossible to hold onto the separate little chunks of information that later become the whole of learning. For example, a student with a working memory deficit who is learning the alphabet may have difficulty remembering the individual sounds that the letters represent and may therefore have a delay in learning how to read later on.

Working memory issues affect approximately 15% of children. More than 80% of these children struggle to learn in both reading and mathematics. There is some evidence to suggest that this group of children has academic difficulties which do not typically get identified for special education intervention. These children may have issues with sustaining attention, solving problems and planning for long- or short-range projects or goals. These students may benefit from direct interventions in the classroom and direct working memory interventions (Holmes et al., 2010).

What Is It Like to Have Working Memory Issues?

Name: Josh
Age: 21
Age at diagnosis: 19
Career: College student. Studying software development

I remember that in 2nd grade they taught us using a program where we learned multiplication tables and I could not get my head around it. I couldn't get the rudiments down fast enough. Everyone else went past it at lightning speed and I just did not have the fundamentals down. Of course, from there came the more complex math and because I had missed those fundamentals, everything just got harder and harder. I think that part of the problem was that I was in the advanced academic program since kindergarten. Even though I had a lot of anxiety even back then, especially about not being good at math, they continued me on that track anyway which was not especially helpful. I remember that I insisted that I just couldn't do math, which was probably just the tip of the iceberg for my working memory issues, but no one really explored it. They just kept telling me that I could do math, that I was really smart and that I just had to keep trying. At the very least, this was frustrating, but mostly it was anxiety inducing.

I also remember in first grade when we were learning to read more complex things, I wanted to be reading further ahead of where I was. My brain was ready for more but since my working memory was lagging, it was just not coming together. I remember going to my teacher in tears

Memory Issues **69**

and saying, "I can't read" and the teacher said, "Yes you can," but it wasn't that I couldn't read. It was that I knew that I wanted to know more but I couldn't get what I wanted out of the books I was reading. I wasn't catching on to reading as quickly as I wanted to, or based at least on what everyone was telling me, as quickly as I should have been. Once I gained the knowledge I needed to read more, I moved ahead but it was the absorbing that gave me a lot of stress. New material did not jump to me as easily as old material did. As I found out when I got my psych testing done a few years ago, there is a significant difference between my processing speeds and my other skills.

I had a lot of moments that I was really anxious about not being able to do things as well as I would have liked. I would tell my teachers and they would respond with "but look how much you have done already." It was a point of serious frustration. Everyone else would learn much more quickly but when I finally got it, I ran with it. I was an above-average kid learning at a below-average pace and because I couldn't articulate that to anyone, my frustration just continued to grow.

In terms of organization, there is some disconnect between my willingness to be organized, my understanding of what it means to be organized and my implementation of it. I would start off great, but my grades usually fell toward the end of the year. There were assignments I would not do because of the anxiety about my slow learning. This was around the time that a narrative started about me from both my parents and my teachers. Basically, the narrative was that I didn't care about learning unless I found things interesting. The truth was that it was anxiety based. The interesting things were the things that were easier to learn. The things that I claimed were not interesting were just the things I found difficult. My parents did not help because they used the narrative to allow me to think that I was smarter than all of my teachers and administrators. This only helped to reinforce and reproduce the faulty narrative that had already been put into place.

In middle school, by the time I was in 7th grade, I did not want to deal with the advanced math classes anymore. I got called lazy and I was proud to be lazy. I never thought I was stupid, I just thought I was inept or not able to do things. I just thought I couldn't do skills—I couldn't absorb them as fast as other people. Eventually, I fell out of the advanced track because I was not able to stay focused. At this point, I became completely socially focused and not really engaged in school at all. It was a willful disengagement. There was a part of me that knew that I was pretending that I was making a choice to be disengaged. That part of me knew that pretending not to care was better than admitting or doing things that were actually hard to do. There were some classes I was doing well in like languages, history and science. As long as it was not math based, I found the classes to be interesting.

70 Related Disorders

By the time I got to high school, the picture got additionally clouded because of my home situation. My dad passed away, I had a disabled older sister who was also having a difficult time and there was just general dysfunction at home. All of that overshadowed the fact that I was having real learning problems. At school, I did minimal work and had started to develop a casual approach to cheating. There were no consequences for it at home so what difference did it make? But now, in high school, it had much more of an impact. I was being called out in class and teachers were much less lenient. Before that point, they had been much more understanding, I would copy peers' work and do a lot of not doing anything and it started to have a more serious impact. In the beginning of high school, I really did want to succeed but that only lasted as long as things did not become too difficult. My working memory kept me from being able to learn as quickly as I needed to in high school and it just made me more and more disengaged. People kept bringing up my lack of organizational skills and the narrative then became "he is lazy." I knew what I had to do to stay organized, I knew that being organized would help me academically, but I just could not do it. People kept trying to teach me how to keep my folders and my backpack and my locker organized but no one really dove into why this was happening. They just kept trying to teach me these skills that I already knew but I just could not implement, and it turned me off.

At this point, I was having a lot of trouble at home. I was fighting with my siblings and getting into trouble everywhere and I ended up in a treatment program for troubled youth. I stayed there for about 15 weeks and from there, I went straight to a residential treatment center in Utah that also had an academic program. I did my work there despite having several fits of intense anxiety about math. I did it anyway because, in this place at least, I was scared of the consequences. At home I was never scared of consequences. In treatment, my issue with math was overshadowed by everything else and was pushed out of the way by the consequences. Since the consequences mattered, I did my work. I was there for 1½ years. It did help but not as much as the first program did. Residential treatment was a place to be because I couldn't go back home at that point. It did manage to improve my self-image and I was able to see that I could get my work done. It was empowering because I had to do all kinds of things like snowboarding and mountain biking that I hated but I did anyway. I get choked up in the idea that people there were proud of me. The recreational director saw me struggle with the things he made me do, like snowboarding and mountain biking. I hated every minute of it and was bad at it but did it anyway. The fact that he saw me struggle and never said anything other than he was proud of me was powerful. He saw me for who I was and supported me anyway. It was incredible.

Memory Issues **71**

I did get academic credits from the wilderness program but there were things there that I did not want to do. Up until then, I had been empowered by my parents to not have to do things that I thought were dumb but there, they kicked my ass about stuff like that. Tough love to a high degree helped me in that case. I could not run away from things there.

After that, I got sent to a boarding school and did my work except for in precalc. I started off okay because it started with a review of things that I already knew but after the review everything started to slide downhill. I didn't know what I was doing and I didn't ask for help. It moved so fast and I felt like I was so slow in that class. When I was with people who could explain it to me at a pace that I could understand, I did great. The problem was that since my working memory was impaired and I was slow to learn these things, I was scared to ask the questions I needed to ask because I was scared that I would slow the class down. Since I didn't ask the questions I needed to ask, I didn't do well. Since math is cumulative, the worse I did, the more I was lost so the more I did not ask questions. My teacher decided to interpret my behavior as being disengaged and he had a hard time dealing with that. Early on, he started refusing to answer the few questions that I did ask and that just continued a cycle that led to my actually becoming disengaged.

There was continuous fallout from all of this and I started to just not do my work. The working opinion was that I was lazy and did not see things as valuable. But I did see things as valuable and I wasn't lazy. It was just hard. Things that did not require a lot of new learning came easily to me. Like stats, which I took and loved even though everyone else was way apathetic about it.

By the time I got to senior year, I had finally found my peer group. Finally, everyone had the senioritis that I had all along. Lazy became the narrative. I did see the counselor on campus. But she was bad and we did not talk about academics at all. Mostly we discussed my other issues. To her credit though there were so many other issues that it was probably kind of difficult to deal with all of them at the same time.

When it came time to start thinking about college, I was at a standstill. My mom and I kept talking about trade school, but I really didn't want to think that I could not go to college. I ended up going to a college that my headmaster recommended. It was the only school that I applied to. My headmaster actually drove me up there and introduced me to the people at the school and I figured that since he thought I was worthwhile enough to do this for, I should go there. So that is where I went. I ended up in Boston and I was holding on and prioritized my work for a while but then fell apart for emotional issues. I left there and now I go to community college. I still have working memory issues and at times it feels as if it is somewhat willful because I start with the full intent of doing something and then I get distracted.

72 Related Disorders

About 2 years ago I went and had psychological testing done. That is when I found out that I had these working memory issues. The testing showed that I scored highly in every other area but working memory and processing skills. There is a significant discrepancy. It makes me feel like I am stupid when I am presented with something new. I never had an IEP or a 504 because I didn't even know that there was anything wrong until so recently.

I think that it would have been great to have someone to push me along when I was younger. When I would get my work done when I was really little, my parents sat with me and "helped" me—it was just them sitting there but it made me do my work. Having someone sit there with me doing nothing but poking me to make sure I'm still working is really helpful. Providing me with a "not tutor" would have been great. I never wanted a tutor and never advocated to have one but in hindsight, it would have been good to have it forced on me. When I was forced to do things, I was able to get them done. If at any point, one of my counselors or teachers would have tried to understand me better it would have helped. It probably would have averted a lot of behavioral and academic issues. If I had felt that I was capable I might not have felt so insecure. Everything I did was a symptom but no one ever caught on to that.

What Are Some Symptoms of Working Memory Issues?

- Quiet affect in large groups
- Inattention and distraction
- Issues with executive function
- Difficulty with planning
- Problem-solving difficulties
- Issues with sustaining attention
- Trouble with following through on directions even if the directions are understood
- Difficulty with multiple-step math calculations
- Word problem difficulties
- Reading comprehension issues
- Writing composition difficulties
- Difficulty with higher order thinking tasks

(Holmes et al., 2010; Kail & Hall, 2001)

What Helps Someone With Working Memory Issues?

- Compensatory strategy instruction
- Written sequential steps for problem solving

Memory Issues **73**

- Written schedules
- Connecting new ideas to older and more familiar ones
- Chunking information into smaller segments
- Extra time for review
- Extra academic support for new learning tasks
- Modeling steps
- Checking for understanding

Short-Term Memory

What Are Short-Term Memory Issues?

Short-term memory issues are problems with retention of information that is only needed for a short period of time (Learning Disabilities Association, 2018). This kind of information, such as the recollection of a verbal telephone number, can be held for a short time or can be repeated and committed to memory to be accessed through long-term memory. Short-term memory is different from working memory in that it is just one component of working memory (Baddeley, 1966). Working memory is more about the entire process of taking pieces of information and converting them into learning. Short-term memory, however, refers to the process of short-term storage of information. This information could be temporary or could become incorporated into long-term memory as well. Students with short-term memory issues will have difficulty learning new concepts if there is a deficit in short-term memory (Gathercole, Hitch, & Martin, 1997).

What Is It Like to Have Short-Term Memory Issues?

Name: John
Age: 20
Age at diagnosis: middle school
Career: College student

My short-term memory issues definitely affect me. I will have someone tell me something and I instantly forget it. I don't really remember a lot of things from elementary school but I remember that in middle school it affected me in socializing. People would be talking and I would forget what they just mentioned and I would get embarrassed bringing it up again. I didn't want anyone to feel like I wasn't listening, so I would shut down and stay to myself. Middle school was better than elementary but it was still hard.

In high school and beyond, things started to evolve. I was more in tune with my issues. I don't think I was as afraid to ask about what just had

74 Related Disorders

happened, so I wasn't as isolated. There are still instances where I prefer to be by myself in social situations. A lot of times when people around me are talking about things and I can't contribute, I'll just listen but not know what they are talking about.

In college things are much better. Last semester there was one class where the teacher would not write things on the board and I had some difficulty. Luckily, she talked slowly so I had time to write it down. Usually if there is something I don't catch I will ask someone else, so I make sure to get everything I need. In terms of self-advocacy, I've been able to get rid of the embarrassment. It is much easier to advocate for yourself when you are not embarrassed. Now that I've come to terms with it, I am able to cope with it. I will let my professors know about my deficits in a meeting at the beginning of class. I find that they understand but it helps when I explain it to them in order to give them a better idea. I think that the professors are pretty open to what I have to say and they are willing to help me in any way that they can.

I think that the best thing that any teacher or counselor in a high school can do is to try their best to understand what these kids are going through. I think that if you truly understand what someone is going through that is the best way to help them.

What Are Some Symptoms of Short-Term Memory Issues?

- Difficulties in speech and language
- Difficulties with multistep math problems
- Difficulty remembering what was just heard

(Alexander, 2004)

What Can Help Someone With Short-Term Memory Issues?

- Lists/checklists
- Calendars
- Mnemonic devices
- Open-note or -book exams
- Multisensory teaching approach
- Use of computers
- Routines and habits
- Repetition

References

Alexander, T. (2004). *Memory/recall difficulties*. Retrieved from https://scips.worc.ac.uk/challenges/memory/

Baddeley, A. D. (1966). Short-term memory for word sequences as a function of acoustic, semantic and formal similarity. *Quarterly Journal of Experimental Psychology, 18*(4), 362–365. https://doi.org/10.1080/14640746608400055

Cowan, N. (2008). What are the differences between long-term, short-term, and working memory? *Progress in Brain Research, 169*, 323–338. https://doi.org/10.1016/S0079-6123(07)00020-9

Gathercole, S. E., Hitch, G. J., & Martin, A. J. (1997). Phonological short-term memory and new word learning in children. *Developmental Psychology, 33*(6), 966.

Holmes, J., Gathercole, S. E., & Dunning, D. L. (2010). Poor working memory: Impact and interventions. *Advances in Child Development and Behavior, 39*, 1–43.

Kail, R., & Hall, L. (2001). Distinguishing short-term memory from working memory. *Memory and Cognition, 29*(1), 1–9.

Learning Disabilities Association. (2018). *Memory*. Retrieved from https://ldaamerica.org/types-of-learning-disabilities/memory/

Rosen, P. (2018). *Working memory: What it is and how it works*. Retrieved from www.understood.org/en/learning-attention-issues/child-learning-disabilities/executive-functioning-issues/working-memory-what-it-is-and-how-it-works

PART 4

Our Role as Counselors

12
OUR ROLE

A few years back, one of my interns and I were sitting together at our weekly review session, and we began a discussion about the concept of goals. It was early May, and she had been working with one of our more worrisome students at the time, a bright young woman who, although on the path toward graduating on time, had not yet committed to any plans for September. My intern was focused on getting her to commit to goals. Jokingly, I said to her, "Well, it's okay because at least your goal here is achieved." She looked at me quizzically and I said, "She's graduating. Isn't our goal as counselors to get them out of here with a diploma? Isn't that what she's doing?" At the time, I was just trying to add levity to a very serious discussion. What occurred instead was an opening into a discussion of what our roles as counselors really were. What are our intentions and our goals in our interactions with our students? What are our roles? Do our goals and intentions match our roles?

On a general level, our roles as counselors are easy to talk about. The American School Counselor Association tells us that our role as high school counselors is to:

provide equitable and appropriate services by addressing students' academic, career and social/emotional developmental needs in addition to balancing delivery methods, recognizing students learn in multiple ways. The end result of this work is reflected in improvement in academic, attendance and behavioral outcomes related to academic development, college and career readiness and social/emotional development.

(ASCA, 2017)

80 Our Role as Counselors

We are supposed to provide both direct and indirect services including, instruction, groups, advisement, counseling, referrals, crisis response and consultation. We are supposed to address our students' academic, emotional, career and social needs. When we translate this into the language of working with our students with learning disabilities, the directive is quite clear. We are supposed to be providing "equitable and appropriate services." The 2016 revision of the ASCA position paper on students with special needs states the following:

> *The school counselor takes an active role in student achievement and postsecondary planning by providing a comprehensive school counseling program for all students. As a part of this program, school counselors advocate for students with special needs, encourage family involvement in their child's education and collaborate with other educational professionals to promote academic achievement, social/emotional wellness and college/career readiness for all.*
>
> *(ASCA, 2016)*

In order to help our students with learning disabilities move toward successful transitions to college, we need to begin with a firm understanding of the learning disabilities and related disorders that were covered in the previous section. With this understanding in place, it becomes easier to understand that our role in the college process for students with learning disabilities may be different than our role in the process for students without learning disabilities. Students with learning disabilities, for example, might need us to guide them through special education classes to make sure that the classes that they are taking will allow them to be eligible for college. These students might also need us to guide them toward accessing services through the office of disability services at their colleges or to help them access assistive technology. They may need our help to understand their IEPs or to recognize their challenges and strengths. They may need us to help them decrease their modifications or to explain the difference between an IEP (which they get in high school) and a 504 (which they get in college). They may need us to work with them on developing self-advocacy, or they may ask us to help them find specific programs or specialized colleges that are suited to their needs. As counselors, we are sometimes the last possible stop for this information before they move on, and as counselors, we need to be able to give them this knowledge that they so desperately need.

The push toward getting students with learning disabilities into college has been successful. More and more students with learning disabilities are attending college, but of these students, only 35% of them even inform their colleges of their disabilities (Newman & Madaus, 2014). These students are not accessing services which they so desperately need, and it shows; students with learning disabilities graduate college at almost half the rate of students without learning disabilities (Cortiella & Horowitz, 2014). Given these statistics, these students are coming to us with a definite need, and we have to be able to be knowledgeable enough to help and guide them with the same efficacy we use when we help and guide our students without disabilities.

References

ASCA. (2016). *The school counselor and students with disabilities*. American School Counselor Association. Retrieved from www.schoolcounselor.org/asca/media/asca/PositionStatements/PS_Disabilities.pdf

ASCA. (2017). *Why high school counselors?* American School Counselor Association. Retrieved from www.schoolcounselor.org/asca/media/asca/Careers-Roles/WhyHighSchool.pdf

Cortiella, C., & Horowitz, S. H. (2014). *The state of learning disabilities: Facts, Trends and emerging issues*. New York: National Center for Learning Disabilities.

Newman, L., & Madaus, J. (2014). Reported accommodations and supports provided to secondary and postsecondary students with disabilities: National perspective. *Career Development and Transition for Exceptional Individuals*, *38*(3), 173–181. https://doi.org/doi:10.1177/2165143413518235

13

WHAT COUNSELORS NEED TO KNOW ABOUT WORKING WITH THE CHILD STUDY TEAM

In this part:
- Working with the child study team
- Attending IEP meetings
- Understanding our different goals
- Working together
- Documentation

Our students with learning disabilities have the wonderful advantage of having multiple supports and advocates within their school day. They have us, their school counselors, but they also have a case manager and an entire child study team standing behind them as well. These members of the child study team are tasked with the awesome responsibility of evaluating, assessing, writing and overseeing implementation of the individual educational plans (IEPs) for all students who are classified as having disabilities within the school. They work tirelessly to create the most appropriate program for these students while still staying within the confines of the law and district budgets, and this is certainly no small task. Timelines have to be adhered to, reports have to be written, meetings have to he held and students' needs must be addressed, all within a specific framework of time. These are the people who understand the special education system, and they are an integral part of the academic process for students with disabilities. Together, child study team members and school counselors are the weft and warp of the programming that makes up the academic day for students with learning disabilities. We each come from our respective disciplines with different expertise and different skills, but we are each equal partners in the process of learning for these students.

Working With the Child Study Team **83**

Attending IEP Meetings

As counselors, it becomes very important to have a positive and working relationship with the members of the child study team in order to be able to give our students a complete and seamless route toward success. Since each discipline has something specific to bring to the table, it makes sense that we should work hand in hand to guide the students that we share. In my school, each counselor attends each IEP meeting for each one of their students. It is not mandated that we be there; we are there because it gives a venue for collaboration and dialogue. We know that it is important for everyone to work together to help the student transition to the next place as seamlessly as possible, so we make it a point to take advantage of those invitations for a seat at the table. Unfortunately, from conversations with other counselors in other districts, we've learned that we are somewhat of an anomaly. With too many other responsibilities and far too much to do to fit into a day, an invitation to an IEP meeting that does not need to be attended is sometimes the last thing a school counselor will place importance on. The opportunities for dialogue become more and more infrequent, and school counselors and child study teams seem to continue to live on separate islands.

The best way to understand and to help a student with a learning disability is to have a combination of an understanding of learning disabilities, a knowledge of the student, a knowledge of how to read reading and understand the IEP and, importantly and often neglected, a presence at the student's IEP meetings. Counselors are not required to attend IEP meetings, but these meetings can provide invaluable insight for the counselor across multiple realms.

In order to understand the benefit of attending IEP meetings, it is important to understand the structure of the meetings themselves. IEP meetings are held at least annually to review the student's progress and update the academic program as necessary based on that progress. Every IEP meeting discusses present performance, goals and objectives and what services will be provided. In addition, if the student is up for their triannual reevaluation and testing has been re-administered, the results of the reevaluation are discussed as well. There are guidelines about who must attend IEP meetings, but generally, those in attendance are the parent, the child (if it is determined that attendance is in the best interest of the child), a general education teacher, a special education teacher and a member of the child study team.

The insight that we gain about the student by sitting in on these meetings is invaluable. The IEP meeting is one of the very few times when multiple and important stakeholders in a child's education get to sit around a table and discuss the student in detail all at the same time. At these meetings, we have the opportunity to hear how the parent views the child's progress, how the teachers view the child's progress and how the child themselves views their progress. It is a rare opportunity to explore what might be gaps in these

84 Our Role as Counselors

pieces of information. Exploring these gaps with the student later on may help us give them more effective insight into themselves and their academic path. Conversely, this information could lead to more informed conversations with the student's teachers as well.

If psychological and educational testing is done and the results are discussed at the meeting, this information too is helpful to the counselor. Getting a glimpse of quantifiable levels of intelligence, achievement or processing speed can give counselors insight into what may be at the root of their specific academic issues or what may or may not be realistic goals for their students. If, for example, a teacher complains that a student never answers questions in class and we know from the testing that their processing speed is significantly lower than their intelligence, we can advocate more effectively for that student by explaining this fact to the teacher. We can also use this information later on when we are working with them toward college accommodations by reminding them to request the extra time that they will need. The danger with these tests though, is great. Although the test (and other tests like it) are acceptable tools in assessment, they should never be used in isolation. Children are much more than their scores, and one or two tests, in isolation from any other form of assessment, could give an incomplete or inaccurate picture of the student. When used holistically, in conjunction with a myriad of other forms of assessment, it can be a helpful and useful tool for the counselor and other educators (Sattler, Dumont, & Coalson, 2016).

In addition to using the information that is discussed at the meeting to better help the student, these meetings also allow us to cultivate a relationship with the student's case manager. Partnering with the members of the child study team is a win/win situation all around. The student wins by having a true multidisciplinary team on their side with expertise in all aspects of their plan. The child study team wins by having an extra person with a different kind of knowledge about the student becoming a part of the planning process, and the counselor wins by learning about the student's specific academic needs, which can then be used to make more informed and appropriate decisions about their educational goals and plans.

Counselors, however, should not just be silently sitting back and listening in an IEP meeting. The contributions that we can provide are unique to our positions as counselors and can enhance the entire structure of the IEP meeting itself. We are, for example, one of the very few individuals in the school who can truly and impartially advocate for our students (Erford & Erford, 2007). Teachers may have an isolated view of the student based on their behavior in the classroom, child study team members may be focused on the special education aspect of the meeting, and administrators (if they are present) may not have knowledge of the student at all. Counselors are trained to see a whole picture of a child and can be that impartial advocate that the student may need.

Working With the Child Study Team **85**

In addition, with the counselor's role in the school, the counselor may have insight into the personal and social factors that may impact the academic success of a student. If a teacher complains that the student does not hand in homework, the counselor may have knowledge of a home situation that precludes the student's ability to do work. The counselor, together with the case manager, can then put together a program for the child that takes all of this information into account and still allows the child to succeed academically.

Finally, as high school counselors, we have insight into the college process that child study team members do not have. Although the case manager will have a more thorough understanding of the disability and special education, the school counselor is the one with the knowledge of the college process and the expectations inherent in it. For our students with learning disabilities who plan on attending college, it is important that the goals and objectives in the IEP and discussed at the IEP meeting match the goal of attending college. For example, if at the IEP meeting it is discussed that the student would like to attend college but has been in out-of-class replacement classes with multiple modifications to their program, then this must be addressed at the IEP meeting. For a student like this, either the program would have to change so that the student starts to experience fewer and fewer modifications in preparation for college, or there needs to be a reevaluation of goals and future aspirations. In either case, the IEP meeting is the correct venue to have these discussions. In many cases, the child study team members may not know what kinds of high school coursework might be needed for college attendance. A counselor's presence at these meetings could redirect programming if needed in order to make sure that the student who might want to attend college will have all the necessary coursework to be eligible.

Understanding Our Different Goals

Another issue that arises from this disconnect between the two disciplines is mired within the very different roles that each professional plays in the life of the student and within the school. Typically, child study team members might be responsible for implementing IEPs, sharing that information with appropriate school personnel, conducting annual reviews, consulting with teachers and managing the emotional and social needs of the classified student. In addition to this, child study team members might also be responsible for helping students and families manage the transition from high school to post–high school programs. This transition planning is typically focused on students who may have more severe developmental issues and more intensive programming needs. These students may need long-term planning care or may have to be admitted to vocational training programs. The transition planning that the child study team usually does is not focused on college or university planning. For this type of planning, the responsibility is frequently

86 Our Role as Counselors

left to the counselor, who is assumed to be the expert in college and university planning. This is the point at which a gap seems to open. Child study team members have knowledge about learning disabilities, appropriate accommodations and possibly even about assistive technology, but they do not usually have extensive knowledge about the college process. High school counselors, on the other hand, do have extensive knowledge about the college process but may not have extensive knowledge about learning disabilities and the unique needs of the students who have them. The gap is at that point in the middle of where the child study team expertise ends and the school counselor expertise begins. Child study teams understand and help to set up the accommodations that "level the playing field" for these students in high school. High school counselors, while helping these students move toward college, may have very little sense of what these students may need to succeed on the postsecondary level. The students are left in a situation in which their child study team makes sure that their needs are met in high school, and school counselors make sure that, if their plans include college, they are prepared to go, but no one seems to put the two of those things together. There is little appreciation for the unique needs of these students as they move forward in their education, and many of them enter college without even knowing that many of their accommodations could have (and should have) followed them (Snyder & Dillow, 2012).

Creating a functional system that utilizes both areas of expertise begins with understanding that the specific goals of the child study team are inherently different than the goals of high school counselors. The goals of the child study team center around providing special education services and complying with the law. High school counselors, although bound by the ethical standards of our profession, do not have the same legal obligations that are the crux of special education. This is not to say that our jobs are any less difficult. Our jobs are equally stressful and equally fulfilling, but unless we understand that many decisions that are made about students by child study team members are based on complying with the law, it is sometimes difficult to find a neutral meeting ground. A functional system must start from the space of respecting and understanding what each discipline does and finding the bridge between both worlds in the fact that we are all here exclusively to help our students succeed.

Working Together

For our students with learning disabilities to get the most comprehensive and appropriate services, child study team members and school counselors must be able to have an ongoing dialogue from the beginning about what is in the best interest of the student. For example, at a recent IEP meeting, my student, a ninth grader, expressed his intent to attend a 4-year college.

His mother, who was also at the meeting, agreed that a 4-year college was the optimal choice for him. At this point, the student was in an out-of-class replacement class for math and getting straight A's. This was a major breakthrough for him since he had been having anxiety about his math performance for many years, and it translated into frequent failing grades in that area. His other academic classes were all in-class-support classes in which he was also doing very well. He also expressed interest in dropping out of his Spanish class for his sophomore year. The potential plan, at that point, was to keep him in the out-of-class replacement class in math for the coming year in order to help him to continue to feel good about his math skills. This particular case manager and I had been working closely together for several years, so our knowledge bases, at this point, just naturally intertwined. When I expressed concern about the program plan that was being discussed for him for the coming year, she gave me the space and respect to speak freely in the meeting. I started by informing the student and the mother that most colleges require at least 2 years of a foreign language. They needed to know that dropping the Spanish class after only 1 year might potentially put him at risk for not having all of the necessary requirements for entering college. The case manager and I, together, also encouraged him to understand that although it might be uncomfortable to come out of the in-class-resource environment and that his grades might even go down if he did, it was important to push himself so that he could grow as a student in order to prepare himself for college courses. We addressed the idea that since colleges do not offer out-of-class replacement classes or even in-class-resource classes, it is important for him to, if possible, make a plan to transition out of those classes completely by senior year. Finally, we spoke about standardized testing and had the family sign a waiver so we could apply to get extra time for his SAT/ACT testing. In this scenario, the case manager and I were able to put all of our knowledge about the student and our respective disciplines together in a way that maximized the information that this family and this student needed to know.

Documentation

Another important area to keep in mind for dialogue between child study teams and school counselors is about accessing disability services once the student is accepted to a college. Most schools will not be able to register a student with a learning disability into the office of disability services without the appropriate documentation. This means that although a student would be accepted to college and be able to attend, they would not be eligible for accommodations unless the appropriate documentation was provided to the school. From the counselor's perspective, it is important to understand how this works so that we can best advise our students.

88 Our Role as Counselors

Typically, a reevaluation by the child study team is done every 3 years, but it does not always have to include the battery of tests. If there is enough evidence to support continued special education services without having to retest, then the retesting does not actually need to be done. This means that if a student was last reevaluated in eighth grade, they will have to be reevaluated again in 11th grade. In that 11th-grade reevaluation, if the team sees fit to reevaluate without retesting, that student will continue to get special education services from the school for what may be the rest of their high school career. This sounds great in theory since the student continues to be supported, but in reality, if the student is planning on going to college and will need continued accommodations, then the lack of testing can actually become a detriment and a hindrance in their ability to access services on a postsecondary level. An IEP alone may not usually be enough documentation for accessing services. Many offices of disability services on college campuses require a recent (1–4 years, but it can vary) educational and psychological evaluation in addition to the IEP for receiving services. The most common tests that these schools require are as follows:

For aptitude and cognitive ability:

- Wechsler Adult Intelligence Scale (WAIS)
- Woodcock–Johnson—Tests of Cognitive Ability

For academic achievement:

- Woodcock–Johnson—Tests of Achievement
- Wechsler Individual Achievement Test (WIAT)

In order to make sure that our students with learning disabilities have all that they need for college and accessing services, we do need to make certain that parents are aware of these requirements and that these tests are administered, preferably sometime in their junior year. If a student does not get retested or gets retested with a test that is not normally accepted at postsecondary offices of disability services, some schools may not consider this as sufficient documentation to substantiate their need for services.

Child study team members may not be aware of the documentation requirements for accessing services, or they may disagree with testing for the sole purpose of providing documentation for later down the road. Testing is, after all, expensive and time consuming, and if the student could remain within special education services without having to use up the time and expense to retest, it is easy to understand why the testing would be neglected prior to the student graduating. In addition, many people believe that the responsibility for testing for post–high school planning should be on the family and not the school. The problem, however, is that no matter how true all of these things might be, private testing is exorbitantly expensive and can sometimes cost upward of $5,000 and is infrequently (if ever) covered by insurance. This cost is prohibitive for most families. In addition, many colleges would not look at private testing in isolation and would require some kind of documented history of a disability as well. Testing is also not typically provided by the colleges and universities either. The assumption from many colleges is that these students will be coming to them with a history of disability and testing that has already been done. This means that, in many cases, if the student does not get retested in high school, they will not be eligible for services in college and will be at much higher risk of not completing college.

Sometimes, child study teams opt not to retest a student because they believe that although the student should still receive support from special education, the testing might reveal that there is not enough of a discrepancy to warrant services any longer. In these instances, a team might choose to go with a functional assessment rather than the formal testing in order to justify continued services. Without the testing, however, even if the student will maintain the services in high school, the student may not have sufficient documentation for accessing services in some colleges. Although many colleges and universities will accept older testing and documentation or even no testing results at all, other schools may still request the more stringent documentation in order to consider eligibility. For these schools, the easiest and most seamless solution is that testing should be redone prior to the student graduating high school. If the testing is done and the discrepancy still exists, then there is no problem in any direction. The student will still receive services in high schools and will also still have the appropriate documentation for college services as well. If, however, the testing is done and there is not enough of a discrepancy to continue to qualify for special education, it is a little bit of a trickier issue. The fact that a student with a learning disability may have been remediated enough to be on par with their peers does not negate the fact that they may still need, at the very least, extra time to compensate for possible processing speed issues. Even though a student may have been remediated, their learning disability is a lifelong issue, and they may still need support. In this case, the student will no longer qualify for services in high school but may still qualify for services in college. Colleges do not typically use a discrepancy model and may look at the testing combined with the history of the learning disability and decide that this may be enough documentation to warrant services with the office of disability services on campus.

In terms of the rest of high school, though, this may be more of a problem. What typically happens in these cases is that the student is then offered a section 504 plan to take them through the rest of high school, but this is not always a solution. The problem with offering a 504 plan at this point is

90 Our Role as Counselors

based on a misunderstanding of what a 504 plan actually is. The 504 plan is not a step down from special education. It is not a natural progression from special education into general education. Section 504 is a plan that requires that all federally funded institutions and programs create accommodations for people with disabilities. 504 plans are available for all students from kindergarten to grade 12 and also for students in colleges and universities and beyond. Unlike special education, there is no funding for high school students under section 504, therefore, the accommodations that are available for these students are not as extensive as the ones offered under special education. In order for a student to be eligible for a 504 plan, there has to be some kind of disabling condition which has to have a substantial impact on one or more life activities. In addition, because the law is written in a way that leaves it open to interpretation (after all, what is a "substantial" impact?), some 504 teams may have a different view than others on what can substantiate granting a 504 plan. Many times, child study teams are not even involved in the 504 process, so they may not have an understanding of what might be necessary to document the need for a 504. There are times when students who are declassified are actually found ineligible for a 504. These students are then left with nothing to provide the accommodations they still may need while in high school. If a student has been remediated to the point of being perceived as not needing any more special education services, it is possible that they will not receive a 504, since there is little documentation of the learning disability's impact on life activities.

Many people might continue to question the need for services in postsecondary school or even in high school after declassification in high school. If a child has been declassified in high school and seems to still be showing success, why would they continue to need services in college anyway? The answer is that they may not. They may not need extra time or special tutoring or any special services at all. They may have been remediated to the point of not requiring anything, and if that is the case, that is wonderful. Unfortunately, that is not always the case. The student might be showing success because they have gotten used to the environment and found workarounds toward that success because of familiarity. Or the student may still be being given extra time or extra help by well-intentioned teachers. Or the student has found a group of supportive friends to help them on a regular basis. Regardless of what the reason is, while declassification may be appropriate in high school based on the legalities involved, it does not mean that the student will not continue to need supports, both in high school and beyond.

If the psychological and educational tests are not done a student with a learning disability who might still require some kind of services might have to find a creative solution to continue to get needed services in college. Without current testing, many colleges may not consider older testing enough to warrant services in college and this leaves a student who will always have a learning disability, in a position that seems to encourage failure. As a side note, even for students with a diagnosis of ADHD, some, but not all, colleges still require that psychoeducational testing still be done.

So, what are the options if our students fall into these categories? The possible solutions to these potential pitfalls lie in the unfortunate truth of comorbidity. For many students with learning disabilities and related disorders, there is also a high likelihood that they may have other comorbid conditions that also affect their academic, emotional and social functioning (Mammarella et al., 2014). Anxiety and depression in children with learning disabilities, for example, are far more prevalent than in children without learning disabilities. Despite the fact that the student's IEP may have been based on the learning disability, it does not negate the other forces at play in the child's emotional and educational health. The anxiety, depression, attentional issues (or whatever other comorbid conditions may be present) may have been having an impact on the student's educational functioning alongside the learning disability all along. Although they may not have been the main issue in the student's IEP, teachers, counselors and other school professionals may have been aware of these issues as the student progressed through school. As long as the comorbid condition can be verified and corroborated by educators and other professionals (such as psychologists, psychiatrists or other medical doctors), it could, potentially, become the basis of the 504. For students who do not get granted 504s for learning disabilities, basing the 504 on the comorbid condition allows the student to still access the services they will need. For students who may have been granted a 504 in high school, the reason for looking outside of the learning disability for the 504 is purely for documentation reasons. Issues such as anxiety and depression do not require psychological or educational testing in order to receive services from the office of disability services in college. For these types of conditions, a psychologist, neurologist, psychiatrist or other relevant medical doctor would provide a formal diagnosis. This diagnosis of the comorbid condition, rather than a diagnosis of a learning disability, in conjunction with the history of the condition, the history of the learning disability and whatever other input might be available, could be used as appropriate documentation for both the 504 and accessing services on the postsecondary level. Although legislation has been introduced to make it easier for postsecondary students to access services without the testing such as the RISE act (Casey, Hatch, & Cassidy, 2016), for the foreseeable future, the fact remains that students with learning disabilities who are trying to access services on a postsecondary level will most likely have to provide current educational and psychological testing. Until legislation actually changes and makes it less cumbersome and onerous for students with learning disabilities to document their disabilities, child study teams and high school counselors will have to continue to work in concert to find ways to help these children get what they will need to access curriculum in college.

92 Our Role as Counselors

References

Casey, B., Hatch, O., & Cassidy, B. (2016). *Respond, innovate, succeed, and empower act of 2016.* Retrieved from www.ncld.org/wp-content/uploads/2016/12/RISE-Act-Updated-Text-12.6.16.pdf

Erford, B. T., & Erford, B. T. (2007). *Transforming the school counseling profession.* Columbus, GA: Pearson Merrill, Prentice Hall.

Mammarella, I. C., Ghisi, M., Bomba, M., Bottesi, G., Caviola, S., Broggi, F., & Nacinovich, R. (2014). Anxiety and depression in children with nonverbal learning disabilities, reading disabilities, or typical development. *Journal of Learning Disabilities, 49*(2), 130–139. https://doi.org/10.1177/0022219414529336

Sattler, M., Dumont, R., & Coalson, L. (2016). *Assessment of children: WISC-V and WPPSI-IV.* San Diego: Jerome M. Sattler.

Snyder, T. D., & Dillow, S. A. (2012). *Digest of education statistics, 2011.* NCES 2012-001. National Center for Education Statistics.

14

WHAT COUNSELORS NEED TO KNOW ABOUT COLLEGE READINESS

In this part:

- College readiness
- Asking for academic help
- Understanding learning needs and study styles
- Understanding the difference between an accommodation and a modification
- Understanding the disability
- Knowing which accommodations work best
- Knowing how to study
- Being organized and self-motivated
- Being able to self-advocate
- Understanding the difference between an IEP and a 504
- Case study: college readiness

College Readiness

Having asked many students over many years what they believe "college readiness skills" actually are, I have heard a wide variety of answers. Some students tell me that college readiness skills are aligned with getting good grades in high school. Others tell me that college readiness skills have to do with their readiness to leave home and live away from their parents. Some tell me that college readiness is more of a mindset than a skill set. Regardless of what their answers are, the truth of college readiness is both concrete and abstract. It is based on the academic, social and emotional readiness for the challenges that college might bring. College readiness skills are the skills that college students need in order to meet the demands of college life and attend college successfully. Students with good college readiness skills will be more ready to work independently and responsibly, live on their own (if that is to be the case), manage their finances, maneuver new social situations and access help if they need it.

As counselors, we need to be aware of the fact that, for our students with learning disabilities, the notion of college readiness skills becomes that much more complicated. Whereas a student without a learning disability may still struggle once they reach college, a student with a learning disability may have additional aspects to that struggle. As an example, researchers have found that high school students' expectation of their first-year experiences in college do not frequently align with the reality they experience (Smith & Wertlieb, 2005). For students with learning disabilities, this discordance between their expectations and reality might wreak havoc with what may already have been a shaky self-esteem related to their ability and intelligence (Goleniowska, 2014). Therefore, the better prepared with college readiness skills our students with learning disabilities are, the higher the likelihood that they will be able to overcome the challenges that they may end up facing. As high school counselors, charged with the responsibility to nurture the academic, social and emotional well-being of all of our students (ASCA, 2017), it is important to remember that this is not a one-size-fits-all concept. Students with learning disabilities may have unique needs when it comes to college readiness skills, and high school counselors can be an important tool in helping these students assess and evaluate what they will need in order to be successful in college.

One way to assess a general concept of college readiness skills for our students with learning disabilities is to take a closer look at what the expectations of college life actually are. In college, students are expected to attend class, stay organized, manage their time well, take good notes, know how to study, know how to read a textbook and know how to take tests (UC Santa Cruz, 2016). In addition, some of the realities of college include the fact that:

- Classes may be multiple hours long
- Classes may have hundreds of students
- Classes may be taught by graduate students
- Classes may require that good notes be taken consistently
- Professors may not be interested in cultivating relationships with students
- Readings of several hundred pages may be assigned weekly
- Work is expected to be completed outside of classroom time and done independently
- Papers with works cited may be expected with frequency
- Papers will be expected to be well written
- Exams may be given infrequently and include an entire semester's worth of work

Although these expectations and realities should come as no surprise, many students with learning disabilities are not prepared to meet these expectations. This means that they are not prepared with college readiness skills and may be at risk for not succeeding in college. Therefore, our roles as high school counselors need to be aligned with helping these students garner as many college readiness skills as they can.

Asking for Academic Help

All students in college need to be prepared to ask for help if they need to access it. It is not a surprise that many students, both with learning disabilities and without, have a difficult time approaching professors and asking for help. The difference for students with learning disabilities is the fact that avoiding academic help may be based in the stigma of having a learning disability (Lyman et al., 2016). It is important, therefore, to help these students overcome the stigma of having a learning disability and find empowerment in getting the academic help they might need. Another reason students with learning disabilities may not be comfortable asking for academic help may be rooted in the help they may have been used to receiving in high school. In high school, the IEP states what the teachers must do to modify the curriculum or accommodate the student. Educators who do not abide by what the IEP dictates are actually breaking the law. The steps for helping the student may be laid out and obvious and may set up a scenario in which the student may not have to be responsible for assessing their own need for help. This could translate into a lack of awareness of even requiring assistance and could leave the student in a difficult and academically dangerous spot. In this case, it is important to encourage the student to practice asking for help before it is given.

Understanding Learning Needs and Study Styles

For students with learning disabilities, an understanding of how they study best and what they need in order to learn is essential. Since students with learning disabilities may have a more difficult time acquiring new knowledge, self-knowledge about how new information best gets integrated is of utmost importance. Helping students understand how they learn is as important as the learning itself. It is important to note that we are not talking about "learning styles" here. The idea of specific "learning styles" as a match toward effective teaching has been disproved again and again (Kirschner, 2017). Just because a student prefers to be taught in a kinesthetic manner does not mean that this is the most effective learning style for that student. In fact, in college, professors are not prone to assessing the learning needs of their students and adapting their teaching style to those needs. What the

96 Our Role as Counselors

term "learning needs" means in this context is completely student directed. Questions such as, "Do I need to record this lecture so I can listen to it at my own pace later?" or "Do I need to sit in the front of the class so I can sustain my attention," or "Do I need to write my notes on my laptop to make sure I can read them later?" are the kinds of questions students need to be encouraged to ask themselves in order to assess their learning needs.

Students should also be encouraged to explore what works best for them in terms of exploring study styles. Do they need total silence? Do they need music? Do they study better when they are surrounded by other people? Do they study better when they study with other people? These are the kinds of questions that students need to be able to ask themselves while they are still in high school. Counselors can encourage students to take some time to reflect and assess what does and does not work as their study style.

Understanding the Difference Between an Accommodation and a Modification

Many educators seem to use the terms "accommodation" and "modification" interchangeably, but the difference between these two terms is enormous. Understanding the difference between an accommodation and a modification (and helping students to understand this difference) is an important component of helping a student with learning disabilities transition to college.

An accommodation is a change to how a student accesses curriculum or assignments. It does not change the curriculum or academic expectations of the student in any way. Accommodations accommodate the students' learning disabilities and allow them access to a curriculum that they might not otherwise be able to access. For example, if a student has a reading disability with a slower processing speed, an accommodation for that student might be that they could access the reading material through a format other than written text and that they might have extra time to complete a test. Some common accommodations in college might be the use of assistive devices, books on tape, use of a computer, extended time or testing in a separate room, recording lectures, speech-to-text programs, text-to-speech programs or note takers. Since accommodations allow a student with a disability to access what might otherwise be inaccessible or inordinately difficult in comparison to their peers, accommodations help to avoid discriminating against students who have disabilities. Accommodations are a way of leveling the playing field so that access to the curriculum is equitable.

In contrast to accommodations, modifications actually do change the curriculum, assignments and academic expectations. Modifications modify existing programs. For example, a high school student who is not able to read at grade level but is in the tenth grade might be placed into a tenth-grade resource program which might require significantly less reading and writing assignments from the other students in that class. Tests might be modified to require less intensive responses than those expected from students in general education. Fewer questions might be asked on the test. Assignments might be modified so that the expectations of the student would actually be different than for students without these modifications. The assigned book may even be different. Modifications change the curriculum in concrete ways, and because of this, modifications for students with learning disabilities are never offered on college and university levels. The students on a college campus are all expected to learn the same information and do the same assignments. The curriculum, assignments and expectations for students in college are never altered.

For students with learning disabilities who are used to receiving modified tests, assignments or even whole classes, the fact that there are no modifications on the college level could be something of a shock. Counselors need to advise students early on about these kinds of expectations. Students who express interest in college need to be advised early that it is in their best interest to work toward diminishing and eventually doing away with any modifications in their program. Struggling in a course without modifications is inherently better preparation for the rigors of college than is getting straight A's in a modified program. Many colleges require placement tests prior to entrance to their programs. For students who do not meet the minimum requirements of the school, remedial courses, at a cost and with no credit attached, are required before the student can begin the entrance-level coursework. For students who have been in a resource room or have had modified course work in high school, there is a likelihood that they may not have acquired all of the necessary skills to pass these placement tests and may have to take these remedial courses several times over before they can begin their college curriculum.

Understanding the Disability

As counselors, we often find ourselves in the role of motivating our students to reach and do better. We are often the people who they come to for that push that they may need to sprint to the finish line. We do it, and we do it gladly because that is a big part of what the job is. What we may not be able to do as well is to help our students with learning disabilities with that same push.

It is sometimes astounding to me (although it happens far too frequently) when I meet with a student who has an IEP and does not understand or know the reason why they were given one to begin with. They may have no actual knowledge of their disability and may not understand at all why they might be in special classes. They may know that they have some trouble in school, but the specifics of it are a mystery to them.

98 Our Role as Counselors

When we meet with these students, part of helping them to acquire those college readiness skills involves giving them that same motivating push that we give to other students. The push that we need to give students with learning disabilities to help them acquire college readiness skills is the push that will lead them toward accepting and understanding their disability. Students who go to college with shame about their disability are much less apt to reach out to the office of disability services for the accommodations that they may need (Lyman et al., 2016), and these students have a much higher likelihood of not meeting success in college. Students who don't understand what their disability is will not be able to verbalize what their challenges are or what accommodations help them to manage these challenges. This puts these students at a disadvantage as well. Our role with these students is to push them toward an understanding and positive acceptance of their disability so that they will be able to ask for and receive what they need to learn and succeed. Helping these students to develop a sense of self-empowerment, helping them to lose shame over having a disability and helping them be able to understand themselves and their own needs in the process is at the core of this aspect of college readiness skills.

Knowing Which Accommodations Work Best

Once a student is able to understand and accept their disability, the next important college readiness skill is based on the student being able to assess what accommodations actually work for them. In this skill, there is an important aspect of self-knowledge that counselors are uniquely equipped to help students explore.

A student with a learning disability who has been given an IEP for much of their school career may not have had any need or even opportunities to assess for themselves what accommodations work best in helping them to learn and to study. For these students, it is important to help them explore the accommodations that they are already receiving and think about what else they might need later on. Asking simple questions such as "how often do you use your extra time for tests?" is a great start, but for some students, helping them assess themselves may take a little more digging and work on the part of the counselor. For example, if a student has a reading disability but has always managed in class because someone at home may have helped them by reading aloud to them, this needs to be explored as an accommodation on the college level. This student may benefit from text-to-speech programs, which many offices of disability services may offer. However, if the conversation never starts and the student is not encouraged to explore and question which accommodations work or do not work for them, they may enter college without the knowledge that this is something they may actually need, even if it was not an actual accommodation in their IEP on the high school level.

College Readiness **99**

In another example, a student may have an IEP for attention deficit disorder and may be getting an accommodation that gives them extra time for testing. Since students with ADHD may have a slower processing speed than other students, the extra time makes sense. However, students with ADHD are also frequently easily distracted by things that might not distract other students, and although they may be managing in high school without an accommodation to address this, college might be more difficult. For this student, a conversation exploring this possible distraction may be necessary. If the distraction is a factor that the student can pinpoint, then having the student assess their needs and explore possible and appropriate accommodations that might work for college is an important goal. Counselors might mention that colleges frequently offer distraction-free settings during testing for students who need this kind of accommodation.

Knowing How to Study

In addition to understanding what accommodations work best, there is also the ancillary college readiness skill of understanding what methods of studying work best for the individual student. Although this study skills in general will be explored in more depth in a later chapter, helping students develop an understanding of what methods of studying work best for themselves is at the epicenter of college and academic success (Gettinger & Schurr, 2002). Good study skills and habits have been shown to have a significant impact on student success (Mortimore & Crozier, 2006) but students with learning disabilities seem to be at a distinct disadvantage when it comes to understanding or using study skills appropriately (Ebele & Olofu, 2017; Mortimore & Crozier, 2006), and this disadvantage has a direct impact on their ability to finish their postsecondary studies (Kosine, 2007; Swanson & Deshler, 2003).

For many students with learning disabilities, independent learning and study skills seem to be a missing piece of their educational puzzle (Swanson & Deshler, 2003). This lack of independence in learning and studying could potentially keep these students from ever having to learn study skills at all. After all, if you are never required to spend the time studying or completing homework on your own at home, why should learning study skills be a need at all? Over the many years of my practice as a high school counselor, I have had too many of my students in replacement resource classes or in-class-support classes (co-teaching) tell me that they never have to do homework at all and that they never study.

Our role with these students is clear. For these students, we are a reliable source of information about college expectations, which include the ability to study and learn independently. Our conversations with them must insist that they look at themselves realistically as students and assess their ability and willingness to put in the time for studying and learning. Students who do

100 Our Role as Counselors

not learn how to study will not be able to succeed in college (Mortimore & Crozier, 2006). School counselors can help these students become aware of their needs and help them start building the study skills that they will need to succeed.

Being Organized and Self-Motivated

The importance of the college readiness skills of organization and self-motivation for all students (but especially for students with learning disabilities) cannot be overemphasized. For many high school students, life is planned and organized for them. The days begin at the same time and end at the same time. There may be a bus or a parent that picks them up from school and brings them home. There may be activities or appointments that parents or other adults have set up and taken care of. There may be wonderful teachers who push students and extend deadlines or send home reminders just to make certain that the students remain successful. In college though, many of those things may no longer be true. For many high school students with learning disabilities, the shift from high school to college in relation to these skills is enormous. In high school, many students with learning disabilities have IEPS that allow them to hand in late assignments or retake failed tests. These students are also, by sheer default of being in high school, in a situation in which the expectations of each day are fairly similar; you get up, you go to school, you come home, you eat, you sleep and you start again. There is little need for a high degree of organization because most of the organizational needs of high school students are taken care of. Once these students get to college, the playing field becomes completely different. In college, a schedule may be different every day, and classes may only meet once a week. In college, appointments might need to be made and remembered by the students themselves, and students may need to figure out how to get somewhere on their own. In college, parents do not have access to grades, and students are left on their own to make sure that their work gets done and handed in on time. Each day may be different, and each semester, things change again. The lack of intrinsic structure means that most days bring with them large chunks of time within which the student is responsible for organizing their obligations completely on their own. For college students, a deficit in these skills could be disastrous to their studies. Losing papers, handing in late projects, forgetting to study for tests and missing class are not acceptable on a college level.

For many students with learning disabilities, this lack of organization is actually based in an executive function disorder that adversely affects the ability to plan, organize, pay attention and develop coping strategies (Gettinger & Schurr, 2002; Swanson & Deshler, 2003). This disorder has correlations with many different types of learning disabilities and related disorders such as ADHD (Willcutt, Doyle, Nigg, Faraone, & Pennington, 2005), dyscalculia (Askenazi & Henik, 2010) and nonverbal learning disability (Wajnsztejn, Bianco, & Barbosa, 2016), to name just a few. This means that for these students, this lack of organization goes beyond just being a little messy or a little late to class. Luckily though, these students all benefit from direct instruction in organizational methods (National Center for Learning Disabilities, 2005).

Counselors can help students explore their organizational and self-motivation skills in an honest and forthright manner in an effort to address executive function skills. Instruction on how to use planners and calendars is not very time consuming, but for some students, this may be the first direct instruction they may ever have received in the uses of these items. It is important to note that many educators and parents make the erroneous assumption that students understand and know how to use these tools but just don't use them. Although this may be true for many students, it is not true for all, and this dangerous assumption makes these conversations more about laying blame then helping these students gain the skills to succeed. Teaching a student something as simple as the concept of adding a long-term assignment not just to a planner end date but to the daily function of a planner can be invaluable to a student who has never used a planner before.

Being Able to Self-Advocate

The college readiness skill of being able to advocate for oneself will be explore in more depth in a later chapter, but the necessity of this ability as a college readiness skill is important to note. Students who have been taught self-advocacy skills have a much higher likelihood of college retention and success than students who have not been taught how to advocate for themselves (Roberts, Ju, & Zhang, 2016).

For our students with learning disabilities, who are much less likely to be independent learners or have good study skills (Mortimore & Crozier, 2006; Swanson & Deshler, 2003), well-intentioned teachers and parents (and case managers and counselors too) may be more likely to want to make sure that this student continues to feel success and engagement over wanting them to struggle with work. This would mean that, potentially, their every academic need might be met before these students are even aware that they might have a need at all. There is little need for a student to learn how to advocate for themselves if there is nothing that they think they need to be asking for. If, for example, a student with a learning disability is starting to struggle in a class and a parent or teacher or other adult sees this struggle and enlists help before the student is given the opportunity to do it for themselves, then we have taken away the need for the student to practice or even understand the need for self-advocacy. On a college level, this inability to self-advocate,

102 Our Role as Counselors

especially for a student with a learning disability, leaves the student unable to verbalize or understand what they will need in order to succeed.

It is important to remember that, as counselors, we may have to place ourselves in the uncomfortable and unpopular position of pointing these things out to parents and students. This gives us the opportunity to work with the students and practice skills such as approaching teachers for help or even recognizing that they may have some unmet academic need to begin with. Students must be given opportunities to practice and understand the importance of self-advocacy while they are still with us in high school so that they have these skills intact as they move forward.

Understanding the Difference Between an IEP and a 504

For students with learning disabilities, understanding the difference between their high school IEP and their college 504 is an important readiness skill for college. Students need to understand the differences between these two documents and how they will ultimately affect them as college students in order to both prepare for and be prepared for college. Since high school counselors are frequently the students' agents between high school and college, the responsibility for disseminating this information could, quite frequently, fall on our shoulders, but if we don't understand this information ourselves, explaining it to our students becomes an impossibility. It is important that we are familiar with these documents and also understand how the differences in them could affect our students. Just like with anything else associated with the college process, giving accurate facts about these differences will give the students the information that they will need to make their transition to college as successful as possible.

Important things to understand about the difference between a high school IEP and a college 504:

- In high school, students with disabilities are identified by the school, and the school is responsible for evaluating and documenting the identified disability. In college, the student is responsible for identifying themselves.
- In high school, the school is responsible for creating and implementing modifications and accommodations for the student's program. In college, the student is responsible for requesting that modifications be implemented when they are needed.
- In high school, the school creates a program based on the IEP. In college, although eligibility may be determined, there is no actual program for the student. Typically, the only things that the schools provide are the accommodations that allow the student with the learning disability to access the curriculum at the same level as students without learning

disabilities. These accommodations are provided only when the student requests them.

- In high school, parents must give permission for any decisions regarding changes in the program. Parents must sign off on the IEP and are encouraged to attend yearly review meetings as the academic needs of their child change. In college, students over the age of 18 are considered adults, and parents are not allowed access unless the student permits it. This means that no matter what grades a student might receive in college, parents will not be notified if the student is having a difficult time academically.
- In high school, special classes and placements are available. Students with learning disabilities may be placed in classes that offer curricula that is different from the general education curriculum. In addition, in high school, students who are placed in general education settings may, through their IEPs, have different work expectations than their peers without learning disabilities. In college, students with learning disabilities are expected to participate in the same classes as students without learning disabilities. These students are also expected to produce the same type of work at the same level as their peers without learning disabilities.
- In high school, special education law mandates that an IEP (individual education plan) meeting be held annually to review progress and address any program changes. In addition, the special education law also mandates that the student be reevaluated every 3 years. In college, the 504 is granted based on the documentation provided, and yearly meetings and reevaluations are not required.
- In high school, psychological and educational testing for reevaluation or for initial evaluation for students suspected of having learning disabilities are conducted by the school at no cost to the family. In college, if a student suspects that they have a learning disability, the student and/ or the student's family are responsible for procuring psychological and educational testing at their own cost in order to provide documentation for the existence of a learning disability.
- In high school, special education law is based on the statute known as the IDEA (Individuals with Disabilities Education Act). The IDEA is based on the requirement to provide equity for students with disabilities from the elementary level all the way through the high school level. In college, the 504 that replaces the IEP is based on the ADA (Americans with Disabilities Act). The ADA was enacted in order to end discrimination aimed at people with disabilities in any public place, including colleges and universities.
- In high school, the IEP is based on the concept of success. Students under the umbrella of special education are given the tools to succeed academically at their level. In college, the 504 is about access. The school is responsible for making the curriculum equally accessible to all students

104 Our Role as Counselors

regardless of disability. Success after access, however, is entirely up to the student.

Case Study: College Readiness

Andrew is a 17-year-old high school junior. He has expressed continued interest in going to college to study business. He and his parents have explored and visited many of the colleges that he is interested in attending. He has a GPA of 3.57, and he and his parents have been careful about choosing schools that are a close match to his GPA. Although he has not taken his SAT or ACT yet, he has told his counselor that he is really anxious about it because he believes that he is not a very good standardized test taker. His friends have told him about some nearby schools that are test optional as long as his GPA is above a 3.0, and he has added these schools to his list of potential colleges he would like to apply to. He is on track to fulfill all of his requirements for graduating high school. At his last IEP meeting, which took place at the end of his sophomore year, it was decided that he would start his junior year in an in-class support environment for his English class, a small-class resource environment for his math class and a general education environment for his history class. His IEP includes extra time, retakes of tests, no penalty for late assignments, modified tests, a supported study period in which a special education teacher sits near him and helps him with homework and teacher reminders to stay focused in class. Andrew completes most of his homework in his supported study and rarely, if ever, brings work home. In meetings with his counselor, Andrew admits that although he has sat in on his IEP meetings every year since he was in elementary school, he "zones out" during those meetings because it is always "pretty boring." When asked about how he feels about having an IEP, Andrew has a hard time acknowledging his disability. All he seems to know is that he was "bad at school" before but now he is not. In class, Andrew's teachers say that he is a diligent but very quiet student. He seems to do his work but struggles on his own instead of asking questions. They frequently come to help him when they see that he is struggling. Both the teachers and his parents have noted that his backpack and locker are a mess. His parents have tried to help him by emptying his backpack every Friday and helping him organize his notes and folders, although his father admits that most of the time, it is he and his wife who seem to be doing all the work while Andrew sits near them with his phone in his hands. Andrew is excited to be starting college in the fall and cannot wait to see what the future has in store for him!

What Can the Counselor Do to Help Him Acquire Appropriate College Readiness Skills?

Andrew's counselor, Mr. Zachary, knows that he has done a great job of choosing schools that match his GPA and agrees that adding test-optional schools are also a good idea for him. He tells him that he is very proud of him for staying motivated and doing so well, but he is also worried that there are many things in his academic program that may need to be explored in order for him to be as prepared as possible for college. Mr. Zachary starts by encouraging Andrew to take the SAT or the ACT anyway. Mr. Zachary has seen Andrew's other standardized test scores from some in-school tests and knows that Andrew is not as low as he thinks he is. Mr. Zachary wants to help Andrew leave as many doors open for college as possible. In terms of his program at school right now, Mr. Zachary knows that Andrew is comfortable in his classes, but Mr. Zachary also knows that there are certain things that are happening that are not helpful in preparing him for college. Mr. Zachary knows that Andrew's resource math class is not rigorous enough to give him the skills he needs for college and that his modifications need to be diminished as well. Mr. Zachary would like to see Andrew move to a general education math class and slowly start to extinguish all of his modifications. When Mr. Zachary meets with Andrew, he encourages his hard work and desire to continue his education but also begins to talk about some of the expectations of college. He tells him that in college, Andrew will most likely be able to get extra time for tests but retakes of tests, no penalty for late assignments, modified tests, reminders to stay focused and supported studies are not typically offered in college. Mr. Zachary and Andrew's case manager are in close contact and have been discussing these ideas even before his meeting with Andrew. He and the case manager have already reached out to Andrew's mother with suggestions to start moving toward being better prepared for college by starting with experimenting with taking unmodified tests. He is told that if he is uncomfortable or does poorly, he can always retake the test, but as Mr. Zachary tells him, it is important to see what he can do without those modifications since he will not have any in college.

Over the course of the next few months, the case manager, together with Andrew, his family and Mr. Zachary, designs a plan to help Andrew transition more seamlessly to college. The plan stipulates that Andrew will continue to take unmodified tests for the rest of his junior year, although he will still be allowed to take retests if he feels he needs them. Since Andrew will need to develop independence, teachers will no longer remind him to be focused in class, and late assignments and papers will be penalized. His supported study will also be dropped, and he will be expected to do his homework and study at home from now on. Mr. Zachary will meet with him periodically and review how things are going and work with him on learning to ask for help, understanding his disability and assessing what he needs to be successful. In addition, his parents have decided that they will no longer be the ones cleaning out his backpack. They have told Andrew that they will stand near him while he does it and give him organizational suggestions, but they realize that he needs to learn to be organized for himself. Finally, because Mr. Zachary wanted to make certain that Andrew was given every opportunity to succeed, Mr. Zachary also met with Andrew's parents and spoke to them about considering looking at some schools that provided specialized programs for students with learning disabilities.

Andrew is aware that his grades may drop, but he also knows that he will be closely monitored by Mr. Zachary, his case manager and his parents to make sure that the plan is working and that he continues to feel successful. His IEP was amended, and it was decided that for senior year, he will no longer be placed in the resource room math class. He will be placed in an in-class support model for math and a general education model for English and history. For math class, which he has struggled more in than other classes, he will still have both a general and a special education teacher, but for English and history, he will only have one general education teacher. He will have an accommodation of extra time (since it was explained to him that he needs the extra time to process what he is learning and thinking) and will still have the modification of being allowed to retake tests. This modification, however, will be diminished as the year progresses. Mr. Zachary feels confident that Andrew will be significantly more prepared for college with this plan in place.

References

ASCA. (2017). *Why high school counselors?* American School Counselor Association. Retrieved from www.schoolcounselor.org/asca/media/asca/Careers-Roles/WhyHighSchool.pdf

Askenazi, S., & Henik, A. (2010). Attentional networks in developmental dyscalculia. *Behavioral and Brain Functions, 6*(1), 2. https://doi.org/10.1186/1744-9081-6-2

Ebele, U. F., & Olofu, P. A. (2017). Study habit and its impact on secondary school students' academic performance in biology in the federal capital territory, Abuja. *Educational Research and Reviews, 12*(10), 583–588.

College Readiness **107**

Gettinger, M., & Schurr, J. (2002). Contributions of study skills to academic competence. *School Psychology Review, 31*(3), 350–365.

Goleniowska, H. (2014). The importance of developing confidence and self-esteem in children with a learning disability. *Advances in Mental Health and Intellectual Disabilities, 8*(3), 188–191. https://doi.org/10.1108/AMHID-09-2013-0059

Kirschner, P. A. (2017). Stop propagating the learning styles myth. *Computers & Education, 106*, 166–171. https://doi.org/10.1016/j.compedu.2016.12.006

Kosine, N. (2007). Preparing students with learning disabilities for postsecondary education. *Journal of Special Education Leadership, 20*(2), 93–104.

Lyman, M., Beecher, M. E., Griner, D., Brooks, M., Call, J., & Jackson, A. (2016). What keeps students with disabilities from using accommodations in postsecondary education? A qualitative review. *Journal of Postsecondary Education and Disability, 29*(2), 123–140.

Mortimore, T., & Crozier, W. R. (2006). Dyslexia and difficulties with study skills in higher education. *Studies in Higher Education, 31*(2), 235–251. https://doi.org/10.1080/03075070600572173

National Center for Learning Disabilities. (2005). Executive function fact sheet. *Retrieved, 8*(15). Retrieved from www.ldonline.org/article/24880/

Roberts, E., Ju, S., & Zhang, D. (2016). Review of practices that promote self-advocacy for students with disabilities. *Journal of Disability Policy Studies, 26*(4), 209–220. https://doi.org/10.1177/1044207314540213

Smith, J. S., & Wertlieb, E. C. (2005). Do first-year college students' expectations align with their first-year experiences? *NASPA Journal, 42*(2), 153–174. https://doi.org/10.2202/1949-6605.1470

Swanson, H. L., & Deshler, D. (2003). Instructing adolescents with learning disabilities: Converting a meta-analysis to practice. *Journal of Learning Disabilities, 36*(2), 124–135. https://doi.org/10.1177/002221940303600205

UC Santa Cruz. (2016, July). *What to expect in college?* Retrieved from https://orientation.ucsc.edu/what-to-expect.html

Wajnsztejn, A. B. C., Bianco, B., & Barbosa, C. P. (2016). Prevalence of interhemispheric asymmetry in children and adolescents with interdisciplinary diagnosis of non-verbal learning disorder. *Einstein (São Paulo), 14*(4), 494–500. https://doi.org/10.1590/S1679-45082016AO3722

Willcutt, E. G., Doyle, A. E., Nigg, J. T., Faraone, S. V., & Pennington, B. F. (2005). Validity of the executive function theory of attention-deficit/hyperactivity disorder: A meta-analytic review. *Biological Psychiatry, 57*(11), 1336–1346.

15

WHAT COUNSELORS NEED TO KNOW ABOUT IEPS

In this section:

- Models of identification
- Reading an IEP
- Interpreting test scores
- Reading and interpreting the WISC-V
- Reading and interpreting the Woodcock–Johnson Test of Achievement

The first time I was presented with an IEP that I actually read cover to cover was at my own daughter's first IEP meeting. Although I had been a teacher and a counselor for many years, I had never read through an entire IEP. I had seen enough of them to know that this was not going to be a short read. I had just never actually done it. At the meeting, which was not then nor would ever be attended by a school counselor, the case manager took his time and explained every aspect of the long and complicated document. He explained what the testing results meant, how the teachers' narratives fit into the picture and how the fluidity of the goals and objectives was based on how quickly or slowly my daughter was able to reach them. Despite having seen so many IEPs, I realized, as I asked question after question about the one that was attached to my daughter, that I knew nothing. The more he explained things to me, the more questions I seemed to have, and by the end of the meeting, I had both more information and more confusion about special education and IEPs than I ever knew existed. As a parent, this was understandable. None of my children had ever been classified before, and this was all new. It made sense that I didn't know much about what went into an IEP. As a professional, however, that day a wake-up call. What I thought I knew about IEPs was turned upside down. I felt like I was looking at an IEP for the very first time and realized that I had missed so much for so many of my students. The information that I learned from my daughter's IEP was invaluable in helping me to understand her needs and her limitations. Learning to read the psychological and educational testing evaluation results gave me an insight into her academic struggles that let me help her much more effectively than I would have been able to without them. I realized that if I now knew how to do this for my own daughter, then I could easily translate this to my students, and I did. I read every single IEP cover to cover, and what I found was that the information from those documents enhanced my understanding of my students in a powerful way.

When our students with learning disabilities are struggling academically, considering what colleges to apply to or thinking about what classes to take, having an in-depth understanding of their IEPs and the process through which they are acquired is an extra and important tool in our ability to guide them appropriately.

Background

In order to understand the IEP, or the individual educational plan, it is important to have an understanding of the law that is at the crux of it. The federal law known as The Individuals with Disabilities Education Act (IDEA) is the law under which special education operates. It is this law which determines who is and who is not eligible for special education services in public schools. Based on this law, there are 13 categories of disability under which a student can be classified within the auspices of special education (IDEA, 2004). These categories are as follows:

- Autism
- Blindness
- Deafness
- Emotional Disturbance
- Hearing Impairment
- Intellectual Disability
- Multiple Disabilities
- Orthopedic Impairment
- Other Health Impaired
- Specific Learning Disability
- Speech or Language Impairment
- Traumatic Brain Injury
- Visual Impairment

For children with learning disabilities and related disorders, the classifications are frequently found under the categories of Specific Learning Disability

110 Our Role as Counselors

(SLD) or Other Health Impaired (OHI). The IEP is the legal document that delineates the educational plan, services and goals for each and every student who has been identified as having one of those 13 categories of impairment. The IEP must contain several very important pieces of information including the students' levels of academic achievement and their functional performance, a statement of how the disability manifests and affects progress in general education, information about academic and functional goals for the student, progress goals for the student, a listing of any related services and supplementary aids that the student might be receiving and a listing of the accommodations and modifications that the student is receiving (IDEA, 2004).

Models of Identification

When a student is suspected of having a learning disability, they are frequently identified through a multidisciplinary team using multiple sources of information including observations, progress reports and standardized tests (Gartland & Strosnider, 2011), but there are three main models to determine eligibility for special education under the SLD umbrella. One model is known as the severe discrepancy model, the second is known as the RTI or response to intervention model and the third is known as the processing deficits approach.

The severe discrepancy model is based on a mathematical discrepancy between intellect and ability. In this model, the discrepancy between intellect and achievement is seen as proof of a learning disability. Students are administered an achievement test, such as the Woodcock–Johnson Achievement Test, and an IQ test such as the Wechsler Intelligence Scale for Children (WISC-V) (Wechsler, 2014). If enough of a discrepancy is found between achievement and intelligence, then the student is considered to have a learning disability. Typically, a student whose achievement test score is 1.5 standard deviations or more below their IQ score, that student may be considered to have a learning disability. Although this model seems to do a great job of quantifying a learning disability, there are many intrinsic problems that it presents as well. For many early elementary-aged students, testing between achievement and IQ may not show a discrepancy if the student has enough support at home. The discrepancy model depends on initial failure in order to identify and does not account for factors that might mask academic struggles early on. This means that early elementary students, who benefit the most from interventions, do not get identified easily with the use of this model. This model also does not take into account the quality of instruction that might affect the achievement or guide teachers in how to teach these students once they have been identified. Despite these issues, and despite the fact that this model has actually been disallowed from being used on its own since 2004 (IDEA, 2004), this is the model used most frequently nationwide (Schultz & Stephens, 2009).

The RTI model is based on tiered prevention levels that increase in support as needed by the student. This model starts with an initial universal screening in the early grades that is used to identify students who may be struggling early on. Students who are identified in that early screening are then given evidence-based interventions, and their progress is monitored continuously. Students who do not respond are then moved to a more intensive tier of intervention. There are typically three or four tiers of intervention, and all instruction is based on the data from continued progress monitoring of each individual student (Hughes & Dexter, 2011). RTI is frequently used in conjunction with the discrepancy model.

The processing deficit approach hinges on specific learning disabilities to processing deficits. This method of identification tests for processing deficits in areas that might affect learning (such as visual, auditory or phonological) and uses these deficits as the basis for detecting students with specific learning disabilities. This method is not used as heavily as the other two, although several states have adopted it as their sole methodology for identification (Schultz & Stephens, 2009).

It is important to note that although IDEA is a federal law, special education law codes do vary state by state. Each state can determine what model it will use for identification, and each state can also individually determine what the guidelines for eligibility will be under the umbrella of specific learning disability. This means that while a student with, for example, dyscalculia is eligible for special education in one state, they may not be eligible for it in another if dyscalculia is not within that state's guidelines for eligibility.

Reading an IEP

The IEP is the legal written contract that delineates the services, goals and objectives that will make up the academic plan for the student with special education. A counselor's ability to read and understand the IEP is helpful in understanding the student but also important in helping students and their families make informed decisions in moving forward successfully in college. Although every part of the IEP is important, for counselors, there are a few areas that are specifically relevant and should be reviewed:

Present levels of performance—this is the portion of the IEP that will indicate how the student is performing at the present time. Many times, this section will actually be a written narrative by each one of the student's teachers. This portion is an important addition to our knowledge base about the student. Although we may have access to grades, the grades themselves do not paint the whole picture. A student may be getting good grades, but those grades may be based on extensive interventions and modifications in the

112 Our Role as Counselors

classroom. If this is the case, postsecondary school choices may have to be informed by this knowledge.

Special education and related services—In this section, the program for the student is spelled out. It is here that you will find out if the student is in a general classroom or a special education classroom. You will also find out if the student is receiving any related services such as speech or occupational therapy. Again, this is important information to know for the college process. If the student is in all special education classes, it may affect their ability to find success on the college level. If they are receiving any related services, it is important to find out how the need for these services impacts the student and what the family plans for these services once the student leaves high school.

Modifications and accommodations—In this section, the student's modifications and accommodations are listed. Since modifications are never done on a college level, it is important to discuss this fact with the family at the IEP meeting and consider changing the program to lessen the amount and/or intensity of the modifications. Accommodations, however, are supplied in college. This list of accommodations could be the crux of accommodations moving forward in college as well. The use of this portion of the IEP in conversations with the student is an important precursor to college as well. Many students have little or no idea of the items listed in this section. Reviewing this with them and addressing each one realistically and with an eye toward the future in college can help our students understand what they may actually need once they graduate high school.

Interpreting Test Scores

Since many states do not use test scores in relation to special education, we will focus on two of the most commonly accepted forms of testing (both for special education and for use on the college and university level). The WISC-V is a commonly used intelligence test for children, and the Woodcock–Johnson Test of Achievement is a commonly used achievement test for children. As stated previously, when both are administered in schools that use a discrepancy model, a significant discrepancy between the two may be used as an identifying factor for special education.

The purpose of understanding how to use these test scores is to have a deeper understanding of how possible deficits manifest themselves in an academic setting. It may be useful to know that a student who is struggling in a math class had a significantly lower score in math ability, working memory or processing speed. Not only can we then take time to engage the teacher in a meaningful dialogue about how this might affect the student, but we can also use this to help the student develop appropriate compensatory skills to address the deficits.

An important thing to note is that evaluations done with these tests can vary in depth. Some evaluations are extensive and filled with results for every nuance of intelligence and achievement, while others are more broadly based. A private evaluation, paid for by the family, would most likely be much more comprehensive in scope, while an evaluation done by a public-school child study team may have more basic information. For our purposes as counselors, this section will only review the more basic test results.

Reading and Interpreting the WISC-V

The WISC-V is composed of ten subtests, each of which produces five separate measures of ability in the tested area. The scores are given in the areas of verbal comprehension, visual spatial, fluid reasoning, working memory and processing speed. The full-scale IQ (FSIQ) is the average of all of these scores. The scores are scaled according to the chart below:

Table 15.1 IQ Chart

130 and above	Extremely High
120–129	Very High
110–119	High Average
90–109	Average
80–89	Low Average
70–79	Very Low
69 and below	Extremely Low

It is important to remember that although the FSIQ is important, it does not tell a full story. A student might be extremely gifted in one area and struggle in another. Working memory and processing speed issues can have a serious and overarching influence on acquiring learning, so if those are very low but the others are very high, the FSIQ will be average.

The report may provide a quantitative summary chart as well as a narrative explaining the testing and the results. For our purposes as counselors, reading the narrative may be helpful but also very time consuming. The quickest way to understand the results is to compare them to the chart above. Understanding that deficits in any of these areas have specific impacts on how a student is able to perform in school and what their needs may be in college is extremely important. The chart below shows examples of how a deficit in each area tested may impact a student in high school or college.

114 Our Role as Counselors

Table 15.2 Deficit Chart

Verbal Comprehension	Affects how we are able to interpret communication. May affect students by making it difficult for them to convey basic knowledge, problem solve or express themselves appropriately.
Working Memory	Affects the ability to hold something in short-term memory and in order as a pathway toward using the information at a later point. May affect ability to take notes, write extensive papers, follow directions and reading comprehension.
Fluid Reasoning	Affects the ability to think creatively and problem solve in novel ways. Difficulty organizing thoughts in writing, applying math skills to new situations and making generalizations and connections.
Processing Speed	Affects how quickly information is used to perform tasks. Affects work rate and completion, reading fluency and writing speed.
Visual Spatial	Affects the ability to perceive where objects are in space. Affects ability to align numbers and letters, which leads to issues with math and reading.

Reading and Interpreting the Woodcock–Johnson Test of Achievement

The Woodcock–Johnson Test of Achievement tests the academic achievement of students in the following areas: reading, math, written language and academic knowledge (which includes science, social studies and humanities) (Kaufman, Flanagan, Alfonso, & Mascolo, 2006). The reading, math and written language portions contain sections that test fluency, application and the basic skills related to that subject. Within each subject, different clusters are teased out as well. For reading, there are seven reading clusters, which are then broken down into even more distinct measures. There are also four math and four written language clusters, which are also broken down into more distinct measures.

The test is scored in three different areas for each testable measure. The first area is the level of development, the second is the comparison with peers and the third is the degree of proficiency of the student. The level-of-development section includes the age equivalent and the grade equivalent. The age equivalent shows the student's level of performance compared to other students based on age, while the grade equivalent shows the level of performance as compared to other students based on grade. So if a 15-year-old student who is in the 10th grade has a reading age equivalent of 10.2 that means that their reading level is comparable to most children who are 10 years and 2 months old. If that same student also has a grade equivalent of

5.1, that means that this student is reading at the same level as most students in early 5th grade.

The comparison-with-peers score shows a standard score and a percentile rank. The standard score describes the score in comparison to the average of the comparable group, and it is scored on the same scale as an IQ test (see chart above). If in a particular math skill a student scored an 85, then this student is considered to have low average ability in this skill.

The percentile rank score places a student in comparison with their peers on a scale of 1 to 100. This means that if a student scores a 40, 40 out of 100 of their peers would score a 40 or less.

The degree-of-proficiency score is based on the relative proficiency index (RPI) and predicts how proficient a student might be in a particular area. The student's score is based on the level of proficiency they are expected to get compared to average peers who would score a 90% on the same test. This means that if a student scores a 90/90 on the RPI then they can be expected to score the same as an average peer on this test. If this student scores a 20/90, this means that they can be expected to score a 20% while their average peer would score a 90%. A student scoring anywhere from 0 to 67 would most likely exhibit great difficulty in these academic areas. A student scoring 67 to 90 would most likely find the subject difficult but not impossible, and a student scoring 82 and over would most likely not have any difficulty at all.

References

Gartland, D., & Strosnider, R. (2011). Comprehensive assessment and evaluation of students with learning disabilities: A paper prepared by the national joint committee on learning disabilities. *Learning Disability Quarterly, 34*(1), 3–16. https://doi.org/10.1177/073194871103400101

Hughes, C. A., & Dexter, D. D. (2011). Response to intervention: A research-based summary. *Theory into Practice, 50*(1), 4–11. https://doi.org/10.1080/00405841.2011.534909

Individuals with Disabilities Education Act [IDEA] of 1997 (2004), Pub. L. No. 105–117, 111 Stat. 37.

Kaufman, A. S., Flanagan, D. P., Alfonso, V. C., & Mascolo, J. T. (2006). Test review: Wechsler intelligence scale for children, (WISC-IV). *Journal of Psychoeducational Assessment, 24*(3), 278–295. https://doi.org/10.1177/0734282906288389

Schultz, E. K., & Stephens, T. (2009). SLD Identification: An analysis of state policies. *Academic Exchange Quarterly, 13*(4), 29–34.

Wechsler, D. (2014). *Wechsler intelligence scale for children-fifth edition.* Bloomington, IN: Pearson.

16

WHAT COUNSELORS NEED TO KNOW ABOUT SELF-ADVOCACY

In this part:
- Understanding disability and learning needs
- Why students may not understand their disabilities and learning needs
- Self-esteem
- Assistive technology
- Understanding of rights
- History of IDEA/504/ADA
- College and disability services
- Effective communication skills
- Passive/aggressive/assertive
- When to disclose and why
- Case study: self-advocacy

Most children do not walk into high school with an innate ability to advocate for themselves. I know that for my own practice, when I meet with my students, especially my freshman students, most are scared to ask questions in class let alone advocate for their own needs. It is a learning process for them, as it is for most people. As counselors, we work with these children and teach them the skills and strategies that they will need in order to access this ability to advocate for themselves. For example, if a student who is struggling in a class has not gone to the teacher for extra help because of anxiety about asking for the help, we may spend time discussing the source of that discomfort first. If the student is truly not ready to speak directly to the teacher, we may strategize alternate plans that will still get their needs met but might not involve face-to-face contact with the teacher. We might suggest that they underline or highlight the questions they might have and then email them to the teacher later. If the student is farther along, we may use our time to help them practice what they might say when they do approach the teacher. Whatever the case, working with our students on self-advocacy is something that is very familiar to high school counselors, but adding a learning disability to the mix changes the playing field significantly.

For students with learning disabilities, learning the skills of self-advocacy can be the difference between success and failure. When these students are taught self-advocacy skills, there is a significant and positive effect on college retention (Roberts, Ju, & Zhang, 2016), and they are more likely to be successful in college than students who have not been taught these skills (Field, Sarver, & Shaw, 2003). Unfortunately, many students with learning disabilities still leave high school without having learned the skills of self-advocacy (Izzo & Lamb, 2002). For these students in particular, the skills they need for self-advocacy are skills that will most likely have to be specifically taught to them (Arkeny & Lehmann, 2010). For these students, self-advocacy skills are not just about being able to approach a teacher and ask for help. The self-advocacy skills they need are specifically tied into their learning disability and must include instruction on understanding their disability and their learning needs, understanding their rights as people with disabilities and understanding how to wrap that all together to communicate their needs effectively.

Understanding Disability and Learning Needs

In order for students to understand their learning needs, they need to be able to understand themselves as learners first (Test, Fowler, Wood, Brewer, & Eddy, 2005). What this means is that students need to be able to understand and talk about what kind of a disability they have, how it affects their ability to learn and what kinds of compensatory strategies they might be able to use to bypass the disability and still access the learning. Yet for many students, there is no understanding of their disability at all. These students may be coming to us with a frame of reference of failure and find it painful to acknowledge the fact that they have a disability. For other students, there may never have been a real discussion or explanation about what their learning disability is and how it affects them. They may only know that they have trouble reading or doing math. When students don't have these skills intact, they lack the knowledge and vocabulary to ask for what they need. These students become stuck and may not even know why. One simple example of this is to imagine that you have never felt the sensation of hunger before and suddenly you feel some sort of discomfort in your body. You know that you are uncomfortable, but when you try to get help, the words you are using don't match up with the problem. You might say, "I feel dizzy" or maybe

118 Our Role as Counselors

"There are strange noises coming from my stomach." In an effort to help you, people around you might have you lie down or maybe give you something to drink, but none of these things are working to solve your problem, and it just seems to be getting worse. Perhaps you even start to feel frustrated at everyone around you for not being able to meet your needs, but all you know is that you still have a problem and you don't understand why. Much like this example, students with learning disabilities seem to have a difficult time making meaning of their experiences as learners. Many students with learning disabilities do not understand their disabilities and do not understand their learning needs (Cortiella & Horowitz, 2014). Many of these students leave high school without an ability to explain what their learning needs are, what their strengths are or even what kinds of accommodations they need in order to succeed (Izzo & Lamb, 2002). This possible disconnect between their experiences as learners and their learning disability can become a huge barrier toward getting the help that they need to learn effectively.

Regardless of what the reason for the lack of knowledge about it, helping students become aware of and accept the nature of their disability helps to give them multiple opportunities to succeed and move beyond the possible limits that their learning disabilities might impose. For example, if a student has a reading disability, an acceptance of that disability would allow them to understand that they might benefit from a text-to-speech technology that could expand their access to otherwise inaccessible material. The self-advocacy needed for this student to get to this point hinges upon an understanding of their disability. Having a working knowledge of their disability and how it affects them makes them far more likely to experience success on a postsecondary level (Durlak, Rose, & Bursuck, 1994), yet these students are still leaving high school without this basic knowledge.

Why Students May Not Understand Their Disabilities and Learning Needs

The very nature of how public education manages learning disabilities is a significant reason why students with these disabilities don't seem to have an understanding of them. The school takes complete responsibility for managing the learning program of the student. The student never has to ask for anything. Accommodations and modifications are put into place automatically because they are incorporated into their program through the IEP. Students don't need to have any understanding of their disability because it is completely managed for them. In early school, this is appropriate and helpful, because the students may not have the understanding to ask for what they need, but by the time these students get to high school, this complete dependence on others for their educational needs starts to work against them. By the time they get to college, when they are completely responsible for their educational needs, this lack of knowledge about their learning disability becomes a serious hindrance.

Another reason why students may be leaving high school without a complete understanding of their disability may have to do with how they view themselves. These students may believe that they have far worse or far better abilities and skills than they actually have (Anastasiou & Michail, 2013). A student who believes that they are skilled at nothing may not access help because they may lack hope that accessing help will make any difference. A student who believes that they have skills in writing when in reality this is not one of their strengths may also be much less likely to access help. Both underconfidence and overconfidence do not allow for a student to get to a point where they can self-advocate. Thinking that getting help is fruitless or thinking that there are skills present that do not exist both lead to the same lack of self-knowledge and lack of self-advocacy skills that lead to poor outcomes in college. This failure, added to an already shaky self-esteem, is the potential beginning of a vicious cycle of continued failure. This disconnect, in either direction, creates a difficult situation for counselors. While we want to promote our students' self-esteem and help them feel good about themselves, we also want our students with learning disabilities to be able to see what their actual real strengths and challenges are and to be realistic about what their needs are as well. This delicate balance between self-esteem and reality can be a real challenge for school counselors.

The student who views themselves with an inappropriate sense of achievement may be feeling so good about themselves that having knowledge about their disability may feel irrelevant. This student may feel as if they are already doing well and are not affected by their learning disability. While this student might be receiving excellent grades and accolades from teachers, these grades and accolades may be based on extensive modifications to the curriculum. The student may be doing well, but the danger is in what happens after high school. For this student, a lack of understanding of their disability could lead them to be completely unprepared for the rigors of college. Since no modifications to the curriculum are provided in college and this student's success is based on modifications, this student may not be able to access the college curriculum. Working with a student who has a false sense of confidence presents multiple challenges to the counselor. No one wants to be the kind of person who tears students down, but counselors still have to be able to help their students see themselves through a realistic lens. There is a fine line that exists between confidence and reality and sending students off to college with a false sense of confidence is irresponsible. For this student, discussing the differences between high school and college expectations and working with them to start diminishing modifications would also be a good way to start the dialogue.

For the student who views themselves as much less capable than they actually are, their negative view of themselves has been solidified over many years

120 Our Role as Counselors

of having difficulty with learning. While we may know that it is the dyslexia and not the intelligence that has gotten in the way of their learning, convincing them of this is no small task. At this point, this student has spent a lifetime learning to see themselves as someone who is not "smart" and may have already shut down to the point of not caring. For this student, understanding their learning disability may seem like a pointless task. Counselors faced with this type of attitude from a student might shy away from working with this student on understanding their disability. After all, there seem to be so many other things at play. Focusing on helping the student to understand their disability may seem to be the least important part of what needs to be done, but the truth is that teaching an understanding of their disability is the foundation for everything else. When a student like this begins to understand that their learning disability does not define their intelligence or that there are ways to access learning that they may not have explored yet, the rest may follow.

Negative self-esteem and self-concept may be another reason why students with learning disabilities may not understand their learning needs or their disability (Goleniowska, 2014). Young children who enter school learn very quickly that being "smart" in school is valued. They also learn that "smart" is fairly easily measured. The classmate who always gets 100% on every test is "smart." The other classmate who never forgets to do their homework and always does it right is also "smart." Students who have been identified as having learning disabilities started off their academic careers by not being able to do any of those things well. For these students, there had to be a "problem" that led to their being identified to begin with. This "problem" meant that they may not have been able to get good grades on tests or complete their homework well. They may have seen teachers lavish praise on their peers for their abilities and success while they, struggling to do the bare minimum, may have gotten (at best), "don't worry. It will come." Once these students get identified, they are finally able to get the help that they need to learn. In theory, this should solve the problem, but it doesn't. They have already learned that "smart" is good and that they are something other than "smart." Now, in order for them to be able to learn, they have to be taught differently than their peers. Perhaps they are placed in a resource room or replacement class, and perhaps this is the place where they finally are able to learn, but something has already happened to their sense of self. They have already internalized the fact that they are not "smart." Even getting the help that they need is still a reminder of the fact that they are not succeeding. For these students, learning about their disability and their learning needs might just be another unwanted reminder that they have a disability at all.

Another common hurdle our students with learning disabilities face while learning about themselves and their disability is dealing with the stigma and embarrassment of having an IEP and a learning disability (Eccles, Hutchings, Hunt, & Heaslip, 2018). The emotional problems associated with dyslexia are significant (Livingston, Siegel, & Ribary, 2018). The shame, stigma and isolation that students feel is also significant (Horn & Moss, 2015). These students might want to free themselves from the identity of having a disability, and rather than wanting to understand and know more about it, they may prefer to ignore it. The shame and isolation that students may have felt all throughout early school are great motivators in shedding any involvement in special education by the time they reach college. This shame may be why students with learning disabilities frequently do not access disability services on campus (Lightner, Kipps-Vaughan, Schulte, & Trice, 2012). Students may feel that they no longer need or want to think about their disabilities or be involved with any services that mark them as "special." The problem is that without the accommodations that they need, students with learning disabilities frequently do not succeed in college. Just because these students have left their IEP behind in high school does not mean that they have suddenly been "cured" of their learning disability. We know that learning disabilities are lifelong afflictions and do not ever go away, but the shame and embarrassment that students might feel about having this kind of disability may preclude their ability or desire to learn more about it.

Self-Esteem

As counselors, one of our many responsibilities is to help nurture the academic, social and emotional well-being of all of our students (ASCA, 2017). This means that one of the tasks we are charged with is helping our students with learning disabilities develop and understand themselves and their learning disabilities. Helping students develop a positive sense of themselves as learners, inclusive of their disability, is a necessary step in helping them begin to understand themselves as a path toward self-advocacy. How students perceive themselves based on their abilities can affect academic achievement (Hampton & Mason, 2003), and our ability to work with these perceptions can have a huge and positive impact. When we work with students with learning disabilities, our job is to help them accept, understand and become aware of what they need in order to be successful. Our students need to be able to use the knowledge that they have about themselves, their learning needs and their disability in order to help them make a realistic assessment of themselves. The fact of having a learning disability is a reality that does not go away. A child with dyslexia becomes an adult with dyslexia. The gift we can give these children is the path toward compensatory skills and information that will light the way for their needs in moving forward.

As counselors, one of our hardest jobs is helping students to find self-acceptance. While we might work with all students on self-acceptance, students with learning disabilities have additional needs. While students without learning disabilities may struggle within the norm of self-acceptance,

122 Our Role as Counselors

students with learning disabilities report that it is their learning disabilities that make them feel frustrated, disappointed, sad and embarrassed (Davis, Nida, Zlomke, & Nebel-Schwalm, 2009). The connection between self-esteem and self-advocacy is a direct one. When a student with a learning disability is able to embrace and understand their disability, they are able to see both their strengths and challenges without judgment. They may understand that they may have to work harder or they may have to have extra help, but they may also understand that these things do not mean that they are bad students or that they are not capable of learning. For students like these, who feel good about themselves despite their learning disability, self-advocacy comes naturally. For these students, asking for help or for needed accommodations is done without question. Self-advocacy, for students who understand themselves and feel good about themselves, is just a natural part of their academic path. For students who do not feel good about themselves, however, the outcomes are not as positive. The negative emotions these students feel about themselves because of their learning disabilities have a distinct and negative impact on their academic success in college (Newman & Madaus, 2014). Helping students find ways to cope with these feelings is an important tool in their ability to find continued success.

One method of helping students with this mindset is to teach them how to reframe the negative into something positive. Reframing is the ability to perceive events in a different way. Most events are not intrinsically positive or negative. We interpret events based on our experiences. So, for example, a student with dyslexia who had trouble learning to read might interpret that difficulty as something negative or something to be embarrassed about. It might make them feel like they are unsuccessful or perhaps even not as bright as other students. On the other hand, having to find different ways of learning may have made them able to see things in a more creative way. It may have made them more patient with other people. It might make them better visual thinkers or better at spatial knowledge. In fact, having dyslexia has actually been linked to having better visual spatial talent (von Karolyi, Winner, Gray, & Sherman, 2003). Helping students acknowledge the negative interpretation of their learning disability and showing them that there are other ways to look at it is pivotal in helping these students accept themselves for the learners that they are.

Assistive Technology

Self-knowledge may be the basis for the self-advocacy that students with learning disabilities need in order to find success in college, but it is also the basis for assessing needs based on assistive technology. For many people, the idea of assistive technology conjures images of wheelchairs, frequency modulation (FM) devices or hearing aids. Assistive technology, however, is also for students with learning disabilities. Much like wheelchairs, FM devices or hearing aids, assistive technology for students with learning disabilities exist to help these students access what would otherwise be difficult or inaccessible. Just as a wheelchair allows mobility to a person who might otherwise not have mobility, assistive technology for students with learning disabilities allows access to learning that they otherwise might not have either.

Although assistive technology for students with learning disabilities is not a new concept, many elementary schools, high schools, parents and even students shy away from its use. I've heard many parents and teachers say that they would prefer that their child or their student keep "trying to learn" before resorting to the technology. Accessing information through assistive technology (AT) does not mean that the student has given up on reading. What it does mean is that the student is now able to gain the information that the other students have accessed and that this information was gained in a way that is facilitated by some form of technology. This access to previously inaccessible information breeds more success and builds upon itself in a way that might not have happened otherwise (Lindeblad, Nilsson, Gustafson, & Svensson, 2017). Continuing to grow skills can happen concurrently with learning about assistive technology. In fact, students with learning disabilities who use assistive technology learn to access the information they need for learning while also increasing their self-concept and self-esteem (Lindeblad et al., 2017). Assistive technology for students with learning disabilities is a tool that provides success (Jing & Chen, 2017). For many students with learning disabilities, however, access to helpful assistive technology is not available. Despite the fact that not all useful assistive technology has to be "high tech," this lack of availability seems based on a combination of a lack of comfort with the assistive technology, a lack of resources and lack of training (Graham & Richardson, 2012).

Types of Assistive Technology That Can Help Students with Learning Disabilities

Table 16.1 Types of Assistive Technology

Dyslexia:	speech to text, text to speech (for writing), word prediction software, reading pens, smart pens, spelling and grammar software, talking word processors, OCR programs, audiobooks, note-taking apps
Dyscalculia:	graph paper, talking calculators, calculators, electronic math worksheets, computer-assisted instruction, math simulations
Dysgraphia:	speech to text, slant boards, mind maps, graphic organizers, typing tools, word processors

(*Continued*)

124 Our Role as Counselors

Table 16.1 (Continued)

Processing disorders:	noise-canceling headphones, FM devices, visually clean worksheets, wide-ruled paper
Nonverbal learning disorder:	laminated daily routine card, graphic organizers, word-prediction software, spell checker, math simulation
ADHD:	electronic calendar, text to speech, mind maps, list apps, timers, distraction-limiting devices and apps, note-taking apps
Dyspraxia:	Mind maps, scanner pens, speech to text, slant board, oversize trackball mouse, robotic arm
Executive functioning:	electronic calendar, timer, mind map, reminder app, list app, scheduling app, note app
Memory:	electronic calendar, checklist, timer, electronic reminders, graphic organizers, smart pen recorders

Understanding of Rights
History of IDEA/504/ADA

Another step in the process toward self-advocacy is making sure that both we as counselors and our students have an understanding of disability rights. Until 1975, most students with serious disabilities were not being educated in the public schools. Students with disabilities did not have rights in the public educational system. Public schools did not have to teach students with disabilities at all, and parents were forced to either pay for services on their own, not educate the child at all or institutionalize them (West, 2000). Students with less visible disabilities such as learning disabilities were frequently thought of as "slow" or incapable of learning. If they were among the lucky who were kept in school, no extra effort was made to educate them. In 1975, everything changed when the Education for All Handicapped Children Act, which later was amended in 1997 and became the Individuals with Disabilities Education Act (IDEA). IDEA insured that all students had a right to a free and public education in the least restrictive environment (LRE). This law brought a majority of students with disabilities into the general education classroom with modifications, accommodations, and support services in order to facilitate their learning (McFall & Fitzpatrick, 2010).

Under IDEA, students with disabilities must be identified by the school districts and must be taught in the least restrictive environment possible. The IDEA requires that all public schools create an IEP (individualized education plan) for all students who qualify for special education. These IEPs are developed by a specialized team that creates a plan that is specifically geared to meet the educational needs of the individual student. These laws were created to ensure that all students in grades K–12, including ones with disabilities, are able to access public education.

The Rehabilitation Act of 1973 brought what is known as Section 504 into the spotlight. This act helped bring the spirit of the IDEA further into the lives of students with learning disabilities. It required that all federally funded institutions and programs create accommodations for people with disabilities and was intended to create equity and access for people beyond school age. One subpart of the act applies to K–12 schools, and another is specific to colleges and universities. The difference between a 504 and an IEP for a K–12 student is the special education component. IDEA is tied to special education, whereas a 504 requires accommodations that are not tied into special education.

Finally, the Americans with Disabilities Act of 1990 (ADA) helped to bar discrimination based on a person's disability. Under the law, in any public place, including places of education, people with disabilities are entitled to the same accommodations and services that are given to people without disabilities.

The combination of these three antidiscrimination laws creates the equity and access that is the crux of the necessary accommodations and modifications for students with disabilities. What is important to remember is that the IDEA is solely intended to ensure the education of students with disabilities from kindergarten through 12th grade (to the age of 21 if necessary). It is the responsibility of the school to identify these students as well as to provide the evaluations and services to ensure their success. For the IDEA, the concept of success is at its base; students with learning disabilities who are covered under IDEA should (barring extreme circumstances) be able to successfully learn how to read, how to write and how to compute numbers. Once that success is achieved and a student leaves the K–12 environment, they are no longer covered by the IDEA and success is no longer the goal. At this point, when the ADA and section 504 take over, the goal is about access. As long as a person with a disability is given the same access to the same education as students without disabilities, the laws have been followed. Once the access is granted, success in college is up to the individual student with or without learning disabilities. There is no guarantee of success for any student, and just because a student attends college does not translate into their being successful at it. In fact, for college students without disabilities, the national average for college completion in 2011 was just over 56% (Shapiro et al., 2017).

College and Disability Services

In order for a college student to access services for their disability, the student must make contact with the office of disability services or whatever office on campus provides services for students with disabilities. In order to assure a

126 Our Role as Counselors

smooth transition, this contact should be made well before the student starts the school year. The student must identify themselves and provide the appropriate documentation (which is typically a recent psychological and educational evaluation). The evaluations and all accompanying documentation are reviewed and evaluated by the office of disability services. If approved, the student is then eligible to receive accommodations in college. Unlike high school, only accommodations, not modifications, are granted in college. This means that only services that can accommodate the students and provide access are typically given through the office of disability services. Modified tests, curricula or homework are not provided. The courses, coursework and expectations are not changed. Also, unlike in high school, college students who receive accommodations must request them each time they are needed. For example, if a professor has announced an upcoming test and the office of disability services has determined that the student is eligible for extra time, the student, not the professor, must contact the office of disability services and let them know that they will be needing extra time for the test. The office of disability services then arranges the exam.

Although there is an office of disability services on each college campus, the services that they provide might vary from one campus to the next. Whereas one campus may provide assistive technology to its eligible students, another campus may not have the means to do so. The term "reasonable accommodations" is the basis of the difference in services. For students with learning disabilities, it is strongly suggested that they visit the office of disability services during any college tour. This visit could give the student information about what kinds of services the office of disability services might be able to provide. Some typical accommodations for students with learning disabilities might include:

- Extra time
- Limited distractions for testing
- Readers
- Note takers

The goal of any office of disability services is to create equal access to all students with disabilities. This is done by providing training to staff, collaborating with all stakeholders and providing individual services for students with disabilities (Council for the Advancement of Standards in Higher Education, 2015; Office for Civil Rights, 2011).

Effective Communication Skills

The third and final leg of self-advocacy is built into the ability to communicate effectively. Now that we know about teaching students about understanding themselves and understanding their rights, it is time to teach them how to get their thoughts across. No matter how well versed the students are about themselves and their rights, without good communication skills, the students will not be able to advocate for themselves effectively. Knowing what they need in order to learn, knowing what their legal rights are regarding their needs and being able to put it all together through effective communication are the essential steps toward self-advocacy and success in college and beyond.

Passive/Aggressive/Assertive Communication

Students with learning disabilities need to be able to communicate their learning needs in an effective way in order to receive them but asking for accommodations in college (or anywhere) can be a terrifying prospect. Approaching new people in a new environment and requesting things that used to be given automatically is daunting on multiple levels. Although some people may be naturally good at communicating, the skills of effective communication are easily taught. In the end, whether you are one of the lucky naturally good communicators or you have had to learn the skills, the result is the same: effective communication skills. The best way to understand communication skills is by breaking down the different styles of communication. Helping our students understand the difference between passive, aggressive and assertive communication can help them become skilled and effective communicators.

Passive communication is a style of communicating that does not overtly express feelings or needs. People who use passive communication tend to let other people make decisions for them and will try to avoid confrontation at the expense of their own needs. For students with learning disabilities who are trying to advocate for themselves, this method of communication can make it almost impossible to get their needs met. Imagine a scenario in which the student needs to remind a professor about an accommodation, such as extra time, that the professor may have forgotten. This student, who may fear upsetting the professor and whose desire to avoid confrontation is overwhelming, may not even remind the professor that they require extra time. This student may start to ask for their accommodation and may apologize continuously throughout the request. This student might also back down if confronted. This passive method of communicating is a way of avoiding uncomfortable situations and will end up hurting more in the long run.

Students should know that they may be passive communicators if they:

- Never assert themselves
- Apologize frequently for stating their opinions or feelings

128 Our Role as Counselors

- Allow other people to be the ones to make decisions for them regardless of what they want for themselves
- Feel conflicted by the things they need and their difficulty in asking for them
- Feel as if others tend to "step all over" them frequently

Aggressive communication is marked by an expression of feelings or needs that can actually violate the rights, feelings or needs of others. This style of communication can be verbally, physically or even emotionally abusive. Unlike passive communication, in which the needs and rights of the individual are not expressed at all, aggressive communicators express their needs and rights overtly. This type of communication can be viewed as intimidating and violent and can actually become the cause of a brand-new problem by causing others to feel fearful or intimidated.

Students should know that they may be aggressive communicators if they:

- Ask for their needs in a loud and demanding voice
- Use blame to get their needs met
- Use threats to get their needs met
- Make others feel fearful of them
- Feel that they are entitled to always get their way

Assertive communicators use respectful words and actions to communicate their needs and rights in a clear and firm manner. They will advocate for themselves decisively, even in situations that they may feel nervous about. Assertive communicators understand their rights, their needs and their ability to get their point across. Assertive communicators know that what they are asking for is necessary and appropriate and will ask to get their needs met even if they are in uncomfortable situations.

Students should know that they may be assertive communicators if they:

- Can state their needs clearly
- Can state their needs respectfully
- Listen to other points of view
- Feel a sense of respectful control
- Feel confident

It is important to note that good communication skills, just like any other skills, are best learned when there is ample opportunity for practice. It may feel silly to a student to be in their counselor's office and be practicing asking for extra time or a decrease of services, but without opportunities for practice, students will not become comfortable with the skill. Students can be given these opportunities either one on one with their counselor or in small

Self-Advocacy **129**

groups. Each student will have their own level of comfort regarding how best to practice. Regardless of how it is done, this practice is a necessary component of teaching effective communication skills.

When to Disclose and Why

Effective communication skills also involve a knowledge and understanding of when it is appropriate to disclose a learning disability. There is no shame in having a learning disability, but the sad truth is that not everyone understands what having a learning disability means. This translates into the fact that disclosing a learning disability needs to be thought through and done purposefully. In general, unless the sharing is being done with friends and family, disclosing a learning disability is usually only done in order to receive accommodations in a new setting. This means that if a student with a writing disability is starting a liberal arts college education, they should disclose their disability in order to receive the services they will need in order to access the curriculum. On the other hand, if a student with a writing disability is starting a program that is completely hands on, such as an art program, or certain kinds of technical or vocational programs, they may not need to disclose their writing disability. If no writing will be expected of them in the program, there is no reason to disclose. Disclosure is only necessary when the disability will have an impact on the student's performance.

Disclosing is an active form of self-advocacy and uses all three core facets of it. If the purpose of disclosure is to receive appropriate and reasonable accommodations, then this means that the person doing the disclosing needs to understand their disability and know what accommodations work for them (knowledge of self), they need to know their legal rights and what they are entitled to (knowledge of rights), and they need to be able to communicate their needs in an effective and assertive manner (effective communication skills).

As these students begin to be a part of the workforce, they should also be aware that disclosing in that arena may become an issue as well. Employees who have learning disabilities that impact their ability to get their work done are entitled to reasonable accommodations. Once again, disclosing to an employer when the learning disability has no impact on the job performance is probably not necessary or appropriate, but disclosing the learning disability when it has a direct impact on the job performance is definitely appropriate.

People with learning disabilities are a protected class under the ADA. An employer cannot discriminate against an employee because they have a learning disability. The law protects employees with disabilities in two ways. It does not allow employers to discriminate against employees or potential employees with disabilities, and it requires the employers to provide

130 Our Role as Counselors

reasonable accommodations for employees with disabilities. In addition, employers are not allowed to ask if an employee or potential employee has a disability. Despite this protection, there is still some ambiguity when it comes to interpreting the law. If, for example, the accommodations that are being requested are not considered "reasonable accommodations," they may not be granted at all. For people with learning disabilities, although the law protects them, disclosing must be a personal and well-thought-out decision.

Once a person decides that disclosure is necessary, they should use appropriate communication skills to ensure that the disclosure is handled in a manner that will provide the necessary accommodation. Using assertive communication skills can make the process run more smoothly and more effectively and can help to create the path toward getting the necessary accommodations.

Case Study: Self-Advocacy

Sydnee is a shy and reserved 17-year-old high school junior who has had an IEP since third grade, when her teacher grew concerned that she was not reading at the same level as the rest of her class. The narrative highlighting her educational history shows that she was identified in third grade after still struggling with reading and math even after being pulled out for basic skills instruction. She was evaluated by the child study team and found eligible for special education services under the category of specific learning disability. The educational and psychological tests that are outlined in the IEP showed that Sydnee has a high-average full-scale IQ combined with below-average processing speeds and that she was almost on grade level for math but not at all for reading. At that time, she was placed in a resource room environment and given replacement reading and math classes. Sydnee had worked really hard in the resource room, and by middle school she was pleased when she was placed in the math general education classroom with one general education teacher and one special education teacher. She was told that the special education teacher was there to support her if she needed it, but she found that she never really had to ask for the help. The special education teacher always explained things to her again anyway, and Sydnee was happy with that because it helped her grades a lot.

She did moderately well in middle school, and by the time she got to high school most of her classes, except for English, had only one teacher. She still struggled in reading and found, as time went on, that she struggled with writing as well, but her extra special education teacher in her English class helped her frequently. Both English teachers have noted that her comprehension and her ideas are wonderful. They note that she seems very shy and quiet and does not contribute frequently, so they make certain to call on her when it seems that she is sure of the answer. They have continuously said that when she speaks in class, her ideas are superb. They have also said that she does not do her work consistently. They have said that they think that her slow reading speed and her challenges with writing seem to have shut down her desire to participate in school. Most of her teachers have corroborated and said that she has the ability to get better grades, but she seems disengaged in class, does not always do her homework and seems to read and write as little as possible for any given assignment. She has a low B to C average in most of her classes.

Sydnee's current IEP shows that there are still discrepancies in her abilities and her skills in reading and writing. Sydnee is getting multiple accommodations and modifications. Right now, she is allowed to retake tests and is getting modified tests and assignments in all of her classes. She is also receiving extra time on tests, quizzes and assignments, but she does not want to ask for the extra time and will not use it when it is given to her. She claims that it makes her "feel more stupid than she already is." She is also very resistant to going for extra help and does not like to ask questions in class either. She verbalizes that going for extra help and asking questions are both reminders that she is "dumb." In the past, she has shared that when she was in elementary school, she was bullied for her reading ability, and since that time she has verbalized on many occasions that she is embarrassed to have an IEP and does not want to draw attention to herself.

Even though she does not like having an IEP, Sydnee is aware of her modifications and accommodations and knows that she has difficulty with reading and writing. She also admits that she is disengaged in school and claims that it is because she is "lazy." She states that her parents and teachers think that she is lazy as well.

Sydnee states that she wants to go to college and wants to be a lawyer. She has expressed interest in a specific college that is about 4 hours away from home and has about 15,000 undergraduate students.

What can the counselor do to help her acquire appropriate self-advocacy skills?

Ms. Cass, Sydnee's counselor, has been a part of Sydnee's academic career since her freshman year. She always makes sure to review Sydnee's IEP and attend her IEP meetings so that she has a better understanding of

132 Our Role as Counselors

her academic needs and challenges. She works closely with Sydnee's case manager to make sure that Sydnee's schedule is appropriately challenging.

Ms. Cass has a good relationship with Sydnee and knows that although she is quiet and withdrawn in her classes, she does much better on a smaller scale. Sydnee feels comfortable with Ms. Cass and talks to her freely. She has told her that she is interested in attending a 4-year college and is also interested in studying law. She has also told her that she has spent every summer working in her uncle's law practice and loves the fast-paced atmosphere and the interesting cases her uncle has shared with her. She seems very interested in politics and, despite her disengagement in school, is very knowledgeable about world events. Sydnee is very fortunate because her school offers many courses in government and law. Each year at scheduling time, Ms. Cass suggests these courses, and each year she refuses, stating that she is "too lazy for those classes." Now that Sydnee is in her junior year, Ms. Cass knows that they have to do more work with helping Sydnee understand and accept her learning disability and her strengths in order to help her prepare for college in a realistic way. Ms. Cass knows that there are several things they need to work on together.

The first thing they need to work on is helping Sydnee understand her learning disability. This means that Sydnee needs to have a working knowledge of her disability and her strengths and what aspects of her learning these might impact. Her slower processing speed in relation to her full-scale IQ needs to be explained to her so that she understands that her difficulties are not based on her intelligence but rather on her learning disability. She also needs to understand that although her learning disability will never go away, her strengths are what will highlight her future and will allow her to find compensatory strategies.

Ms. Cass might also work with Sydnee to understand that her dislike of reading and writing is not based on laziness but is instead an understandable response to something that has never been easy or pleasant for her.

Ms. Cass can also work with Sydnee to help her discard the shame and also find a sense of self-acceptance for her learning disability. Self-acceptance will lead to Sydnee being able to ask for the help she might need without being ashamed. The empowerment that comes with self-acceptance will also allow her to do a realistic assessment of what kinds of things actually help her to succeed. Sydnee's slower processing speed means that she will need to have and to use extra time on her assessments and tests. It also means that she might have difficulty

Self-Advocacy **133**

taking notes and listening at the same time. The fact that there is still a discrepancy between her abilities and skills in reading and writing and that she is still below grade level in these areas means that she may need to find alternate ways to access written material. She may also need compensatory methods to get her thoughts across in written format. Sydnee needs to know that her reading and writing challenges are not going away in college, nor are they going to be managed by an extra teacher in the classroom. Ms. Cass can also remind Sydnee that she has real intellectual strengths by reiterating the positive comments her English teachers have made about her contributions in class.

Ms. Cass can review the accommodations and modifications that Sydnee has been using in high school and help Sydnee to explore the idea of decreasing her modifications. Ms. Cass can explain to Sydnee that modifications are not provided on a college level and that it is in Sydnee's best interest to start getting used to not having them. Ms. Cass can begin to work with Sydnee and her case manager to start decreasing her modifications in order to start preparing for the realities of college.

Sydnee's lofty goals of attending law school do not match her current behavior. Ms. Cass can begin a discussion with Sydnee about her future goals in relation to current behavior. Ms. Cass can have a reality-based discussion with Sydnee about matching her future goals to her current behavior. If Sydnee wants to go to college and law school, she will need to understand that her academic behavior right now is not aligned with what she will need to do to achieve her goals. Ms. Cass and Sydnee can come up with a plan to help Sydnee start modifying her behavior in order to ensure that she will be successful in meeting her future goals.

It is important that Sydnee be prepared for the realities of the expectations of college. Ms. Cass can give Sydnee an overview of college academic expectations. She can explain what a typical workload looks like and tell Sydnee that she will be responsible for doing work on her own. Sydnee and Ms. Cass can discuss a plan for Sydnee to start completing her homework assignments in preparation for college.

Ms. Cass can arrange for an assistive technology evaluation for Sydnee. This evaluation will give Sydnee an opportunity to explore what kinds of assistive technology will be helpful for her. Sydnee will be able to work with the assistive technology expert from the district to find ways to access reading, writing and note taking. Assistive technology devices are constantly changing and improving, but in general, text-to-speech programs are readily available in many different formats for accessing reading. Writing can be accessed with speech-to-text programs followed by editing programs. Note taking can be helped with mind maps, electronic note taking devices and recorders. Sydnee would benefit from using text-to-speech and speech-to-text programs, and Ms. Cass and the assistive technology expert can work together with Sydnee to help her start using all of these tools. Ms. Cass knows that many colleges have assistive technology available for students who are affiliated with their campus office of disability services and she will discuss the availability of these services at the colleges Sydnee has expressed interest in.

Since Sydnee has never seemed to be very engaged in her IEP meetings, she may not understand her rights as a person with a disability. Ms. Cass can give her information about her rights regarding her disability. Ms. Cass can remind Sydnee that it is Sydnee's disability that causes her to access material more slowly than her peers and that despite this, Sydnee has the same rights as everyone else to access the educational material she will find in college. Ms. Cass will explain that in college, disability services work differently than they do in high school and that Sydnee will need to take responsibility for making sure that she gets what she needs to access the curriculum.

Since Sydnee is so quiet and reserved, Ms. Cass will help her practice assertive communication skills. Since she and Sydnee have been talking about decreasing Sydnee's modifications, Ms. Cass will work with Sydnee to practice speaking with her teachers and case managers to request the decrease. Ms. Cass knows that Sydnee is uncomfortable with speaking her mind, and she wants to make sure that Sydnee's passive communication style does not get in her way. Ms. Cass wants to make sure that Sydnee gets enough time to practice her communication skills before leaving high school and heading off to college.

References

Anastasiou, D., & Michail, D. (2013). Exploring discordance between self-efficacy and writing performance among low-literate adult students. *Learning Disabilities: A Contemporary Journal, 11*(1), 53–87.

Arkeny, E., & Lehmann, J. (2010). Journey toward self-determination: Voices of students with disabilities who participated in a secondary transition program on a community college campus. *Remedial and Special Education, 32*(4), 279–289. https://doi.org/10.1177/0741932510362215

ASCA. (2017). *Why high school counselors?* American School Counselor Association. Retrieved from www.schoolcounselor.org/asca/media/asca/Careers-Roles/WhyHighSchool.pdf

Cortiella, C., & Horowitz, S. H. (2014). *The state of learning disabilities: Facts, trends and emerging issues.* New York: National Center for Learning Disabilities.

Council for the Advancement of Standards in Higher Education. (2015). *Professional standards for higher education.* Retrieved from http://standards.cas.edu/getpdf. cfm?PDF=E868395C-F784-2293-129ED7842334B22A

Davis, T., Nida, R., Zlomke, K., & Nebel-Schwalm, M. (2009). Health-related quality of life in college undergraduates with learning disabilities: The mediational roles of anxiety and sadness. *Journal of Psychopathology and Behavioral Assessments, 31*(3), 228–234. https://doi.org/10.1007/s10862-008-9110-4

Durlak, C. M., Rose, E., & Bursuck, W. D. (1994). Preparing high school students with learning disabilities for the transition to postsecondary education: Teaching the skills of self-determination. *Journal of Learning Disabilities, 27*(1), 51–59. https://doi.org/10.1177/002221949402700108

Eccles, S., Hutchings, M., Hunt, C., & Heaslip, V. (2018). Risk and stigma: Students' perceptions and disclosure of disability in higher education. *Widening Participation and Lifelong Learning, 20*(4), 191–208. https://doi.org/10.5456/WPLL.20.4.191

Field, S., Sarver, M. D., & Shaw, S. F. (2003). Self-determination: A key to success in postsecondary education for students with learning disabilities. *Remedial and Special Education, 24,* 339–349. https://doi.org/0.1177/07419325030240060501

Goleniowska, H. (2014). The importance of developing confidence and self-esteem in children with a learning disability. *Advances in Mental Health and Intellectual Disabilities, 8*(3), 188–191. https://doi.org/10.1108/AMHID-09-2013-0059

Graham, R., & Richardson, C. W. (2012). Levelling the playing field: Assistive technology, special education, and a Canadian perspective. *American International Journal of Contemporary Research, 2.*

Hampton, N. Z., & Mason, E. (2003). Learning disabilities, gender, sources of efficacy, self-efficacy beliefs, and academic achievement in high school students. *Journal of School Psychology, 41*(2), 101–112. https://doi.org/10.1016/S0022-4405(03)00028-1

Horn, J. H., & Moss, D. (2015). A search for meaning: Telling your life with learning disabilities. *British Journal of Learning Disabilities, 43*(3), 178–185. https://doi.org/10.1111/bld.12093

Izzo, M., & Lamb, M. (2002). *Self-determination and career development: Skills for successful transitions to postsecondary education and employment. (White Paper).* NCSET. Retrieved from ncset.hawaii.edu/publications/pdf/self_determination.pdf

Jing, C. T., & Chen, C. J. (2017). A research review: How technology helps to improve the learning process of learners with dyslexia. *Journal of Cognitive Sciences & Human Development, 2*(2).

Lightner, K. L., Kipps-Vaughan, D., Schulte, T., & Trice, A. D. (2012). Reasons university students with a learning disability wait to seek disability services. *Journal of Postsecondary Education and Disability, 25*(2), 145–159.

Lindeblad, E., Nilsson, S., Gustafson, S., & Svensson, I. (2017). Assistive technology as reading interventions for children with reading impairments with a one-year follow-up. *Disability and Rehabilitation: Assistive Technology.* https://doi.org/10.1080/17483107.2016.1253116

136 Our Role as Counselors

Livingston, E. M., Siegel, L. S., & Ribary, U. (2018). Developmental dyslexia: Emotional impact and consequences. *Australian Journal of Learning Difficulties*, 1–29. https://doi.org/10.1080/19404158.2018.1479975

McFall, L., & Fitzpatrick, M. (2010). Mainstream literature for full, inclusive secondary classrooms. *Intervention in School and Clinic, 45*(4), 263–270. https://doi.org/10.1177/1053451209353448

Newman, L., & Madaus, J. (2014). Reported accommodations and supports provided to secondary and postsecondary students with disabilities: National perspective. *Career Development and Transition for Exceptional Individuals, 38*(3), 173–181. https://doi.org/doi:10.1177/2165143413518235

Office for Civil Rights. (2011). *Students with disabilities preparing for postsecondary education: Know your rights and responsibilities.* Retrieved from https://www2.ed.gov/about/offices/list/ocr/transition.html

Roberts, E., Ju, S., & Zhang, D. (2016). Review of practices that promote self-advocacy for students with disabilities. *Journal of Disability Policy Studies, 26*(4), 209–220. https://doi.org/10.1177/1044207314540213

Shapiro, D., Dundar, A., Huie, F., Wakhungu, P. K., Yuan, X., Nathan, A., & Bhimdiwali, A. (2017). *Completing college: A national view of student completion rates—Fall 2011 cohort.* National Student Clearinghouse Research Center. Retrieved from https://nscresearchcenter.org/signaturereport14/

Test, D. W., Fowler, C. H., Wood, W. M., Brewer, D. M., & Eddy, S. (2005). A conceptual framework of self-advocacy for students with disabilities. *Remedial and Special Education, 26*(1), 43–54.

von Karolyi, C., Winner, E., Gray, W., & Sherman, G. (2003). Dyslexia linked to talent: Global visual-spatial ability. *Brain and Language, 85*, 427–431. https://doi.org/10.1016/S0093-934X(03)00052-X

West, J. (2000). *Back to school on civil rights: Advancing the federal commitment to leave no child behind.* National Council on Disability. Retrieved from https://files.eric.ed.gov/fulltext/ED438632.pdf

17

WHAT COUNSELORS NEED TO KNOW ABOUT STUDY SKILLS

In this section:

- Mnemonic devices
- Acronyms
- Method of the loci
- Imagery
- Rhymes
- Organizational skills
- Time management
- Connecting to time
- Making a schedule
- Using timers
- Planning for goals
- Material organization
- Organizing study material
- Cognitive skills
- Study routine
- Metacognitive skills
- General study tips
- Case study: study skills

School counselors are an integral part of helping all students achieve academic success. One of the ways that school counselors can achieve this aim is by helping students develop study skills. Direct instruction on study skills and how to use them has been found to have significant impact on a student's academic progress (Mason, 2018). For some students, these strategies come easily, but for many students with learning disabilities, these study skills seem

138 Our Role as Counselors

to have eluded them completely (Gersten, 1998). Since study skills have been found to be an important component of academic success, it is important that students have a large "bag of tricks" at their disposal and have an understanding of when to use each skill (Gettinger & Schurr, 2002). In general, effective study skills are made up of four basic components: repetition skills, organizational skills, cognitive skills and metacognitive skills (Gettinger & Schurr, 2002). These skills, although seemingly innate for some students, seem to elude others. The good news is that they are teachable skills and can have great and positive impact on all students. For students with learning disabilities, who already have difficulty with learning, teaching these study skills can help make these students feel competent, capable and successful.

Mnemonic Devices

Repetition skills are necessary for the memorization that makes up many kinds of studying. Learning things such as the multiplication table or the table of the elements is not easily done without having a working knowledge of repetition skills. For many students, repetition skills are simple. They can memorize information by repeating it frequently enough for it to "stick." Unfortunately, this kind of memorization does not work for everyone or even for every kind of information. Some students can repeat information over and over and over again and still not be able to remember it. For students with memory issues, this simple act of repetition can become more of an exercise in frustration than a study session. Luckily, there are simple methods that can help these students remember the information regardless of their memory or learning challenges.

Mnemonic devices are memorization and repetition tools that allow people to remember complex things. These techniques help to create relevant and memorable connections to the information that we need to learn by attaching new knowledge to things that are already embedded in memory. These techniques can also be used for remembering many different types of information. For students with working memory issues, mnemonic devices are an integral tool in helping to store long-term information. There are many different types of mnemonic devices, and they can each be used for different purposes.

Acronyms

A typical mnemonic device that may be familiar to many people is the use of acronyms. Acronyms are words or phrases that are formed from the first letter of each word in a list of words that need to be memorized. For example, if a student needs to remember the colors of the rainbow, they may remember the name of "ROY G BIV." Each of the letters of the name stand for each successive color in a rainbow—red, orange, yellow, green, blue, indigo and violet. Another example: "Every Good Boy Does Fine" is used to teach children the names of the strings on a guitar: E, G, B, D and F. For students having difficulty remembering the order of operations for math, PEMDAS, or, "Please Excuse My Dear Aunt Sally," is a common and helpful acronym. It stands for Parentheses, Exponents, Multiplication/Division, Addition/Subtraction. For lists that need to be memorized that have no common acronym, students can be encouraged to create their own. A quick internet search for "random acronym generator" generates multiple websites that will create the acronyms for the students automatically. As long as the acronym has some kind of meaning that is easily remembered, it can give students a tremendous boost in their ability to remember ordered lists.

Method of the Loci

Another method of memorizing items in a list is by using what is known as the Method of the Loci. Loci is the Latin word for "place," and this very ancient and powerful method of memorization uses the concept of place quite literally. This method uses quite a bit of imagination and requires both focus and practice for it to be useful. The first step in this method is to have the student imagine a place that they are completely familiar with. It could be their home, their school, or anywhere they can visualize completely. This place should be so familiar that if they think about it or close their eyes, they can find their way through it as if they were actually there. Have the student visualize themselves navigating through this place in a set order. It might help if the place they visualize has something of a linear concept already embedded into it. For example, if they are visualizing their home, it is helpful to visualize it through routines that they have when they come home (i.e., I enter my house through the front door, open the closet and hang up my coat, go upstairs to my room, put down my backpack, go to the bathroom and then stop in the kitchen for a snack). The set order is an important part of the process because the student will then visualize navigating through the place they have chosen. In each stop (i.e., the front door, the closet, the bedroom etc.), they will visualize placing one item from the list until all of the items have been mentally placed. Ideally, the memorized items can be recalled by visualizing the set path through each of the rooms.

In another version of this type of mnemonic, items in a list are recalled by mentally attaching them to specific words that rhyme with numbers. This method too relies heavily on imagination and the ability to think visually. In this method, numbers are rhymed with simple words such as "One, bun. Two, shoe. Three, tree. Four, door", etc. The items that are meant to be remembered are then attached as mental images to each set of rhyming words. So, for example, if the items to be remembered are pencils, concrete, a laptop and a

140 Our Role as Counselors

ruler, each of these items would become a mental image superimposed into the rhymed words. "One, bun" might become an image of a hot dog bun with a pencil inside of it instead of a hotdog. "Two, shoe" might be an image of shoes walking on a concrete sidewalk. "Three, tree" could be a tree that grows laptops and "four, door" could be a height chart on the side of the door that is measured with a ruler.

Imagery

Imagery in general is an excellent mnemonic tool. Imagery takes new information that might not have enough meaning to be remembered on its own and connects it with something that is already familiar. There are multiple ways of using imagery as mnemonic devices, but the crux of each method is the same; the image is the connector to the information that must be remembered. While for some students, recall of facts may occur through repetition or reading, many other students might spend hours doing the same to no avail. For many students with learning disabilities, new knowledge may take longer to make sense, connect and synthesize than it does for students without learning disabilities. For these students, connections may have to be made in a far more specific manner. Information such as names of people, dates or events remains disconnected and untethered. For these students, tests that require recall of these kinds of details may be impossible to pass. It may seem easy to remember that George Washington crossed the Delaware River by boat, but for many students with learning disabilities, each word may as well exist in a vacuum. To them, the name George Washington may not have any connection to the Delaware River or the boat he used to cross it. There is no reason to attach George Washington to the Delaware River unless you already know that there is a connection, and this may not be the case for students with learning disabilities. These students need to have the connection made in another way. The use of imagery and visualizing techniques as mnemonic tools becomes the connection that ties the events to each other, and it does so in a vivid manner.

Imagery as a mnemonic tool takes the items that need to be remembered and arranges them mentally them in an unusual or meaningful way. As an example, to remember that it was George Washington who crossed the Delaware River in a boat, a student might have to think about what they already know and can already visualize. Perhaps they know who George Washington was and they can visualize him in their mind. Perhaps they have also heard or seen the George Washington Bridge, which spans a large river. Perhaps they also know, as they see George Washington in their mind's eye, that the short pants that he wears are called knickers. Perhaps, as they think about those knickers he is wearing, they also know that the word "knickers" is another word for "underwear." And finally, perhaps as they think about George

Study Skills **141**

Washington's "underwear," they realize how similar to it the word "Delaware" is. Suddenly, they can remember that it was, indeed, George Washington who crossed the Delaware River.

As another example, a student might not remember that Isaac Newton is connected to the laws of gravity. They might, however, remember this fact if they connect his name (Isaac Newton) to Fig Newton cookies (Newton) which they imagine are falling from the sky (gravity). This connection helps to solidify the idea that Isaac Newton (Fig Newtons) had something to do with gravity (Fig Newtons falling from the sky). Perhaps they may be having trouble remembering the name of the first colony founded in the United States. Perhaps, though, they are also lucky enough to have a friend named James. They might imagine James (James) coming in first (first colony) in a race in a town (town) not too far away.

If, for example, a person has difficulty matching names to faces, a mnemonic device can be used to attach the person's name to a certain attribute that they possess and can also visualize. A simple example of this could be that someone named Jane might dress in very simple style. Attaching her name to an image of a simple outfit she may have worn would be the visual mnemonic device. The name Harry might remind a student of the word "hairy." If Harry has a beard or a mustache, this would be a useful connection for remembering his name, but even if he didn't, creating a visualization of Harry with a beard is also useful.

In math, some students have difficulty remembering which axis is the "x" axis and which is the "y." One of my students shared that the only way they could remember which was which was by thinking about pirates. When I seemed confused (and I was), they said, "you know, like in "x marks the spot!" I had to admit that I was still confused but then they explained themselves. They had connected the concept of the x axis to "x marks the spot" by imagining a pirate following a treasure map to the point where "X" marked the spot. Digging for the buried treasure on that "X" spot would be done on the ground beneath the "x," and since both the ground and the "x" axis are horizontal, that was where the connection was made. While it seemed that this student had done an awful lot of storytelling and image generating to create this connection, it worked for them.

Another student was having difficulty memorizing the table of the elements. For this student, the chart was mostly just a bunch of letters. While some of the letters matched up to the elements easily (such as "He" for Helium or "O" for oxygen), many of the others seemed to have no connection to the elements that they were supposed to represent. When this student learned how to use imagery as a mnemonic device, they were able to memorize the entire table in one night. This student used images such as a thickly spread peanut butter sandwich that is so heavy from the peanut butter that it falls to the ground like a lead weight (Pb = lead), a surprise gift of a beautiful gold

142 Our Role as Counselors

necklace that makes people say, "Aw, that is so sweet" (Au = gold) and the iron bar that closes across the seat on a Ferris wheel to keep people from falling out (Fe = iron). The idea, with this kind of imagery, is to create some kind of meaningful connection where there has been none before. The imagery could be fanciful and unusual, like my student's pirate image or the images associated with the table of the elements, or it could be more commonplace. If the imagery helps the student to make the connection, then this mnemonic tool has worked.

Rhymes

Although the use of rhymes as a mnemonic device is a popular technique for memorization, it must be noted that it may not be the most appropriate method to use with students with learning disabilities. Students with dyslexia might have difficulty identifying rhymes, so using a mnemonic device that is based on recalling a set of rhymed words may be difficult if not impossible and might defeat the purpose of using a mnemonic device. If rhyming is not a problem, using rhymes as mnemonic devices entails creating a rhyming word of phrase to connect with the information which needs to be memorized. Examples of well-known mnemonic rhymes are:

> Thirty days hath September, April, June, and November;
> All the rest have thirty-one,
> Save February, with twenty-eight days clear,
> And twenty-nine each leap year.
> or
> In fourteen hundred ninety-two
> Columbus sailed the ocean blue.
> or
> "I" before "E" except after "C."

Some important points to remember when using mnemonics:

- The mnemonic device creates relevance when there does not seem to be any inherent in the information that needs to be recalled.
- Vivid or unusual mental images may take some practice or time to create but can be excellent mnemonic devices.
- Many mnemonic acronyms already exist and can be easily found with a little bit of research. Alternately, acronym generators can be used as well.

Organizational Skills

Organizational skills, in terms of study skills, are the skills which allow students to organize their time, their minds and the materials they will need in order to study effectively. Organizational skills allow students to have a direct and clear path toward the end goal. These skills act like a roadmap toward the assimilation of the material the student is trying to study. A student might have all the intentions of studying, but if they have not set aside enough time, have not brought home the right books for studying or keep getting distracted by other things, they will not be able to study effectively. Many students with learning disabilities and related disorders have challenges with organizational skills, so it is important that we address organizational skills and habits early on and discuss the different components, including time management skills, material organization and cognitive skills.

Time Management

Although for many students (and adults) time management seems like a challenging skill to master, it is an integral organizational skill that allows students to stay focused on the task at hand and not get lost in their day. It is also a skill that needs to be specifically taught and practiced in order for students to master it. But teaching time management skills is not just a matter of showing students how to create checklists or set timers. The question of why these students lose track of time so easily needs to be explored before the solutions are suggested. How these students experience time is something that needs to be addressed first. For most people, a connection to time is not as straightforward as we might believe. It is easy, as so many of us have experienced, to find that we have lost hours of our day to things such as internet surfing or games on our phones. For students, the distractions are even more powerful than the ones that we fall prey to. Social media, for example, is just a click away and can be a powerful time sucker/avoidance tool. Despite the fact that there are 60 minutes in an hour and 24 hours in a day, there are still moments when time seems to move much more quickly or much more slowly than usual. Even in my memory of it, my very first job (as a receptionist) seemed to make the days stretch longer than I ever thought was possible. Good time management skills allow students to still engage in the activities they enjoy with the limits necessary to make sure that they are still doing the things they need to do.

Connecting to Time

Students with certain related learning disabilities such as ADHD or executive function disorder might feel the passage of time like this at all times. One of my students once explained to me that school and studying felt like 100 years had passed, whereas when they played video games, for example, the only way they would know that hours rather than minutes had passed was their parents telling them how many hours had passed since they had started to play. We can't teach a student to use time management skills when

144 Our Role as Counselors

they have such little connection to time to begin with. For these students, we need to start more slowly. These students need to have some concrete connection to time that will become the basis of the other skills. Without this basic connection to time, these students get lost inside of it. There is little wonder why a student with no sense of time at all would forget to study or would not be able to get their homework done. Telling a student that they will need to make time to study is not as effective as exploring their connection to time, helping them set up a schedule and then showing them how to set timers for each activity in the schedule.

Helping students connect to time is a way of giving them some control. If time disappears and they don't have any way to account for it, they are not the ones in control of their day. Helping them to make time more concrete gives them the ability to take back some of that control and allows them to make decisions about what they will be doing with the time that they now have. Assuming that the student in question is actually bringing home the materials they need to study and do homework and also has the time and a place to do it, we can start with exploring what happens in the time between when they get home and when they go to sleep. What time do they get home? What time do they go to sleep or eat dinner? What are the things that they are actually doing in the time between they get home from school and the time they go to sleep? Are they coming right home after school? Are they eating a snack, watching TV, playing video games? Do they have other responsibilities such as making dinner or caring for a younger sibling? Once we get the answers to these questions, we can begin to help them concretize their afternoon. There are only so many hours between the time they get home and the time they go to sleep. By figuring out how many hours are in between those times and what activities besides homework and studying need to fit into those hours as well, we can start to help them to make a more concrete connection with time. Let's imagine that this student, after answering all of the questions, realizes that they have seven hours between the time they come home and the time they go to sleep. I have had many students who, after running through this exercise, have been shocked to realize that they have been playing video games for six hours or more a night. This skill of connecting with time roots students into their day and lets them see their behavior with a little more clarity.

Making a Schedule

Once there is some connection with time, we can help the student make a schedule. We already know how much time the student has in between the time they come home and the time they go to sleep. We might also know what, if any, responsibilities they might have besides schoolwork during this time. In order to help them create a schedule, we have them write a list of

Study Skills **145**

all of the activities and responsibilities, including homework, that they have to do after school. I find that the more concrete it is, the more of an impact it seems to have, so I like to have them write it as a list and then cut each activity into a separate strip of paper. The student then physically arranges the activities in the order that they believe will work best. There are times that I will need to step in and help them rearrange some of the items, but for the most part, the list is theirs, and they need to own it. At this point, the student assigns time frames to each of the activities, i.e., snack from 3:15–3:30, video games from 3:35–4:30, etc. The student checks to make sure that everything they want or need to do fits into their afternoon, makes adjustments as needed and then creates their calendar either electronically or on a planner. (For some reason, as adept as they seem to be electronically, many of them do not seem to know how to use their phone's calendar so there are times when using that calendar is presented as a tutorial as well.) In general, creating an actual written schedule (on paper or electronic) is not just helpful but necessary. It is important to remember that the schedule must be both rigid enough to be able to make sure that it avoids distractions but flexible enough to account for the unexpected. For homework and studying purposes, this might mean making sure to embed extra time just in case there is a need for it (Gettinger & Nicaise, 1997).

Using Timers

Again, making a schedule means nothing if the student has no sense of time to begin with. The schedule has to be tied to a concrete tool that signifies the end of one activity and the beginning of another. Otherwise, the student who gets lost in time will still get lost in time. A timer is a simple and effective tool for setting the beginning and end of activities. For scheduling purposes, if the student is using their phone calendar for their scheduling needs, timers and alarms can be set up that can be attached to each activity and can be set to repeat automatically. Otherwise, timers or alarms would have to be manually set for each activity beginning and end. The timer reminds the student to stop one activity and then start on another.

For the student who is reluctant to start working on something that seems difficult or distasteful, timers can be used to create realistic parameters as well. Since many students with learning disabilities do not have that innate connection with time, getting started on schoolwork could feel like they are falling into an abyss. The timer can be set as a definitive parameter. The student is told that they can decide how much time they will spend doing the task. The timer is set to that amount of time, and when the timer goes off, they can stop, no matter how much they have accomplished. What this does is twofold. If the student sees an end to a task that they find very distasteful, they may be more apt to start doing it. The concept of allowing them to stop

146 Our Role as Counselors

working even if the work is not completed gives them a way out if they need it. Even if they do not complete the task but have, at the very least, gotten started on it, they are more engaged in their academics than they had been previously. At the same time, many of my students who use this method find that the amount of time that they have set aside for accomplishing this academic task is actually enough anyway.

Planning for Goals

Good time management also involves the creation of goals. Goals are not just about stating what you want for your future. Anyone can say that they want to be an NFL star, but if all they do is sit in front of the television and eat ice cream, wanting to be an NFL star is not a goal, it is just a fantasy. Having goals does not mean having a desire for something. Having goals means deciding what it is that is wanted and then figuring out what the steps will be for getting it. In terms of study skills, an appropriate goal might be that a student would like to get a good grade on an upcoming test. Just wanting the good grade is not enough. The student needs to be encouraged to create a path or a plan that leads to this goal. The goal has to be attached to behavior, and that behavior needs to be aligned to the goal. Perhaps, for the student whose goal it is to get a good grade on an upcoming test, the plan for achieving this goal will be to put 30 minutes of study time aside each night for a whole week prior to the test. This would be an example of a plan that is aligned to the goal. If, on the other hand, the goal is to get a good grade and the plan to achieve the goal is to study for 10 minutes the night before the test, then this plan is not aligned with the goal and would probably not lead to achieving it.

When working with students on planning for goals, it is important to help them understand the realities associated with planning for goals. First, the student must be made aware of the fact that their goal needs to be realistic. They cannot, for example, have a goal of getting an A as a final grade in a class where they have been getting low grades all year long. Secondly, they must also be made aware of the fact that their plan needs to be realistically aligned to the goal. A plan of minimal study time with a goal of a good grade is not a realistically aligned plan. Finally, students need to be aware of the fact that sometimes, no matter how good your plan is and no matter how hard you try, goals may not always be achieved, and that too is okay.

Once the goal and the plan to achieve it have been identified, the next step is to determine the actual amount of time it will take to achieve the goal. A realistic assessment of the time involvement is very important, and for students who may not have experience with goal setting, this may be difficult, and they may need extra guidance. At this point, the student's schedule needs to be revisited in order for the plan for achieving the stated goal to be incorporated.

Material Organization

It is important for students to know that being prepared for studying and homework is as important as the studying itself. Spending 20 minutes searching for a pen or a charger for your computer wastes time and can be a frustrating endeavor. An organized spot with study material ready for use creates a more efficient study time. It also allows the students to free their minds from having to search for the materials they need to study and gives them, instead, the time to actually study.

Organizing Study Material

Good study habits are difficult to have without good organizational habits, and good organizational habits start inside a student's backpack and locker. Backpacks and lockers are meant to help students be prepared in their classes. When students are more prepared in their classes, homework and studying become inordinately easier as well.

Although I see students walking the halls with backpacks so heavy that it makes me wonder how these children are still standing upright, the purpose of lockers is to store books and binders while they are not being used. Encourage students to clean out their lockers at least once a week. This will keep the garbage that they might store in there (for lack of finding an actual garbage can) to a minimum. Since so much of what goes into a backpack is also what goes into a locker, the tips and tricks for much of the organization are similar for both.

Students should be encouraged to have separate binders or notebooks for each subject. These binders and notebooks should each have their own particular color in order for students to be able to find them easily both in a backpack and in a locker. If books are to be covered, then the book cover for the book pertaining to the particular subject should, ideally, be the same color as the notebook and/or binder. Any folders should be the same color as well. This means that if a student has decided that their English binder will be red, then their English folders and book covers should be red as well. Every subject and their related folders, book covers, and binders should have their own separate colors. This color-coding system makes it easy to quickly find, both in their backpack and their locker, what a student might need for a class.

Students also need to understand that they will need to make sure that their backpacks are always prepared for the day as well. Paper, pens, pencils, sharpeners, computers and whatever else they need for the day should be fully stocked in their backpacks every single day. Having a separate pencil case with extras of everything is always a good idea. Finally, backpacks and folders should be cleaned out every night if possible. It is astounding how much paper students can collect in a single day, and all of it can add to less focus, more chaos and more distraction.

148 Our Role as Counselors

Students should have planners. Let me say it again. Every student everywhere should have a planner. This planner should be used to write down assignments in every single class every single day, and these assignments can then be added to the schedule. Even if the teacher posts assignments online, students should still get into the habit of keeping all of their information in one place. Students should also get into the habit of using the information in that planner to check what they might need from their locker for the night. At the end of the night, not in the morning, students can use that planner again to make sure that they have packed up everything they will need to be prepared for the next morning.

Encourage students to pick a specific location in their home as their study place. Ideally, the spot should be in a location where they will not have significant opportunities for disruption. Sitting near a loud television or in the middle of a busy kitchen are not ideal locations for studying. The space should allow for comfortable writing both on paper and on a computer.

Any item that the student will need for studying should be stored in or near the spot they have chosen for studying. Items such as pens, pencils, sharpeners, erasers, paper, hole-punches, tape, glue, scissors, staplers and highlighters should be accessible nearby. Students can be taught to place the most frequently used items, such as pens, pencils, erasers, sharpeners and highlighters, in a separate and easily retrieved canister.

Students should also be encouraged to develop good habits regarding their computers. If students get into the habit of charging their laptops at the same time of day that they charge their phones, they will always have a charged and prepared laptop. If students make sure that their charging cable is always left in the same spot (preferably near their study area), they will always be able to find it. Finally, just like their binders, books and folders should be organized and easy to find, their computer files should follow suit as well. Each school subject should have its own aptly named folder on their computer, and all documents related to that subject should be dropped into the appropriate folder.

Cognitive Skills

Cognitive skills can be defined as the skills that allow us to think. These skills can include things such as the ability to pay attention, the ability to remember things and the ability to find logic or patterns. They are the skills we use to take information that comes in through our senses and translate it into knowledge and understanding. Without these skills, we are just experiencing our lives through our senses without any understanding of the meaning behind what we are experiencing. Good cognitive study skills help students to organize their thoughts and become active learners. When students have learning disabilities, some of these cognitive skills can be at somewhat of a deficit, and this could make organizing their thoughts or becoming active learners a bit more of a challenge. When students with learning disabilities study for school, these deficits might put them at a disadvantage if their abilities to learn new concepts, keep sustained attention or remember facts are not as strong as they need to be. Luckily, and despite these possible deficits, there are skills that these students can learn in order to compensate for the deficits they might have in this area. A student with a learning disability may know that they have cognitive deficit when it comes to remembering facts. This student could be encouraged to use mnemonic devices to compensate for this deficit. Another student may know that learning new information might take them longer than many of their peers. This student could be encouraged to find connections between what they are currently learning and any prior knowledge that they may have about the topic in order to help solidify the learning a bit more quickly. All of these students should be given a "bag of tricks" that they could pull out to use when they find that their basic cognitive skills may be lagging. Some examples of these tricks might be:

- Rewording new information in their own words to check for their own understanding
- Reading chapter and section headings prior to reading a whole chapter to make sure that focus is maintained and that the main ideas are understood
- Taking notes during class to stay actively involved in the learning process
- Creating outlines from readings to remember what was read
- Reviewing information daily to reinforce long-term memory
- Studying while moving to maintain attention and focus
- Speaking aloud while studying to help with retention
- Dividing long assignments into shorter chunks in order to aid memory and create manageable goals
- Studying in a quiet and distraction-free place in order to maintain focus

Study Routine

Time management skills also involve the ability to create a study routine. Helping students to create a study routine will provide them with the structure needed to complete work effectively. Without a routine, habits are untethered and easily neglected. A study routine solidifies habits that make it easier and quicker to get into the practice of getting the work done. If the student knows that at 4:00 p.m. they have to get to work, there is no reinventing the wheel, and time is actually saved by having this part of an automatic

150 Our Role as Counselors

routine already in place. Parts of a study routine might involve turning off distractions such as phones, taking scheduled breaks with specific time limits and creating realistic schedules. Below is a more complete list of potential parts of a good study routine:

- Working in a dedicated place for working (not a bedroom etc.)
- Completing difficult work at times when you are most alert and least distracted
- Reviewing notes every day
- Starting writing assignments even if there is uncertainty about how to start
- Highlighting notes if there are specific questions
- Leaving phones in another room
- Taking planned breaks
- Checking planner or to-do list
- Doing hardest assignments first
- Checking deadlines for assignments

Metacognitive Skills

So many times over a school year, a student will come to my office in tears after doing poorly on a test for which they have studied for hours. The student is distraught, the parents are disappointed, and the teacher is convinced that they are just not trying hard enough. The poor student does not understand why all of the time they have spent studying did not translate into a better grade. They might tell you that no matter what they do, they fail. They might blame the teacher for testing them on things they "did not teach" them. Students with learning disabilities (who may already have experienced failure and frustration) may shut down even further when these kinds of things happen. What these students might be missing is that despite the amount of time they might have studied, it is possible that their "studying" was done with a lot of quantity but not a lot of quality. It is possible that these students were focused on rote memorization when what was needed was a deeper understanding of the material. They may have been reading the words associated with the material over and over and over again, but those words may never have come to mean anything. They may even have memorized some facts associated with the material, but the understanding eluded them.

How is it possible that this situation happens so frequently to so many students? The answer is that, no matter how much time these students are putting into studying, they are not engaging with the material in a meaningful

Study Skills **151**

way. These students may not even realize that they are working from a shallow knowledge of the material. They know that they have spent hours "studying" but do not understand that studying involves more than just rereading the material. These students are missing the metacognitive strategies that help make the information that they are learning more meaningful and more fully understood.

Metacognitive strategies allow students to question the goals and purposes of what they are currently doing and bring forth a deeper understanding of the material they are studying. Metacognitive strategies involve having students ask themselves questions while they are studying such as "Why is this important to know?" "Does this make sense to me?" and "What can I do to understand this better?" These strategies allow students to delve into the topic being studied in a way that solidifies understanding in a manner that simple rote memorization cannot achieve (Gettinger & Schurr, 2002).

The concept of metacognition is based on the ability to be able to understand one's own thought processes and how these thought processes translate into learning (Flavell, 1979). This type of understanding precludes simple memorization. It moves beyond memorization into a realm in which students actively create a study and learning plan that is based on identified needs and continuously assess themselves and strategize their learning based on those assessments.

Students who use metacognitive strategies would not rely on the same study techniques that they have used in the past just because it is what they are used to. Metacognition involves a thoughtful plan of study based on what needs to be learned. "How will I learn this best?" is the question that begins the metacognitive process. As the studying progresses, the student may ask "Is this working for me?" These self-assessments about the studying process allow students to change gears as needed to another more appropriate study behavior.

Metacognition in studying and learning involves planning for the learning, monitoring the learning, reflecting on understanding or lack or of understanding and strategizing to resolve any remaining confusion (Flavell, 1979). Students who use metacognitive skills are not just following directions when it comes to learning. They are actively engaged in the learning process and take ownership of it. A student using metacognitive strategies who is preparing for a test may plan their time for studying far in advance of the test, use all resources available to study (PowerPoints, notes, books etc.), make mental and physical notes of anything they may not understand and actively seek help for filling in any gaps in their knowledge. These students are not just memorizing facts, they are continuously asking themselves if what they are

152 Our Role as Counselors

learning makes sense or if there is something else that they can connect to the information to make it even more meaningful. A student who is reading might ask themselves, "What is happening in this section?" A student who is taking notes in a class may ask themselves, "Do I understand this?" or "Is this important?" A student who is studying may ask themselves, "Does this make sense to me?" This ability to ask themselves these types of questions enable the student to make adjustments to their studying and learning behavior as warranted by the tasks they are engaged in. This gives these students the power to know that they do or do not understand what they are learning, and this understanding gives them the locus of control for accessing help and getting answers to their questions.

For students with learning disabilities, metacognition skills have been shown to have a significant positive effect on their learning (Trainin & Swanson, 2005). Students with learning disabilities who use these skills and strategies can become successful when they rely on them to compensate for the cognitive deficits they may have that are related to their disability. These skills are fairly easily taught. Counselors can teach their students to use metacognitive strategies by breaking down the studying into three distinct parts and having the students ask themselves questions associated with each part:

Planning
- When should I start studying for this test?
- How much time per day will I devote to studying for this?
- What is the best way to study for this test?
- Should I study in a group or by myself?
- Do I have all of the materials (books, notes, presentations etc.) that I will need to study for this?

Studying
- Do I actually understand this?
- Is this connected to anything else I have learned in this class?
- Why is this important to know?
- Am I using the best study strategy for this?
- Can I explain this to someone if they asked me what this was about?

Resolving confusion
- What questions do I have about this?
- Where can I get answers to these questions?
- Where else can I get answers to these questions?
- Who can I ask to help me?

Table 17.1 General Study Tips

Use mnemonic devices
  Create mental images to help in remembering things
  Create relevance for things that are hard to remember
  Create rhymes to help in remembering things
  Create acronyms
  Create unusual connections or visualized images
Be organized
  Create a specific study space
  Use a planner or calendar
  Use colored folders
  Clean out backpack daily
  Pack necessary material for the next day prior to going to bed
  Set specific time aside for studying for tests and doing homework
  Have a plan for long-term assignments
  Write daily to-do list
  Write down assignments
  Write neatly on tests or use computer if possible
Create good study habits
  Do homework every night
  Use flashcards
  Take practice tests
  Study during most productive time
  Study more difficult subjects first
  Review notes every day
  Study in a quiet, distraction-free place
  Do an overview before reading to make sure you are focused
  Pick one site to find information to avoid getting lost in the internet rabbit hole
  Change your mind-set about work—a challenge is different than an impossibility

Vary study tasks (e.g., do reading and then writing and then studying or study while moving or speaking aloud)
Reward yourself
Turn chapter headings into questions that get answered as you write an outline
Take tests smarter
  Cross out answers you already know are wrong
  Answer on your own before reading the choices on multiple-choice tests
  Read all of the choices on multiple-choice tests
  "Brain dump" on scrap paper prior to test starting (write out all remembered information)
  Answer tests questions even if you aren't sure
  Read directions carefully on tests
  Find hints or key words in questions
  Answer everything (partial credit is still credit)
  Keep your first answer
  Review answers before handing in test
  Mark unsure responses to questions to come back to them later
Take better notes
  Create a shorthand for note taking
  Leave room for questions in the margins of notes
  Use different-colored pens and highlighters to help differentiate ideas
  Highlight missed points in notes
  Listen for important points
  Underline while taking notes
  Take notes while listening actively

154 Our Role as Counselors

Case Study: Study Skills

Maya is a 16-year-old high school sophomore. She is a bright young woman who seems to be well liked by all of her teachers and peers. Although her teachers consistently say that she adds invaluable information and discussion points to every class, her test scores are always lower than what the teachers believe she is capable of. Maya claims that she studies for tests but that when she gets to the test day, she seems to forget everything she has studied. She admits that she does not always get her homework done and acknowledges that she forgets to do it frequently. Maya tells her counselor that she is frustrated, because no matter what she does, she cannot seem to do well on her tests and quizzes.

What can the counselor do to help her acquire appropriate study skills?

Mr. Scott, her counselor, knows that Maya really does want to succeed and wants to help Maya figure out what is getting in her way. Mr. Scott can help Maya assess what she is actually doing when she is studying. If Maya is spending 3 hours repeating information from a book with little understanding of what any of it means, she is not studying. Mr. Scott can ask Maya to take him through her study routine step by step so that they can figure out where the breakdown might be. Once Mr. Scott has an idea of where Maya's study skills are lacking, he can show her alternative and more appropriate strategies for studying.

After speaking to Maya, it may become clear to Mr. Scott that Maya may be putting a lot of time into studying, but she is not engaged on a cognitive level. Mr. Scott can explain to Maya what metacognitive skills are and why they are important for studying and learning. He can give Maya a list of good metacognitive questions to ask herself while studying and even have her practice using the questions in different study situations. These practice techniques can help her learn to assess her learning while it is happening in real time.

Mr. Scott can also help Maya set up a study routine BEFORE the night before a test. Since Maya has admitted that she does not do her homework in any consistent way, it is clear that Maya does not see that her lack of a consistent homework routine is actually hurting her study habits. Maya does not seem to see homework as an actual form of studying, so she does not see the need to put the time into getting it all done. Mr. Scott can explain to Maya that doing homework is both a way to study and also good way to assess whether or not she knows the material before it is time for a test. Mr. Scott can help Maya see that if she has an idea of what she is unsure about, she can approach her teacher with questions prior to taking the test.

Based on the fact that Maya reports that she has difficulty remembering things when it comes time to take a test, Maya may have some difficulty with memory. Mr. Scott can teach Maya some mnemonic devices and when to use them.

Finally, if Maya is only engaging with her work on a very superficial level, then it would make sense that she is having difficulty passing tests. Mr. Scott can work with Maya to help her use metacognitive skills to help her assess when she does and or when she does not understand something.

References

Flavell, J. H. (1979). Metacognition and cognitive monitoring: A new area of psychology inquiry. In *Metacognition: Core readings* (p. 8). Boston: Allyn and Bacon.

Gersten, R. (1998). Recent advances in instructional research for students with learning disabilities: An overview. *Learning Disabilities Research and Practice, 13*(3), 162–170.

Gettinger, M., & Nicaise, M. (1997). Study skills. In *Children's needs II: Development, problems and alternatives* (pp. 407–418). Bethesda, MD: National Association of School Psychologists.

Gettinger, M., & Schurr, J. (2002). Contributions of study skills to academic competence. *School Psychology Review, 31*(3), 350–365.

Mason, H. D. (2018). Evaluation of a study skills intervention programme: A mixed methods study. *Africa Education Review,* 1–18. https://doi.org/10.1080/18146627.2016.1241666

Trainin, G., & Swanson, H. L. (2005). Cognition, metacognition, and achievement of college students with learning disabilities. *Learning Disability Quarterly, 28*(4), 261–272. https://doi.org/10.2307/4126965

18

WHAT COUNSELORS NEED TO KNOW ABOUT CHOOSING COLLEGES AND UNIVERSITIES

In this part:
- Searching for appropriate schools
- Levels of support
- Schools with programs for students with learning disabilities
- Understanding the role of the office of disability services
- Disclosing and accessing services

Students with learning disabilities have unique needs when it comes to choosing colleges and universities. These needs extend beyond just choosing schools that provide the career or study path that students might consider. For students with disabilities, the path to finding the right school must include an acknowledgment of their disability as well. These students must be able to understand that their disability might have an impact on their postsecondary studies and this potential impact might have to inform their search process. For example, a student with extensive support needs must make sure to explore schools that will provide the kind of support that they will need. This means that students need to have guidance in understanding the different types of disability support programs that schools provide. In addition, students must have an understanding of the function of the office of disability services, and they must have an idea of the specific kinds of questions they might need to ask. Finally, these students must also be comfortable disclosing their disabilities appropriately.

As high school counselors, we are in the unique position of having insight and knowledge about colleges and universities that we then share with our students. For the majority of our population, we use this knowledge to help them make informed decisions about their postsecondary education. For

Choosing Colleges and Universities **157**

our students with learning disabilities, it is important the we also have an understanding of the schools, programs and offices of disability services that provide these students with what they will need.

Searching for Appropriate Schools

One of the many things we might do as high school counselors is visit and get to know the schools and programs that might be of interest to our students. In my career, I have visited with many universities, colleges, technical programs and armed forces representatives. I have gotten to know the representatives, have gotten to know the programs and have used this knowledge to inform my practice with my students. On many occasions, I have called students out of class to meet with a representative from a program I believed might be a good fit. I make it a point to visit and learn as much as possible about the programs that might be of interest to my students and use this knowledge to help my students make good and informed decisions. When we work with students with learning disabilities, it is just as important to have a thorough understanding of the programs and services that these students will need to use to help access their postsecondary education.

To make sure that we are servicing our population inclusive of students with learning disabilities, we also need to make sure that we have that same kind of insight into the potential differences in services offered by the different schools. Because schools are only required to provide a basic level of service, it is important to encourage our students to explore what each school might be able to offer. There is no uniform requirement for schools to service students with learning disabilities outside of providing "reasonable accommodations." Unfortunately, the term "reasonable accommodations" can change its meaning based on financial or even physical resources that each individual school might have. For some schools, "reasonable accommodations" for students with learning disabilities means little more than facilitating extra time on exams. For other schools, "reasonable accommodations" might mean providing assistive technology tools or specialized and professional tutoring. To help students be more informed in the search process, there are certain key things that they should be looking out for:

- Specific programs. Many schools provide separate programs within the schools for students with learning disabilities. If there is a specific program, these might have separate applications, different criteria for admission or extra fees.
- Freshman orientation. Some programs allow students who are registered with the office of disability services (ODS) to attend an earlier orientation in order to have a little more time to acclimate.

158 Our Role as Counselors

- Documentation. Each school might have slightly different requirements for documentation necessary to register with the ODS.
- Cost for services. Although most schools do not charge for basic services, many schools with intensive programs do charge an extra fee. This fee can be upward of several extra thousand dollars per semester.
- On-campus mental health. Many students with learning disabilities also suffer from comorbid anxiety and depression. Knowing that there is accessible mental health service on campus can make the difference between success and failure for many students with learning disabilities.
- On-campus or nearby pharmacy. For students living far away from home, necessary medications may have to be filled while they are at school. Having a pharmacy on or near campus that can fill these prescriptions on a regular basis may be a real necessity for some students. For these students, coming home just to get ADHD, anti-anxiety or any other medication may be a real disruption. Having a pharmacy close by and accessible makes it easier for students to manage their medication needs without disrupting their studies.
- Class size. For many students with learning disabilities, learning is more readily accomplished in a smaller setting. Overwhelmingly large classes may be too difficult for some students. Many colleges and universities, when talking about class size, will disclose information that is based on an average rather than a range. The problem with this is that this number is an average that takes into account all of the classes that the school has to offer. The real question is not "What is the average class size" but rather "How big is your biggest class?" "How many classes are offered that are close to that size?" "Are any of those classes mandatory?" and "Are any of those classes mandatory for my prospective major?"
- Tutors. Most colleges and universities will offer some sort of academic tutoring. Frequently, this tutoring is peer-based tutoring and is offered to all students free of charge. The ODS, however, may provide specialized tutoring. If there is specialized tutoring for students with learning disabilities, it is important to know if this tutoring is provided by tutors who have specialization in learning disabilities. Although many students with learning disabilities will be perfectly fine with any kind of tutoring, many others may need this higher level of expertise. It is important to have the students and families ask the schools if the tutoring is fee based or free, if it is done individually or in a group and if it is drop-in or prearranged. In addition, for students with writing-based needs, it is important to find out if there is a writing center on campus and, if there is, how is it accessed, who does the tutoring and is there an extra fee.
- Advising. Most universities assign specific advisors to each incoming student. These advisors usually help students navigate through the maze of choosing classes and picking a major and support the student through

Choosing Colleges and Universities **159**

college. For students with learning disabilities, the ODS may assign an extra advisor to support the student in getting the accommodations that they are entitled to. Meetings with either advisor may be mandatory, and students should ask about the frequency and/or accessibility of these advisory meetings.

- ODS services and accommodations. Since not all schools can provide the same kinds of accommodations, students and their families should be advised to research the services that the ODS at each prospective school might be able to provide. Students who are preparing to enter college but continue to struggle with time management, social skills or study skills could benefit from programs that might provide these services for them on campus. Assistive technology services also vary from campus to campus, so students who could benefit from assistive technology should also make certain to ask about the availability and type of assistive technology that will be available to them. Students who receive extra time and/or distraction-free settings should also ask if there is a specific place for them to take exams. Finally, students need to make sure to understand the process is for making professors aware of their accommodations.

Levels of Support

Students should understand that for the most part, disability support services for students with learning disabilities are not the same across the board. Some schools have intensive, 4-year programs that employ learning specialists as tutors or mentors, while others offer extra time and peer tutoring. For the most part, these levels seem to fall into three different categories, which we will refer to as basic, intensive and complete. Every school in the United States is obliged to offer disability support services. This service is offered at no cost to students at every single college and university in the United States, and this is considered a basic level of service. Although basic services provide support to students with learning disabilities, there is no uniform formula, and all colleges differ in the exact kinds of support that they offer, even at this level.

Another level of support, for students with more intensive needs, is the intensive level. At this level of support most but not all, programs charge an extra fee over and above the tuition fee. Schools that offer these intensive programs will also have a general office of disability support that still provides the basic and free-of-charge support for students who are not involved in the intensive program. These more intensive programs sometimes require an additional application. Some may even have different criteria for admission to the university. For the most part, these intensive programs offer students services such as access to mentors, counseling services and help with organization and time management. Many are 4-year programs, but some are only

Table 18.1 Levels of Support

Basic Services

Basic services are appropriate for students who require the fewest accommodations. This structure of service might be best for students who might have seen some success in high school with few to no modifications and minimal accommodations. Basic services:

- May have the most basic level of services
- Offer few services outside of "reasonable accommodations"
- Require documentation in order to receive services
- Differ from college to college
- Are based in the federal mandate to provide "reasonable accommodations"
- May be based on different interpretations of the term "reasonable accommodations"

Basic services may be appropriate for students who:

- Do not require extensive accommodations
- Are self-motivated and independent learners
- Can voluntarily request their accommodations as they are needed

Basic services may provide:

- Extended time on tests, separate testing room, alternative testing formats, note takers, text to speech for textbooks

Intensive Services

Intensive services may be more appropriate for students who may require more support and accommodations than most basic services provide. These programs may be helpful for students who may have received some modifications in high school in addition to their accommodations. Intensive services:

- Provide significant levels of services for students with learning disabilities
- May have at least one certified learning disability specialist on staff
- May require documentation in order to receive services
- May require a separate application
- May have additional fees
- May have admissions criteria that are flexible and separate from the general university

Intensive services may be appropriate for students who:

- Can voluntarily request their accommodations as they are needed
- May have received some modified tests and curricula in high school
- Required some assistance in high school
- Were able to request some services as needed in high school

Intensive services may provide:

- Extended time on tests, separate testing room, alternative testing formats, note takers, text to speech for textbooks, early registration, enlarged print, reduced course load
- Remedial classes (although most do not)

- Tutors and assistive technology
- Access to a staff member trained in helping students with learning disabilities
- Support programs (study, counseling and self-help skills)
- Assistance with advocacy
- Precollege summer program
- Structured advisement
- Weekly meetings with advisor or mentors

Complete Services

Complete services provide the highest level of support services for students with learning disabilities. Students who require this level of service may have required more intensive services while still in high school. At this level, the school itself is designed for educating students with learning disabilities. At this point in time, there are very few schools in the country that provide complete services for students with learning disabilities.

Complete services:
- Have the highest level of services for students with learning disabilities
- Have significant amounts of support for students
- Have staff, directors and professors who are trained and/or certified in special education
- May require documentation in order to receive services
- Are embedded into the school itself

Complete services may be appropriate for students who:
- May have received extensive resource services in high school
- May have received modified tests and curricula in high school
- May have had close academic monitoring in high school
- May need high levels of support to maintain academic standing

Complete services may provide:
- Extended time on tests, separate testing room, alternative testing formats, note takers, text to speech for textbooks, early registration, enlarged print, reduced course load
- Tutors
- Assistive technology
- Access to a staff member trained in helping students with learning disabilities
- Support programs (study, counseling and self-help skills)
- Assistance with advocacy
- Precollege summer program
- Structured advisement
- Regularly scheduled meetings between support staff and student
- Modified courses
- Study skills and academic improvement classes
- Special orientation programs
- Close academic monitoring
- Counseling

162 Our Role as Counselors

offered as a first-year transition service. In addition, although most of them allow students to choose a major in whatever field they are interested in, it is important to note that some may have limitations in the choice of majors.

Finally, the most intensive types of service for students with learning disabilities can be found at the complete level. This level is comprised of colleges and universities that only serve a population of students who have learning disabilities and related disorders. These kinds of schools are for students who might require more than a general college classroom might be able to give them. The professors and teachers at these colleges are well versed in an understanding of learning disabilities and teach their courses with these needs in mind. Support is embedded in the curriculum.

Schools With Programs for Students With Learning Disabilities

The chart below shows a sample of both intensive and complete programs from around the country. The fees are approximate, based on current and available information. Most of the programs require a separate application aside from the school's general application. Many of these programs are also quite competitive. For these programs, the application process for both the school and the learning disabilities program may be quite extensive. There are several programs on the list that work in concert with the admissions staff and might allow for more flexible admissions criteria to the school if it is deemed warranted. Most of the programs offer robust programming. Therefore, the "services offered" column may not reflect the full range of services offered by each individual program. Finally, although the list is extensive, it is by no means exhaustive. With the thousands of colleges and universities in the United States, there are certain to be many more programs for students with learning disabilities. The following list is just intended to be a sample of several of the more well-known programs.

Understanding the Role of the Office of Disability Services

The first and most basic step for getting to understand programs and services for students with learning disabilities is getting to understand the role of the office of disability services. Federal law mandates that each university and college have an office of disability services on campus. These offices are on each campus to ensure that students with disabilities, including students with learning disabilities, are given the opportunity to access their academic goals. Many students with disabilities might not even be aware of the existence of these offices. Many of these students enter college without an awareness of the fact that these offices are the epicenter for the services that they are still

Table 18.2 Specialized Programs

Name of School	State	Name of Program	Fee (US$)	Services Offered
Adelphi University	NY	Learning Resource Program	4,730 per semester	counseling, summer program
American International College	MA	Supportive Learning Services	375–2,775 per semester	professional tutoring, study skills, time management, organization
American University	DC	Learning Services Program	4,700	one-year program, weekly meetings, writing tutor, course advising, mentor
Beacon College	FLA	n/a	N/A	college dedicated to students with learning disabilities
Bethany College	WV	program for academic and social success	Unspecified	learning specialist support
Centenary University	NJ	Project ABLE Program (Academic Bridges to Learning Effectiveness)	Unspecified	learning support specialist, workshops, professional tutors, group counseling, academic monitoring, counseling
Concordia College New York	NY	Concordia Connection Program	6,000 per year	group sessions, study sessions, progress monitoring, counseling
Curry College	MA	Program for Advancement of Learning (PAL) program	Unspecified	biweekly meeting with learning specialist, separate courses, summer program
Davis and Elkins College	WV	Supported Learning Program	Unspecified	supervised study hall weekly, supported learning program instructor, assistive technology, progress monitoring, social skills, study strategies, time management, organization
Dean College	MA	Arch Learning Community	1,750–3,600 per semester	designated courses, career advising, academic coaching

(*Continued*)

Table 18.2 (Continued)

Name of School	State	Name of Program	Fee (US$)	Services Offered
Fairleigh Dickinson University	NJ	The Regional Center for Learning Disabilities	None	metacognitive strategies, learning specialists, tutoring
Hofstra	NY	Pals Program	14,050 for all 4 years	learning specialist, academic coaching
Iona College	NY	College Assistance Program (CAP)	Unspecified	learning specialist, taught strategies and skills, priority registration, counseling
King's College	PA	First Year Academic Studies Program	530–1,390	first year only, peer tutoring, advocacy, academic skills, individual and small group learning consultant, note taking, organization
Landmark College	VT	n/a	N/A	college dedicated to students with learning disabilities
Limestone College	SC	Program for Alternative Learning Styles (PALS)	2,500 per semester	student progress meetings, organization and time management skills, study strategies course, supervised study halls, weekly and midterm progress reports, individual tutoring
Long Island University, CW Post Campus	NY	Academic Resource Program	2,000 per semester	utilizes master's students in special education for working with students with LD
Loras College	IA	Enhanced Program	4,300 per year	weekly advisory meeting, learning strategies class
Lynn University	FLA	Metamorphosis Program (for students with ADHD) Institute for Achievement and Learning	Unspecified	open to all students; tutors with advanced degrees, separate courses
Marist College	NY	The Learning Support Program	Unspecified	competitive, learning specialist, note taking skills, organization, time management, test-taking strategies,

Marshall University	WV	Higher Education for Learning Problems Center (HELP)	Unspecified	learning specialists and graduate assistant tutors, study skills, organization and time management training, skills development, summer prep, psychoeducational testing
Marymount Manhattan College	NY	Academic Access Program	About 3,000 per semester	learning specialist, counseling, academic coaching, priority registration, monthly parent's meeting
Mitchell College	CT	The Bentsen Learning Center Program (BLCP)	1,225–3,700 per semester	counseling, weekly meetings with learning specialist and skills building with learning specialists, assistive technology
Mount St. Joseph University	OH	Project EXCEL	1,800 per semester	professional tutoring, progress monitoring, academic counseling, organization and time management skills, academic success strategies, executive function support, mentoring
Muskingum University	OH	PLUS Program	2,900–8,780	weekly meetings, learning strategy instruction, learning consultants, executive functioning skills
Northeastern University	MA	Learning Disabilities Program	2,900 per semester	regular meetings with learning specialist, test-taking strategies, executive functioning,
Pace University	NY	OASIS Program	Yes but unknown	academic coaches, social workers, social coaches
Rochester Institute of Technology	NY	EMPOWER	760–1,520 per semester	mentor program
Schreiner University	TX	learning support services	About 2,800–3,800 per semester	certified tutors, advisement
St. Thomas Aquinas College	NY	Pathways Program	Unspecified	mentoring, academic counseling, course advisement, priority registration, summer program, assistive technology

(*Continued*)

Table 18.2 (Continued)

Name of School	State	Name of Program	Fee (US$)	Services Offered
University of Arizona	AZ	The Strategic Alternative Learning Techniques (SALT) Center	1,200–2,800 per semester	learning specialists, assistive technology, tutoring, workshops, psychological services
University of Denver	CO	Learning Effectiveness Program (LEP)	1,350 per quarter	weekly academic counseling, tutoring, executive functioning support, organization, time management, social skill building, peer mentoring
University of the Ozarks	AK	Jones Learning Center (JLC)	Unspecified	academic support coordinators, peer tutors and note takers, skills specialists
University of Wisconsin Osh Kosh	WI	Project Success	Unspecified	remediation
Ursuline College	OH	FOCUS Program	760–2,000 per semester	weekly meeting, priority registration, mid-term progress report, disability specialist, academic and social support, grad school advisement
West Virginia Wesleyan College	WV	Mentor Advantage Program	800–2,200 per semester	academic tutoring, organization skills tutoring, daytime and evening check-ins, open access to tutors

Choosing Colleges and Universities **167**

entitled to. The simple act of guiding our students with learning disabilities to these offices can have a significant positive impact on their academic success. For some of my students, I will have them sit with me and help them do a search for contact information for the office of disability services on their prospective campus.

The role of the office of disability services on a campus is to provide students with the "reasonable accommodations" that they are entitled to based on section 504 and the Americans with Disabilities Act. In some very few instances, these offices will provide education or psychological testing on campus for a reduced fee, but this is very rare. The office is there to make certain that students with disabilities receive equitable treatment despite whatever disability they have.

Disclosing and Accessing Services

Talking to students about disclosing their disabilities is a tricky subject. On the one hand, we want our students to view their disability in a positive light and be able to discuss it without shame or embarrassment. On the other hand, it is also important to have the students understand that disclosing their disability needs to be done thoughtfully and for the right reasons. For many students, a learning disability is already a thing to be ashamed or embarrassed about, so the conversation about disclosure needs to be done carefully so as not to exacerbate those potential feelings of shame.

For many students, having a learning disability in high school is something that has been kept so confidential that sometimes the student wonders who they are even allowed to tell. I have actually had students ask, "Wait, I can do that? That's okay to do?" when we discuss disclosing their disability to other people. In that light, it is important to address the concept of disclosure in general before moving to the nature of disclosure for services in college. Students do need to have an awareness that although there is no shame to having a learning disability, the reality is that many people do not really understand what a learning disability, such as dyslexia for example, really is (Furnham, 2013). This could mean that disclosing randomly may not always end with a positive or anticipated result.

Despite the laws protecting people with learning disabilities against discrimination, students still need to be advised to understand when and where disclosure is appropriate. Telling close friends about a learning disability can be empowering and liberating but telling a prospective employer prior to even being offered the job is not necessary. Even disclosing to an employer for a job that does not engage any activities that are impacted by the disability is not necessary. Students might be counseled to consider disclosure of their learning disabilities for reasons such as personal empowerment or for the purpose of accessing necessary accommodations.

168 Our Role as Counselors

When students are looking at their postsecondary academic environment, high school counselors need to have knowledge about the process of and need for disclosure in order to best counsel their students. The first thing to note is that students need to understand that in order for them to get the accommodations and services that they are entitled to and may require at the postsecondary school level, they will need to be comfortable disclosing and discussing their disability. Students will need to know that they will need to disclose both to the office of disability services and to their professors. Disclosing a disability to the office of disability services and accessing services from them has been shown to have a major, positive impact on postsecondary success for students with learning disabilities (Kim & Lee, 2016). This ability to discuss their disability should go beyond just being able to say, "I have a learning disability." Disclosure on this level is about accessing services and accommodations. Since each student has individual needs, just telling the office of disability services that they have a learning disability may not help them access the services that would be most helpful to them. It is also helpful if the students can also verbalize what accommodations have helped them in the past. With an intact knowledge of what kinds of accommodations have already helped them, the students can then meet with an office of disability services counselor and have an honest conversation about what the college or university might be able to offer them.

The specific process involved in accessing services for college students with learning disabilities is different from school to school, but in general, the process may look something like this:

1. The student gets accepted to the college or university they have applied to and accepts the offer.
2. The student calls the campus office of disability services (which they may already be familiar with if they contacted them during the college search process) and requests accommodations and services.

   Typically, a student will contact the office of disability services on the campus of the college or university they have decided to attend and let them know that they have been receiving services at their high school. They will also let the ODS know that they are interested in receiving services in college as well. This initial request sets the wheels in motion. The sooner the student makes contact with the office, the sooner they can begin to gather the necessary documentation they might need. In addition, the sooner the student makes contact with the office, the sooner they can get acclimated to campus once they actually start school. Students do not need to disclose their learning disabilities prior to being accepted. Disclosure is done purely to help the student access the accommodations they may need to access the curriculum.

Choosing Colleges and Universities **169**

3. The office of disability service requests documentation of the disability in order to be able to issue a 504 plan for the student.

A this point, the ODS will most probably request some kind of documentation. For students with learning disabilities, this documentation will typically consist of recent psychological and educational testing. For some schools, recent documentation can go back as far as 5 years, but many schools only accept documentation from within the previous 3 years. In order to ensure that students are aligned with most of the college's requirements, it is advisable to encourage the students and their families to request a complete reevaluation in the student's junior year of high school, inclusive of the psychological and educational testing. It is important to note that child study teams could deny the request to redo the testing or, conversely, redo the testing and find the student ineligible. In either case, it is beneficial for the student to consider any dual diagnosis that might also be used for a 504. If the case is that there is no recent testing, families can be encouraged to call the office of disability services of the colleges and find out if the school provides testing for their students for free or at reduced fees. Some but not many colleges do provide this service for reduced fees for their students.

In addition to the psychological and educational testing, many offices of disability services teams also request that students fill out questionnaires and/or participate in interviews. These interviews and questionnaires are normally designed to help the team assess the needs of the student in relation to the accommodations they might be able to provide. It is important that the student be as forthcoming as possible in the questionnaire and interview in order to get the appropriate accommodations.

4. The student is granted their 504 and is assigned an office of disability services advisor.

An ODS advisor is assigned to the student after the student is granted the 504. This advisor would most probably be the main contact person for the student as they go through their postsecondary education. This advisor would be the person the student would go to for any disability-related issue as it comes up. For students who might require assistive technology, extra time, note takers or whatever the need might be, the advisor would be the "go-to" person.

At this point, the advisor will normally inform the student of what accommodations have been approved and what the protocol is for accessing these accommodations. An important thing to note regarding accommodations is that all of it is on the student. The ODS does not share information with professors, nor does it chase after students to make sure that they are getting what they need. What this means in practice is that after identifying themselves to the ODS, a student must identify what their needs are and then must contact the advisor and find out

170 Our Role as Counselors

what the protocol is for accessing these accommodations. Extra time for exams, for example, usually requires following a particular protocol, and the protocol places most of the responsibility on the student. In many schools, in order to access services, the student is required to contact the ODS every semester and request a letter that outlines the accommodations that the student is entitled to. The student, not the ODS, then must bring the letter to the class so that the professor is aware of the student's needs. At this point, if there is an exam scheduled, the student might have to contact the ODS (usually about 5 business days before the exam date) and let them know that an exam is scheduled. The ODS then schedules the student to take the exam with whatever accommodations the student is entitled to.

The office of disability services functions as the gateway for services for the student. What this means is that a student might disclose their disabilities to the office of disability services and be registered to receive services but can still decide not to use them if they so choose. Conversely, disclosure alone does not begin the process of receiving accommodations. If the student does not follow the protocols for accessing the services, even if the student needs them and wants to use them, the accommodations are not automatically in place. The protocol must be followed each time the student wants to use them. Many schools actually require a reregistration at the start of each semester. Although this does not normally require new testing documentation, it does require that the student contact the office to let it know that they will still be receiving services. There may be an online form or a hardcopy form to fill out. In addition, this initial reregistration still may not engage the accommodations. Unless it is ongoing and constant accommodations, each time the student will need it, the office of disability services will need to be contacted according to the protocol they might have.

5. The student stays in contact with the office of disability services and informs it of any new information or changes that might be needed.

Since college is very different than high school and because students change and grow even after they enter college, their accommodation needs may change depending on their own needs and the classes they might be taking. A student might, for example, realize that testing in a distraction-free environment is something that they may require, or they may realize that they might need computer access in a particular class. When these needs arise, it is important that the student know that they can access their advisor at the office of disability services and discuss any changes that they may need in their accommodations.

6. The student may consider disclosing the exact nature of their disability to their professors at the start of the semester.

Having an honest conversation with a professor of a class at the start of the semester could be both empowering and helpful.

References

Furnham, A. (2013). Lay knowledge of dyslexia. *Psychology, 4*(12), 940. https://doi.org/10.4236/psych.2013.412136

Kim, W. H., & Lee, J. (2016). The effect of accommodation on academic performance of college students with disabilities. *Rehabilitation Counseling Bulletin, 60*(1), 40–50. https://doi.org/10.1177/0034355215605259

PART 5

The Comprehensive Program

19

BUILDING THE PROGRAM

In this part:

- Creating buy-in
- Finding group members
- General instructions for the group
- Pretest

The program presented in this book is meant to be used by school counselors in a school or a clinical setting with 9th- through 12th-grade students. Membership in the group is based on the students' desire to attend a 2- or 4-year college and their having an IEP or a 504 for a diagnosed learning disability or related disorder. Although 9th- and 10th-grade students might get benefit from the group, it is best suited for students in the upper grades. The group is meant to be voluntary and should have anywhere from 4 to 10 members.

Creating Buy-In

Successful programs cannot be built in a vacuum. Buy-in from administrators, supervisors, teachers, parents and students is necessary in order to ensure the success of any program. For programs to be seen as useful by the community, there needs to be a reason for the program to exist. For many counseling programs, justification is found in needs assessments. These needs assessments are useful tools in helping to create programming that is useful, necessary and justified. In this case, however, the need for this program does not become obvious until after the students have left high school.

176 The Comprehensive Program

A needs assessment might not give information that would justify the program. For this reason, it is important to understand that the need for this program is more global in scale. The need for this program lies in the empirical evidence that educational research brings to the table. The global research suggests that students with learning disabilities are not being prepared to succeed in college. Although we are doing a better job getting students with learning disabilities to college, we are not doing a good job of preparing them to stay there. Students with learning disabilities who attend college are almost 20% more likely to drop out than are their peers without learning disabilities (Cortiella & Horowitz, 2014). Researchers suggest that we need to change how we help students with learning disabilities transition to college. Empowering these students with a knowledge of their disabilities and the contents of their IEPs and their legal rights and teaching them self-advocacy strategies and basic facts about how and why to maintain their accommodations through college are significant factors in the success of these students in college (Skinner, 2004).

Creating buy-in with the teachers is also necessary. For teachers to feel comfortable having students pulled out of their class to attend the group, teachers need to be a part of the discussion as well. Explaining the program, getting input about scheduling and just generally being respectful of the teachers' needs in terms of curriculum and testing requirements goes a long way in finding partners in the process. I usually approach teachers who have students in the group and let them know what I am doing. I send an initial email and then follow up with face-to-face contact so they can ask me questions directly. In my school, since there is no common lunch or prep time, students are pulled out of classes in order to attend the group. In order to keep teachers in the loop, create buy-in and be respectful of teachers' time, teachers are told about the group ahead of time and given the schedule (which runs at a different period each week in order to keep disruption to a minimum). Explaining the purpose and the scope of the group to teachers gives a platform for the partnership that we share in helping our students succeed.

Approaching administrators or other stakeholders in the process of creating the program can be daunting, but it can be done. Presenting a well-designed plan with appropriate justification is key to getting buy-in. You will need:

- Justification for the group (significant inequity in college retention for students with learning disabilities)
- An overview of the program itself
- A plan for finding members
- A plan establishing meeting times

Building the Program **177**

Finding Group Members

The next step in the process would be finding the group members. As counselors, we may have access to information about the students, including their IEPs and their classifications. If this information is available, any student with a classification of specific learning disability might be eligible. If that information is not available, consulting with the child study team is a good way to identify the group members as well. Certainly, letting the child study team members know that this group will be running or even inviting them to be a part of it can be nothing but helpful for everyone involved anyway. For the groups I run in my school, I have access to whole-school lists of students that include their classification. I run the list of all students with the specific learning disability and other health impaired classification and speak to the students' counselors and their case managers for input. Since the students in the group need to be both interested and cognitively able to attend college or university, input from anyone who knows these students is helpful in finding members who are appropriate for the group.

At this point, it is time to approach the students. I send out an initial email to both parents and students and ask that anyone who might want more information provide me with their contact information. I also call down any students who may not have responded to the email. I introduce myself, explain the program, answer any questions that they may have and reach out to their parents. I find that these in-person discussion yield a lot more excitement and interest than the initial email. At this point, I usually have large list of potentially interested students, so I send out another email to the parents and the students on the list. This email explains the group in more detail and contains a schedule. I explain that the group will take place over approximately 8 weeks, and in order to diminish time out of class in one particular period, we do a staggered schedule. This means that we may meet during period 1 in week 1, period 2 in week 2, period 3 in week 3 and so on. The email contains specific details about meeting dates, topics and times. A consent form is sent out at this time.

General Instructions for the Group

The lessons in this program are meant to be used as a starting point for discussion, but a counselor's level of comfort and experience can determine where the conversation can go as it unfolds. What is important is to make certain that the research-based topics are always touched upon during the weeks of the group. These topics include empowering students with a knowledge of their disabilities, exploring their IEPs, teaching them about their legal rights, teaching self-advocacy strategies and discussing the benefits of keeping their accommodations in college (Skinner, 2004). The lessons are set up by topic and can be completed as slowly or as quickly as needed based on the individual requirements of your group members. Each lesson is broken down into several subtopics, which allows for extending topics into multiple weeks if needed. Some topics may be completed fairly quickly, while some may take several weeks to complete.

It may be a good idea to supply or request that students bring a folder or three-ring binder to the group. There will be many handouts, and there will be times that students may want to refer to the information at some later point.

A pre- and posttest are included in order to help collect data if needed. Both tests address skills and knowledge the program teaches, but the posttest contains two extra questions addressing the students' perceptions of what they have learned as well. These questions can be deleted or may be kept as a part of the posttest. The pretest is to be distributed to students as they come into the room, collected and kept for the duration of the group.

References

Cortiella, C., & Horowitz, S. H. (2014). *The state of learning disabilities: Facts, trends and emerging issues*. New York: National Center for Learning Disabilities.

Skinner, M. E. (2004). College students with learning disabilities speak out: What it takes to be successful in postsecondary education. *The Journal of Postsecondary Education and Disability, 17*(2), 91–104.

Pretest

Table 19.1 Pretest

	Strongly disagree	Disagree	Neutral	Agree	Strongly agree
1. I know what the academic expectations of college will be.					
2. I am familiar with the differences between high school and college accommodations.					
3. I have read my IEP.					
4. I know what my challenges and strengths are.					
5. I know what kinds of assistive technology might be useful to me.					
6. I know what self-advocacy is.					
7. I know why it is important to be an effective self-advocate.					
8. I am good at time management.					
9. I know how to study effectively.					
10. I know what mnemonic devices are and how to use them.					
11. I know that there are different levels of support available in college for students with disabilities.					
12. I know how to access support services through my university or college.					

Copyright material from Mati Sicherer (2020), *College for Students with Learning Disabilities*, Routledge

20

THE PROGRAM

In this part:

- Part 1: College Readiness
- Part 2: Understanding Strengths and Challenges
- Part 3: Self-Advocacy
- Part 4: Study Skills
- Part 5: Picking the Right School

Part 1: College Readiness Grade Level: 9–12

Materials

- Chart paper
- Markers
- Pens or pencils
- Sheet 1.a. *College Readiness Skills Information Worksheet*
- Sheet 1.b. *Executive Functioning Skill Self-Assessment Worksheet*
- Sheet 1.c. *Accommodation Differences Between High School and College Information Sheet*
- Sheet 1.d. *Accommodations/Modifications* (just one copy). Each line should be cut into separate strips and placed in a box or container.
- Sheet 1.e. *Examples of Accommodations in College*
- Sheet 1.f. *My Modifications*

Engagement

Begin by welcoming the group and explaining that this is a group for students with learning disabilities who are planning on attending either a 2- or

The Program **181**

a 4-year college. Discuss the confidential nature of special education and IEPs and explain to the group that it is very important that everyone feel safe and able to speak freely. Explain to the group that this safety is based on each member of the group maintaining and respecting each other's privacy. Explain that if there is anyone in the group who does not feel safe or comfortable sharing in the group, they are always free to speak with you individually.

Have each member of the group introduce themselves by stating their name, their grade and any career or educational aspirations they may have.

Tell the group that today's discussion will focus on college readiness skills.

Procedures (student behavior in bold)

Have the students break up into one to three smaller groups (depending on size of the group) and hand out 1 piece of chart paper and markers to each group.

Ask the students what they believe the term "college readiness skills" means.

Ask the students to use the chart paper and markers to write down examples of "college readiness skills."

Students will create a list of what they consider "college readiness skills."

Discuss responses and ask each group why they believe the items they chose are college readiness skills.

Explain that college readiness skills are the skills that students need in order to be prepared to be successful in college.

Also explain that college readiness skills include being emotionally ready, academically ready, organizationally ready and, for students with learning disabilities, being prepared to manage their specific learning challenges as well.

Hand out Sheet 1.a. *College Readiness Skills Information Worksheet.*

Ask the students to take a few minutes to read through the worksheet and answer the questions.

Students will read through the worksheet and answer the questions.

Have students follow the directions to score themselves.

Students will score themselves.

When students are done scoring themselves, tell them that, ideally, all the answers should be "yes."

Ask the students to share their scores if they are comfortable doing so.

Students will share their scores.

Ask the students if they have any thoughts or comments about the expectations and questions on the worksheet.

Students will discuss the academic expectations from the worksheet.

182 The Comprehensive Program

Explain that adapting to the academic expectations can be a challenge for a lot of students but that having an idea of what to expect and how to manage it makes the transition much easier.

Ask the students if they have any specific concerns after they have read through the sheet, and ask students how they feel about the expectations from the sheet.

Students will ask questions as needed based on the worksheet.

Make certain to tell the students that they are not expected to be able to know all of this now. Explain that the point of the group is to help them achieve these goals, but also make certain to address any concerns.

Remind students again that the intention of this group is to help them meet these expectations successfully.

Explain again that college readiness involves understanding their learning disability and how it might impact the academic expectations of college.

Explain that this group is going to help them explore all of these things and help them prepare themselves for college success.

Explain that the structure of the group is that we are going to go step by step through many techniques and skills that will help prepare for college and address any concerns they may have.

Tell students that the next topic addressed will be organization and "executive function." Explain that executive function skills are the skills that allow people to organize their days effectively.

Explain that for students, good executive function skills would be things such as using a planner, remembering to study for tests, organizing their time effectively or keeping their folder, notebooks and backpacks organized and efficient.

Ask students to raise their hands if any of them have experienced any issues with organization or executive function.

Students will raise their hands if they have any organizational issues.

At this point, if only a very small percentage of the group raises their hands, or if you know for certain that your students do not have issues in this area, move on to the next topic. However, since this is a frequent comorbid condition, there is a high likelihood that it should be addressed regardless.

Hand out Sheet 1.b. *Executive Functioning Skill Self-Assessment for College*.

Ask students to read through the worksheet and place a check mark in the column that best describes their ability in each area.

Remind students that no one is going to see this but themselves and they should be as honest with themselves as they can be.

Students will fill out the worksheet.

Discuss results as needed.

Explain that a big part of college success is tied into having good organizational and executive function skills.

Explain that college is structured very unlike high school.

The Program **183**

Explain that in high school, classes may meet every day, and there are multiple classes all day long.

Explain also that most of the learning in high school is done in school, and only some of the work is expected to be done at home for homework.

Explain that in college, the exact opposite is true. Classes meet infrequently over the week, and most of the work is expected to be done at home.

Ask students how the structure of college might be affected by poor organizational or executive functions skills.

Students will engage in a discussion about how the structure of college might be affected by poor organizational or executive functions skills.

Ask students if they think that there is anything from their worksheet that they think they might need to work on.

Students will review the worksheet and discuss any executive function or organizational issues that they may not be strong in yet.

Engage the group in a discussion of ideas to address the concerns brought up by the students. Topics might include, using planners, calendars, checklists etc.

Students will share ideas with one another regarding help for organization or executive function skills.

Explain to students that the next topic regarding college readiness will center on their learning disability.

Explain that in order for students to know how to succeed in college, they have to understand that not only are academic expectations different in college, but so is how learning disabilities are addressed.

Ask students if they know what modifications and/or accommodations they are receiving in high school (give examples of accommodations and modifications such as extra time, retaking tests etc.).

If students do not know, tell them that they will be reading their IEPs in the group later on and that, for college preparation, these are very important things to know.

Students will respond with their accommodations and modifications.

Hand out Sheet 1.c. Accommodation Differences Between High School and College.

Tell students that there are some very important differences between high school and college that will have an impact on their success in college.

Give students a few minutes to look over the sheet and have them underline or highlight anything on the sheet that they find interesting or disturbing.

Students will review sheet 1.c. accommodation differences between high school and college and highlight or underline anything they find interesting or disturbing.

Ask the students to share anything they saw on the comparison that surprised them or made them think.

184 The Comprehensive Program

Students will share anything they saw on the comparison that surprised them or made them think.

Explain to students that one of the main differences between high school and college is that there are no modifications in college.

Discuss the difference between accommodations and modifications.

Explain that accommodations accommodate the disability by "leveling the playing field." Modifications actually modify the information being taught or the work being assigned. Modifications are not normally done on a college level. Give examples of each.

Explain that it is sometimes hard to remember the difference between accommodations and modifications, but it is important that they understand the difference.

Explain that they will be doing a short exercise to make sure that they understand the difference between modifications and accommodations.

(Sheet 1.d. should have already been cut into strips and placed into a box or container.)

Tell students that they are each going to pick a strip of paper from the box that has either an accommodation or a modification written on it, and they will have to figure out whether it is an accommodation or a modification. (Counselor can have the students answer independently or as a group.)

Students will take turns picking one strip of paper at a time and decide whether what they have chosen is a modification or an accommodation.

Ask students to explain the difference between an accommodation and a modification.

Students will be able to explain the difference between an accommodation and a modification.

Hand out Sheet 1.e. *Examples of Accommodations in College* and discuss how these are the same or different from what the students receive now.

Students will discuss how the college accommodations may be different than the services they are receiving now.

Ask the students to think about their own modifications or accommodations again.

Explain that modifications are not a part of a typical college program.

The Program **185**

Explain that colleges expect that the curriculum and expectations will be the same for everyone but that how they are accessed might be different based on the students' disabilities.

Ask the students why it might be important to try to diminish modifications through high school.

Students will discuss why it might be important to try to diminish modifications through high school.

Explain to the students that modifications such as out of class resource rooms or even in-class resource (special education support in a general education framework) are still modifications that will not be available in college.

Explain to students that reviewing their modifications (not their accommodations) will be helpful for them to be able to see what they may still have to work on before starting college.

Hand out Sheet 1.f. *My Modifications* and ask students to work on sheet in small groups. Have students share their responses and discuss responses.

Students will fill out sheet 1.f. my modifications in small groups and then share responses aloud.

(It is important that the students understand that their IEPs exist for them. This means that we can empower them to start viewing their accommodations and modifications more critically. We can encourage them to start asking teachers to let them attempt things such as taking the same tests as their peers or advocating for themselves to experiment with fewer supports.)

Ask the group the following review questions:

- What are some college readiness skills you think you have already? What are some you think you might need?
- What are some executive function or organizational skills that are challenging for you? What are some you excel in?
- Why is it important to start decreasing your modifications in high school?
- What is the difference between having a disability in high school and having one in college?
- What is one thing that you took away from today's group that you think you will remember?

The students will verbally respond to the closure questions.

186 The Comprehensive Program

Sheet 1.a.

College Readiness Skills Information Worksheet

For each question, put a check in the box that applies to you. Add up the number of checks in each column.

Table 20.1 College Readiness Skills

	Yes	No
1. Can you read 200 pages in a week?		
2. Do you have a plan for note taking?		
3. Do you take notes?		
4. Can you listen while taking notes?		
5. Can you take notes from an oral presentation?		
6. Can you take notes in a 3-hour-long class?		
7. Can you remain focused in a 3-hour-long class?		
8. Can you write a 3- to 10-page paper with at least 2 sources?		
9. Can you organize ideas in writing?		
10. Do you know what a thesis statement is?		
11. Do you retain the information you have read?		
12. Are you comfortable asking for academic help?		
13. Are you an independent learner?		
14. Can you learn in a class with 100 to 300 other students?		
15. Can you learn with a professor who is not interested in getting to know you?		
16. Do you have a strategy for studying for an exam on a full semester's worth of notes, lectures and multiple chapters of textbook reading?		
17. Can you organize your time?		
18. Do you understand your learning style?		
19. Do you know what modifications work best for you?		
20. Do you understand your learning differences?		
21. Do you know how to advocate for yourself?		
22. Do you know what kind of environment works best for you for taking tests or studying?		
23. Do you know the difference between an accommodation and a modification?		
24. Do you understand the differences between a high school IEP and a college 504?		
25. When you think about the academic expectations in college, are you relatively certain that you can succeed?		
Total		

Copyright material from Mati Sicherer (2020), *College for Students with Learning Disabilities*, Routledge

Sheet 1.b.

Executive Functioning Skill Self-Assessment in Preparation for College

Table 20.2 Executive Function Skill Self-Assessment

Skill	Almost never	When reminded	Most of the time
Time Management:			
• Do you **independently** plan/complete daily assignments?			
• Do you **independently** plan/complete steps for projects?			
• Do you **independently** plan/complete long-term projects (on time)?			
• Is your homework completed on time?			
• Are you prepared with materials in class?			
• Are you prepared with materials at home?			
• Are your papers neat and organized?			
• Do you check your own work?			
• Do you keep track of assignments/deadlines on your own?			

Copyright material from Mati Sicherer (2020), *College for Students with Learning Disabilities*, Routledge

Sheet 1.c.

Accommodation Differences Between High School and College

Table 20.3 Accommodation/Modification Chart

Accommodation/Modification Differences Between High School and College

High School	College
The school identifies students with disabilities and is responsible for evaluating and documenting the identified disability.	The student is responsible for providing documentation about their disability.
The school automatically creates a program based on the accommodations and/or modifications that have been written into the IEP.	Accommodations are provided only when the student requests them. They are not typically added automatically.
The school may modify educational programs; the curriculum and assignments may be altered if it is deemed necessary.	The academic program is not usually modified. Students with disabilities are expected to access and produce the same amount and the same level as students without disabilities.
Parents are involved and must give permission for any decisions regarding changes in the program.	Students over the age of 18 are considered adults, and parents are not allowed access unless the student permits it.
Special classes and placements outside the realm of general education classes are made available if needed.	No special classes are offered.
An IEP (individual education plan) meeting is held annually to reassess placement and services.	Yearly meetings are not required.
The school conducts educational and psychological evaluations at no cost to the family.	The student is responsible for providing any testing and/or evaluation to document a disability.
IDEA is the statute behind special education law (Individuals with Disabilities Education Act).	ADA (Americans with Disabilities Act) is the statute behind providing services for students in college.
IDEA is about success in learning skills.	ADA is about access to the curriculum.
Responsibility for enacting accommodations or modifications lies with the school.	The student is responsible for requesting accommodations.

Copyright material from Mati Sicherer (2020), *College for Students with Learning Disabilities*, Routledge

Sheet 1.d.

Accommodations/Modifications

Counselor cuts each line into separate strips and places them into a box or container.

Table 20.4 Accommodation/Modification Worksheet

Assistive devices	
Braille	
CD/audiotapes	
Computer	
Extended time	
Graphic organizers	These are the accommodations: Changes to how a student accesses curriculum or assignments
Large print	
Magnification devices	
Preferential seating	
Study guide	
Testing in a separate room	
Teacher notes	
Partial completion of assignment	
Changes to curriculum	
Shortened assignments	
Abridged reading assignments	These are the modifications: Changes to curriculum or assignments
Different tests than the rest of the class	
Alternate forms of assessment	
Shorter tests	
Grading that is not aligned to the rest of the class	

Copyright material from Mati Sicherer (2020), *College for Students with Learning Disabilities*, Routledge

Sheet 1.e.

Examples of Accommodations in College

- Recording lectures
- Speech-to-text programs
- Text-to-speech programs
- Ramps and adaptive equipment
- Reduced barriers for physical access
- Note takers
- Extended time
- Braille
- Assistive technology

Reasonable accommodations are used to give students with disabilities the same rights and privileges as students without disabilities while still not changing the curriculum or expectations.

Sheet 1.f.

My Modifications

Make a list of modifications that you or people in your group have used or are using now:

a. _____
b. _____
c. _____
d. _____
e. _____

Modifications are not usually allowed in college. What are some things you can do now to prepare for this?

a. _____
b. _____
c. _____
d. _____
e. _____

192 The Comprehensive Program

Part 2: Understanding Strengths and Challenges
Grade Level: 9–12

Materials

- Blank sample IEP from your school or district
- One copy of each member's individual IEP
- Pens or pencils
- Sheet 2.a. *What Are You Good At?*
- Sheet 2.b. *Assistive Technology*
- Paper
- Computer, laptop or internet connected phone
- Sheet 2.c. *Assistive Technology* part 2

Note: Before this group meets, make sure to meet with each member individually to let them know that they will be looking at their IEP in the next group. Allow the students to decide what their comfort level is in reviewing their IEP, and allow any individual to decline looking at their IEP if they are uncomfortable doing so. You may be able to get the IEP from the case manager, the parent or, in some cases, from the computer program that your school uses. Ideally, parents will have been given a list of topics prior to the start of the group, but some parents may still have a level of discomfort with the idea that their child will be reviewing their own IEP. This is a good time to have an open discussion with parents about the need for their children to have an understanding of their learning issues. If parents are still uncomfortable, respect their wishes, but maintain a dialogue about the need for their children to have accurate information about themselves and their learning challenges.

Engagement

Begin the session by welcoming the group back and reminding the students about the confidential nature of special education and IEPs.

Remind the group that it is very important that everyone feel safe and able to speak freely, and the only way for this to happen is to make sure that each member of the group maintains and respects each other's privacy.

Remind the group that if there is anyone who does not feel safe or comfortable sharing in the group, they are always free to speak with you individually.

Tell the members of the group that although this week's topic is strengths and challenges, we are going to be using their IEPs to start the conversation.

Procedures (student behavior in bold)

Have each member of the group restate their name, their grade and any career or educational aspirations they may have before starting the session.

The Program **193**

Tell the group that today's discussion will focus on strengths and challenges, and the discussion will start with their IEPs.

Explain that IEP stands for individual educational plan, and it is the legal document that drives each of their educational programs.

Explain that understanding what is in their IEP is the best way to understand what they may need for college and beyond.

Ask the group if they know why they have IEPs (many students do not have a full understanding of why they have an IEP).

If they know, students will state the reason they have an IEP.

Explain to the students that the group will start by discussing their IEPs.

Ask the members of the group to raise their hand if they have ever been prescribed any kind of medication from their medical doctor for an illness.

Students will raise their hands to indicate if they have ever been prescribed any kind of medication from their medical doctor for an illness.

Ask the students how they would feel if the doctor prescribed medication for an illness but gave them no explanation about the illness itself.

Ask the students how likely they would be to take medication from their doctor if they did not understand why they had to take the medicine.

Students will discuss how likely they would be to take medication from their doctor if they did not understand why they had to take the medicine.

Explain that just like the doctor gives medication based on a diagnosis, the IEP does the same. Explain that the IEP states the diagnosis, and the "medication" is the student's program.

Explain that just like taking medication without knowing why is not the best way to manage an illness, following the IEP program without knowing why is not the best way to manage a learning disability.

Explain to the students that understanding their IEP is a path toward understanding themselves. Explain that if they can understand themselves and their strengths and challenges, this will help them be more successful in high school and college.

Explain that with a realistic sense of their own strengths and challenges, students can learn to make their strengths work for them while figuring out how to compensate for their challenges. Explain to the students that gaining an understanding of their IEP is a good first step to getting there.

Ask the members of the group to raise their hand if they have ever attended their own IEP meeting.

Ask the members of the group to raise their hands if they have ever read through their IEP.

Students will raise their hands if they have ever read their iep or attended their IEP meeting.

Explain that one of the things the group will be doing today is reviewing both a sample IEP and their own IEP.

194 The Comprehensive Program

Explain that reviewing their IEP will help them to understand their learning needs, and this will help them to better manage their learning and study styles in college.

Hand each student a blank IEP and a copy of their own IEP. Ask the students to take a few minutes to review both documents.

Make sure that students turn to the page in their IEP that outlines their accommodations and modifications, their program and their testing results.

Ask the students if they are surprised by any of the things they have read in their IEP.

Ask the students how they feel about the items in the accommodations and modifications page.

Students will discuss their feelings after reading the accommodations and modifications page.

Ask the students to take a minute and read through their entire IEP. Tell the students to feel free to ask questions at any point.

Students will read through their entire IEPs and ask questions as needed.

Ask the students to share any thoughts after reading through their entire IEPs.

Students will share their thoughts after reviewing their individual IEPs.

Ask the students what they believe an IEP is and what it is used for.

Students will respond with their ideas about what an iep is and what it is used for.

Discuss responses and explain that an IEP is their individual education plan based on their individual needs.

Explain that an IEP dictates the courses and expectations for them in high school.

Tell the students that an IEP is based on a disability and is intended to give students with disabilities the same chances for success that those without them have.

Explain that the laws that govern special education are based on a federal statute called the Individual with Disabilities Education Act (IDEA) and that before these laws were enacted, there were no rights for students with disabilities.

Ask the students why it is important they understand what is in their IEP.

Students will share their ideas about why it is important to understand what is in their IEP.

Explain to students that one of the things they may have noticed in their IEP is that it discusses both their strengths and challenges.

Ask the students to see if they can find where in their IEP their strengths and challenges are discussed (help the students as needed).

The Program **195**

Students will look for and find their strengths and challenges as they are discussed in their IEPs.

Explain to students that it is as important to understand your strengths as it is to understand your challenges. Understanding strengths and challenges helps people to focus on what they are good at while still finding ways to manage their challenges. Explain that today's meeting is about using knowledge about strengths and challenges to devise plans for success in college.

Remind students that they may need to devise new plans for success in college since there are differences between a high school IEP and a college 504 (refer to Sheet 1.c. *Accommodation Differences Between High School and College* and Sheet 1.a. *College Readiness Skills Information Worksheet)* and finding their strengths and challenges is a good way to start configuring their plan.

Remind students that knowing their strengths will help them choose the best ways for them to learn and study through college.

Explain that the group is now going to look at strengths in a somewhat different way.

Explain that sometimes what we think we are good at or bad at may not align with what other people think we are good or bad at.

Ask the students why someone might disagree with what we think our strengths and challenges are.

Students will discuss why people's perceptions of their strengths and challenges may not align with their own.

Hand out Sheet 2.a. *What Are You Good At?* And ask students to take a few minutes to fill out the sheet. Make sure they are following the directions on the sheet.

Students will fill out sheet 2.a. what are you good at?

Allow time to discuss the results. Allow students to add any other strengths that they may have thought of if needed.

Students will discuss responses and add other strengths.

Remind students about why other people may have differing opinions on their strengths and challenges.

Remind students that sometimes things that we perceive as strengths may not be as highly developed as we need them to be, while at the same time, things we are not as confident about may actually be areas of great strength.

Ask students if they believe that any of those differing opinions might have validity and what should they do about it if they do?

Students will discuss if they believe that any differing opinions might have validity and what they should do about it if they do.

Remind students that although sometimes we may not be completely realistic about our strengths or challenges, it is important to know that learning disabilities and related disorders can sometimes mask real strengths.

196 The Comprehensive Program

Explain that a student can be a creative thinker with interesting ideas but may have difficulty putting these ideas down in writing down, but this does not automatically make the student a bad writer.

Explain that the act of writing is the mechanics of the process and that difficulty with that part does not necessarily mean that people have difficulty with all of it.

Ask students if they have ever experienced this kind of challenge.

Students will discuss the challenges they may have had when their strengths are masked by their learning disabilities.

Ask students if a challenge like the one above means that the person is not a good writer.

Students will discuss if having creative ideas but a disability that does not allow you to be able to write them down effectively means that the person is a bad writer.

Explain to students that these strengths are still strengths, but they need to be accessed in a different manner.

Explain that assistive technology is a method of accessing these strengths.

Ask students if they know or can guess what the term "assistive technology" means.

Students will discuss what they believe the term "assistive technology" means.

Tell students that assistive technology is any kind of technology (high or low tech) that assists a person with a disability to achieve equal status with people without disabilities.

Explain that many times when we think of assistive technology, we might be thinking about the kinds of assistive technology that people with physical disabilities use, such as wheelchairs or electronic speaking devices.

Ask the students if they have ever seen anyone with any of these devices or if they can think of any other examples.

Students will share examples of assistive technology.

Explain to students that assistive technology is also for students with learning disabilities. Explain that when people have learning disabilities, assistive technology devices also help them achieve equal status with people without disabilities.

Tell the students that just like for people with physical disabilities, the assistive technology for learning disabilities is only useful if it relates to the specific person's needs.

For example, a person with a physical disability that only affects their ability to walk would have little use for a communication device.

When we are looking at assistive technology to help people with learning disabilities, individual needs also need to be taken into consideration.

The Program **197**

For example, giving someone a calculator as assistive technology for a reading disability would not be helpful at all, but giving that same person a text-to-speech program might be very helpful.

Hand out Sheet 2.b. *Assistive Technology.*

Ask the students to think about their own needs and to place a check mark in the column next to any statement that they believe is true and applies to them.

Students will place a check mark next to any statement they believe may apply to themselves on sheet 2.b. *Assistive Technology.*

Explain to the students that each sentence they marked has a corresponding word in the column to the left of their check mark.

Have students read those words aloud (reading, comprehension, writing, note taking, organization, focus, study skills, math, handwriting and memory).

Students aloud will read the words in the far-left column on sheet 2.b. *Assistive Technology.*

Ask the students to create a list on the bottom of their paper from any of the words from that far-left column they have placed a check mark next to.

Only words that correspond to the check marks should be placed on the list.

Students will make a list of the words from the far-left column they have placed a check mark next to.

Explain that each of these words is a potential academic challenge that they may have that could be helped with assistive technology.

Tell students that we will use each one of these words in a search to find examples of assistive technology.

Explain that each word will require a separate search.

Ask students to share any words which came up on their list.

Students will share words that come up on their lists.

Tell students that they will now be doing an internet search for assistive technology for whatever challenge word came up on their lists.

Ask students to open up their computers, laptops or phones and type the following statement into the search bar: "assistive technology for challenges with."

Explain that the last word of the sentence in the search bar will be a word from their list. An example of the final sentence might be "assistive technology for challenges with *reading.*"

Students will type a search query into the search bar on their phones, laptops or computers that will end with a word from the list they have previously compiled.

Ask students to share what kinds of assistive technology they found in their searches. Allow time for discussion.

198 The Comprehensive Program

Students will share what kinds of assistive technology they found in their searches.

Explain that assistive technology is available for many different kinds of learning disabilities and challenges.

Explain that someone with a reading disability who needs to read 200 pages for a college class would benefit from a text-to-speech assistive technology.

Explain that this kind of technology takes the written word and reads it aloud for people who could otherwise not access it. Tell the students that now they will have an opportunity to look at these assistive technology devices a little more closely.

Hand out Sheet 2.c. *Assistive Technology* part 2.

Explain to the students that they are going to look back at their previous search and choose one or two assistive technology devices from that search that seem interesting.

Tell students that they will be listing these devices on Sheet 2.c. in the box under the heading "device name."

Students will list the devices they have chosen on sheet 2.c. in the box under the heading "device name."

Ask students to fill in the next box, "reason why it might be useful," with one reason for each device for why they think it might be useful for them.

Students will fill in the next box "reason why it might be useful" with one reason for each device for why they think it might be useful for them.

Ask students to fill in the next box, "reason why I might not want to use it," with one reason for each device explaining why they might not want to use it.

Students will fill in the next box, "reason why i might not want to use it," with one reason for each device explaining why they might not want to use it.

Ask students to fill in the final box with a rating number from 1 to 10.

Explain that the lowest number would represent the lowest likelihood of using this device, whereas the highest number would represent the highest likelihood of using it.

Students will fill in the final box with a rating number from 1 (no chance of using it) to 10 (most likely will be using it).

Discuss results.

Students will discuss the results of their searches.

Explain to students that this worksheet is a good way for them to explore more assistive technology devices as they move forward in their academic lives.

Explain that needs change over time, and what they may need today will not be the same in a few years from now, so it is a good idea to reassess every once in a while.

The Program **199**

Remind them that knowing their own strengths and challenges is the best way to find what works well for them.

Ask the group the following review questions:

- Why is your IEP so important?
- Why is it important to understand your strengths and challenges?
- How can using knowledge about your IEP, your strengths and your challenges help you?
- What is assistive technology?
- What does assistive technology have to do with your strengths and challenges?
- What is a good way to find assistive technology that might work for you?

What is one thing that you took away from today's group that you think you will remember?

The students will verbally respond to the closure questions.

Sheet 2.a.

What Are You Good At?

Everyone has strengths, and knowing them makes it easier to find your path. Knowing what we are good at gives us the opportunity to pick careers and majors that will fit us. Some strengths are natural and are just a part of who we are, and some are skills that we can learn and can get better over time. Below you will find a list of statements that show examples of strengths. In the chart below, check off what you consider to be true about yourself and then check what you think your friends, family, teachers and others would say about you.

Table 20.5 What Are You Good At? Part 1

	me	friends	family	teachers	other
1. I am good at organizing myself.					
2. I am good at organizing events.					
3. I am an enthusiastic person.					
4. I have a good sense of humor.					
5. I am a leader.					
6. I am creative.					
7. I am open minded.					
8. Even when things are difficult, I don't give up.					
9. I am athletic.					
10. I always get my work done.					
11. I am honest.					
12. I am a good listener.					
13. I am kind.					
14. I am a team player.					
15. I value originality.					
16. I love puzzles and problem-solving activities.					
17. I am good at math.					
18. I am good at writing.					
19. I am good at social studies.					
20. I am good at science.					
21. I am good at reading.					

Copyright material from Mati Sicherer (2020), *College for Students with Learning Disabilities*, Routledge

Sheet 2.b.

Assistive Technology

Read the sentences below and place a check mark in the column to the left of each sentence you believe applies to you.

Table 20.6 Assistive Technology Part 1

	✓	
Reading		It takes me a long time to read things.
Comprehension		I don't always understand what I read.
Writing		I have trouble putting my thoughts on paper.
Writing		Writing papers for class is really hard for me.
Writing		I have trouble organizing my thoughts and ideas when I have to write papers.
Note taking		The notes I take in class are usually not helpful for me.
Note taking		I have trouble taking notes in class.
Organization		I lose homework frequently.
Organization		My notebooks and binders are messy.
Organization		I can never find anything in my notes and binders.
Organization		I have trouble finding the things I need to do my work (such as pens, paper, books etc.).
Focus		I lose focus easily.
Focus		I have frequent trouble staying on task when things are not interesting to me.
Study skills		When I say I studied for something, it usually means that I read the study guide or notes once or twice.
Math		No matter how hard I try, I don't understand math or math concepts.
Handwriting		My handwriting is so bad that I can't even read my own notes.
Memory		I have trouble recalling facts for tests or for writing papers.

Copyright material from Mati Sicherer (2020), *College for Students with Learning Disabilities*, Routledge

Sheet 2.c.

Assistive Technology Part 2

Choose one or two assistive technology devices from your previous search that seem as if they might be helpful to you.

List them in the box below "device name."

In the first box next to each item, write one reason why using this item might be useful to you.

In the next box, write one reason explaining why you might not want to use it.

In the final box, rate how likely you are to use this device.

Table 20.7 Assistive Technology Part 2

Device name	Reason why it might be useful	Reason why I might not want to use it	Rating: 1 (no chance of ever using device) to 10 (will probably use this from now on)
1.			
2.			

The Program **203**

Part 3: Self-Advocacy Grade Level: 9–12

Materials (include activity sheets and/or supporting resources)

- Sheet 2.a. *What Are You Good At?* (from previous week)
- Sheet 3.a. *Reframing the Label*
- Sheet 3.b. *My Assertive Self*
- Pens or pencils
- Chart paper
- Board
- Masking tape
- Markers (1 for each student)
- Half-filled glass of water
- Sheet 3.c. *Aggressive, Assertive or Passive?*
- Sheet 3.d. *Emily's Story*

Engagement

Begin the session by welcoming the group back and reminding the students about the confidential nature of special education and IEPs. Remind the group that it is very important that everyone feel safe and able to speak freely, and the only way for this to happen is to make sure that each member of the group maintains and respects each other's privacy. Remind the group that if there is anyone who does not feel safe or comfortable sharing in the group, they are always free to speak with you individually.

Tell the students that in a minute, you will be reading a story to them. Tell the students to listen to the story and listen for anything at all that they can relate to.

Read the following story:

> *Emily is at the beginning of her senior year in high school. She has a diagnosed reading disability and has struggled with reading from as far back as she can remember. She was identified as having a learning disability when she was in third grade, and for the rest of her academic career in elementary and middle school, much of her day was spent in a special education class.*
>
> *When Emily entered high school, her classes continued to be special education classes, or what her school called "out-of-class resource." These classes were taught by special education teachers and always had fewer than 10 students. Emily always listened in class and did all of her homework in a special study hall taught by a special education teacher.*

204 The Comprehensive Program

By junior year, her parents and case manager decided that it was time to move her out of most of her small classes. The only small class she remained in was her English class. Her mother had advocated to keep her in the smaller English class because she thought that Emily's struggles with reading had never really gone away. In fact, as time went on, Emily's mother thought that writing and spelling were challenges for her as well. Her placement in the small special education English class gave her teachers continued opportunities to help build her skills in all of those areas.

Emily's math, history and science classes have become a little difficult for her since leaving her small classes. There are so many more students than she had been used to, and there is a lot of information to learn but luckily, the school has made sure that all of those classes are taught by two certified teachers. While one of the teachers teaches the class, the other one is always standing by her side and helping her even before she knows she needs the help. Between them, they give Emily class notes so that she never has to worry about taking notes in class for herself. They even read passages out loud to her if it looks like she is having trouble. They make sure that Emily always gets shorter tests than the rest of the class and even allow her to take her tests over again if she does not do well the first time. She sometimes thinks about asking for the same tests as everyone else in her class, but she is not sure which teacher to ask or if she is even allowed to take the other test, so she never says anything. Her grades are good, but even though she always appreciates the help, she always feels stupid because she is a "special ed" student and likes to imagine what life will be like when she is in college and won't have to be "special" anymore.

Although Emily knows that she has an IEP, she doesn't know much about it. Each year at her IEP meeting, Emily sits at the table with her parents and her case manager and listens to her teachers talk about what a hard worker she is. She likes to hear the teachers say such nice things about her but admits that she stops listening when her case manager starts to read her IEP out loud.

At her last IEP meeting, Emily's case manager encouraged her to get a job, and although Emily has been applying to many local businesses, she has not had any luck. Emily knows that she has a hard time filling out applications. She worries that her prospective employers will see that she is having difficulty, so she makes sure to tell them that she has a learning disability before she even starts filling out the application.

Emily and her family spent the spring of her junior year visiting colleges, and she has already started applying to some of them. She is sure that she will do well in college and is looking forward to saying goodbye to "special education."

Ask the students to answer the following questions:

1. What were some things in the story that you found you could relate to?
2. Are there any problems that you see with anything that Emily and her family are planning?

Allow for a brief discussion.

Procedures (student behavior in bold)

Have each member of the group restate their name, their grade and any career or educational aspirations they may have before starting the session.

Tell the group that today's discussion will focus on self-advocacy.

Tell the students that today we will be discussing self-advocacy in relation to their learning disabilities.

Ask the students to share what they believe the term "self-advocacy" means. Allow for a brief discussion.

Students will discuss what they believe the term "self-advocacy" means.

Explain that self-advocacy is the action of taking control of one's own life by speaking up for oneself and one's own needs.

Provide examples of self-advocacy in the classroom, such as asking for extra time, approaching your child study team to change accommodations or modifications or asking a teacher to give you an unmodified test to explore your abilities.

Ask students to provide examples of their own self advocacy in the classroom.

Students will describe examples of their own self-advocacy in the classroom.

Ask students to share if they have ever wanted to self-advocate but did not.

Students will share if they have ever wanted to self-advocate but did not.

Ask the students why they think self-advocacy might be important now and in college.

Students will discuss why they think self-advocacy might be important now and in college.

Ask students why they think people do not always advocate for themselves.

Students will discuss why they think people do not always advocate for themselves.

Explain that self-advocacy is not easy, and there are many things that can get in the way of self-advocating effectively.

Tape chart paper to wall (or use the board) and create a list from students' responses to the following question:

206 The Comprehensive Program

"What are some things that might get in the way of successful self-advocacy?"

Students will share responses to the question "What are some things that might get in the way of successful self-advocacy?"

List their responses on chart paper or the board, and make sure that the following items are included on the list:

1. Lack of self-awareness
2. Denial of disability
3. Confusion about when to disclose
4. Discomfort with being assertive

Tell students that the group will be addressing some things on the list that may affect the ability to self-advocate effectively.

Tell the group that one thing that might affect our ability to self-advocate is a lack of self-awareness.

Explain that self-awareness is the ability of a person to know themselves and have an honest assessment of their own strengths and challenges.

Ask the students why self-awareness might be an important aspect of self-advocacy.

Students will respond with reasons why self-awareness might be an important aspect of self-advocacy.

Explain (if needed) that the ability to self-advocate involves a knowledge of what a person needs in order to learn effectively.

A lack of self-knowledge or self-awareness could mean that a person might not even be aware of the fact that a need exists.

Explain that there is no way for a person to ask for what they need if they don't even know that they need it.

Ask the members of the group to think back to the theme of last week's group (strengths and challenges).

Ask the students if they remember talking about how to find appropriate assistive technology.

Students will respond with their recollection about what is needed to find appropriate assistive technology.

Ask the students to take out their completed Sheet 2.a. *What Are You Good At?* (from previous week).

If students do not have it, hand out a new copy and review the directions on the sheet.

Give the students a few minutes to write in or review their previous answers.

Students will review or write in their answers to sheet 2.a. *What are you good at?* (from previous week).

The Program **207**

Ask students the following questions to begin a discussion about self-awareness:

1. Why is there room on the answer sheet for input from friends, family, teachers and others as well as from yourself?
2. Will other people always agree with what you think you are good at? Why or why not?
3. Why might other people have a different view of our abilities? How does this affect our self-awareness?
4. What does self-awareness have to do with self-advocacy?

Students will engage in a discussion about self-awareness.

Remind students that self-awareness is the ability to know themselves and be honest about what their strengths or challenges might be, and it is an important skill to have in order to self-advocate effectively.

Ask students to tell you what the next item on the list is (denial of disability).

Students will look at list and respond appropriately.

Remind the students that another reason that self-advocacy might become difficult is that sometimes students are in denial about their disabilities.

Ask the students why being in denial about a learning disability might get in the way of effective self-advocacy.

Students will respond with reasons why being in denial about a learning disability might get in the way of effective self-advocacy.

Explain to students that being in denial about learning disabilities is just another form of lacking self-awareness.

Explain that pretending that learning disabilities do not exist does not make the learning disabilities go away.

Denial only makes it more difficult to access the things that help make the disability more manageable.

Ask the students why a person might want to deny the fact that they have a learning disability.

List the students' responses on chart paper or a board.

Students will list reasons why a person might want to deny the existence of a learning disability.

Explain to students that all of their responses are understandable and that it is not easy to be a person with a learning disability.

Tell the group that in order to be successful, it is important to be able to admit that their learning disability exists.

Tell the students that a good way of doing this is by doing something called "reframing."

Take the glass that is half-filled with water in your hand and ask the class if the glass is empty or full.

Students will state their answers about how much water is in the glass.

208 The Comprehensive Program

Explain that the glass is both empty and full and that both answers are correct.

Explain that one response is positive and one response is negative.

Explain that "reframing" is the skill of being able to take something that seems negative and turn it into something that is positive.

Explain that for students with learning disabilities, reframing can help them see their learning disability a different way.

Explain to students that wanting to deny their disabilities might be understandable, but it is not helpful.

It is natural for people to want to escape from something that might make them uncomfortable, but pretending something is not there does not make it disappear.

Explain that how you view your disability can influence your behaviors and self-worth.

Tell the students that many people with learning disabilities have spent a long time feeling "less than."

Explain that many times, students with learning disabilities may feel like they are not as smart as other students or not as capable as other students.

Ask the group if anyone has ever experienced any of these things.

Students will engage in a discussion about feeling "less than."

Explain that although it is important to accept disabilities for what they are, it is also important to be able to look at the value that certain aspects of the disability actually provide.

Give the following example: "A student with a reading disability could let themselves feel bad about their difficulty with reading, or they could reframe and tell themselves that because of their disability, they have learned to read very carefully."

Tell the students that reframing the negative helps us find the value in ourselves.

Rather than sticking with our negative labels, we can reframe and find what is good about us as opposed to just what is bad.

Draw the following chart on the board or on poster paper.

Table 20.8 Negative/Positive Reframing

NEGATIVE LABELS	POSITIVE REFRAMING

The Program **209**

Ask the students to think of some negative labels that they have heard about themselves or others.

Students will think of negative labels they have heard about themselves or others.

If students have difficulty thinking of labels, give them examples, such as bossy, hyperactive, slow etc.

Write the negative labels in the column "Negative labels."

Ask students to think of ways to reframe these negative labels and turn them into something more positive.

If students have trouble, you can give them examples, such as bossy = leader, hyperactive = high energy, slow = careful.

Students will share responses about reframing the negative.

Write the positive, reframed labels in the column labelled "positive reframing."

Ask students to fill out Sheet 3.a. *Reframing the Label* (in groups or individually). Have students share their responses.

Students will complete the worksheet and share their responses in the group.

Explain to students that reframing allows us to see ourselves in a positive way.

It takes aspects of ourselves that we might have previously interpreted as "bad" or "negative" and shows that they don't necessarily have to be interpreted that way.

Explain that in order to self-advocate effectively, it is important to feel good enough about yourself to believe that you actually deserve to get what you need or are asking for.

Remind students that another thing that might get in the way of being able to self-advocate effectively is being unsure or confused about when to disclose a disability.

Even though the idea of self-advocacy is to be able to speak up for yourself, disclosing inappropriately can actually work against you.

Ask the students to think about how disclosing a disability might work against them.

Students will engage in a discussion about how disclosing a disability might work against them.

Tape a piece of chart paper in each corner of the room.

At the top of the first piece of chart paper, write the following: "Pros to disclosing my disability." On the second piece, write "cons to disclosing my disability."

On the third piece, write "Good idea to disclose my disability when . . ." On the fourth piece, write "Bad idea to disclose my disability when . . ."

Tell the students that they will each take a marker and go around the room to each piece of chart paper and write down their answers.

210 The Comprehensive Program

Students will each take a marker and go around the room to each piece of chart paper and write down their answers.

Have students sit back down and review answers in a discussion format. Use the following questions to guide the discussion:

Can anyone talk about a time that you had to talk about your disability outside of this group?

How did it feel?

Has there ever been a time when no one knew you had a learning disability?

How did that feel?

When is it appropriate to disclose?

When is it not appropriate to disclose?

What happens if you are applying for a job?

(Employers are not allowed to ask if you have a disability but can ask questions about it if you disclose the disability to them.)

What about tests that an employer might give to see if you are right for a job? (You may ask for extra time or a reasonable accommodation, but you may have to provide proof of your disability.)

How does disclosing affect college acceptance? (Colleges cannot discriminate if you decide to disclose before or after acceptance.)

Should you disclose after you get accepted? (If you require accommodations, disclosing is the only way to make sure that you will receive them.)

Students will review their answers in a discussion format.

Explain to students that self-advocacy is only powerful when it is meaningful and is not necessary in every situation.

Explain that having a math disability would probably not require asking for extra time to write an essay.

In that environment, disclosing the math disability would not be necessary.

If, however, you are taking a math test and require a calculator because of your math disability, that would be an appropriate time to disclose.

Ask students if they can think of other times when it may or may not be appropriate to disclose their learning disability.

Students will think of and discuss other times when it may or may not be appropriate to disclose their learning disability.

Remind the students that there is still another reason why people may have difficulty with self-advocacy.

Explain that people might have difficulty with self-advocacy because in order to self-advocate, people have to be able to communicate effectively.

If someone is self-advocating but they are not communicating effectively, they will not get their needs met.

Explain that the most effective way to communicate is to do it in an assertive manner.

The Program   **211**

Explain that self-advocacy is the act of communicating learning needs, and in order for it to be effective, it too has to be done in an assertive manner.

Ask the students what it means to be assertive.

Students will respond with their thoughts about what it means to be assertive.

Hand out Sheet 3.b. *My Assertive Self* and have the students work in groups to answer the questions.

Students will work in small groups to answer the questions.

Have the students return to the large group and ask the following question:

What did the answers to these questions tell you about how assertive (or not assertive) you are?

Students will engage in a teacher-led discussion.

Tell the students that being assertive takes practice and is not easy.

Explain that sometimes people think that they are behaving in an assertive manner, but they are actually behaving in an aggressive or even a passive manner.

Explain that communication can be separated into three distinctive styles.

Explain that assertive communication is honest, direct and respectful.

Explain that aggressive communication is confrontational and intimidating.

Explain that passive communication is avoidant and nonconfrontational to a fault.

Hand out Sheet 3.c. *Aggressive, Assertive or Passive?*

Read each sentence aloud and ask the students to work in small groups to decide which sentences are aggressive, which are assertive and which are passive.

Students will work in small groups to decide which sentences are aggressive, which are assertive and which are passive.

Have the students return to the larger group and review their responses together.

Students will return to the larger group and review their responses together.

Explain that it is important to understand the difference between passive, aggressive and assertive behavior in order to be able to assess your own behavior.

Ask the students which of the three types of communication is most likely to elicit positive responses (assertive).

Students will respond to the question of which of the three types of communication is most likely to elicit positive responses.

Ask the students why assertive behavior is typically the most beneficial (assertive behavior is respectful, honest and unintimidating).

Students will respond to the question of why assertive behavior is typically the most beneficial.

212 The Comprehensive Program

Remind the students that everything we have been talking about refers to self-advocacy, which is an important component in finding success when you have a learning disability.

Remind the students that we have been talking about things that might get in the way of self-advocacy, such as:

- Lack of self-awareness
- Denial of disability
- Confusion about when to disclose
- Discomfort with being assertive

Remind students that in order to be an effective self-advocate, you have to have self-awareness, understand your disability, know when to disclose and be comfortable being assertive.

Remind students that we began this section by listening to a story about Emily.

Hand out copies of Sheet 3.d. *Emily's Story* and read the story aloud.

Ask the students to work in groups and rewrite or discuss) the story in a way that shows Emily using self-advocacy.

Students will reread sheet 3.d. Emily's story and rewrite (or discuss) it as a story in which she uses self-advocacy.

Ask the students how the story has changed and what, if anything, they can relate to in the new version.

Students will discuss the new iteration of the story and relate it to themselves.

Ask the group the following review questions:

1. Why is self-advocacy so important?
2. Why is it important to understand what might get in the way of self-advocacy?
3. What is one thing that you took away from today's group that you think you will remember?

Students will reflect on the lesson by answering the questions.

Sheet 2.a.

What Are You Good At?

Everyone has strengths, and knowing them makes it easier to find your path. Knowing what we are good at gives us the opportunity to pick careers and majors that will fit us. Some strengths are natural and are just a part of who we are, and some are skills that we can learn and can get better over time. Below you will find a list of statements that show examples of strengths. In the chart below, check off what you consider to be true about yourself and then check what you think your friends, family, teachers and others would say about you.

Table 20.9 What Are You Good At? Part 2

	Me	Friends	Family	Teachers	Other
1. I am good at organizing myself.					
2. I am good at organizing events.					
3. I am an enthusiastic person.					
4. I have a good sense of humor.					
5. I am a leader.					
6. I am creative.					
7. I am open minded.					
8. Even when things are difficult, I don't give up.					
9. I am athletic.					
10. I always get my work done.					
11. I am honest.					
12. I am a good listener.					
13. I am kind.					
14. I am a team player.					
15. I value originality.					
16. I love puzzles and problem-solving activities.					
17. I am good at math.					
18. I am good at writing.					
19. I am good at social studies.					
20. I am good at science.					
21. I am good at reading.					

Copyright material from Mati Sicherer (2020), *College for Students with Learning Disabilities*, Routledge

Sheet 3.a.

Reframing the Label

Think about any negative labels you might have about yourself. Labeling our disabilities or our behavior in a negative away affects how we view ourselves and can help to convince us that we are not capable.

Reframing those labels flips them into a new light and can remind us of the special gifts we have to offer.

In the box below, write some of your negative labels and then flip them around to reframe them in a more positive light.

Table 20.10 Reframing the Label

Negative Label	Reframed
Example: Slow	Careful
1.	
2.	
3.	
4.	
5.	

Sheet 3.b.

My Assertive Self

How do you . . .

1. Ask a teacher you don't know well for help?
2. Say "no" to something you don't want to do?
3. Tell someone that you are annoyed at them?
4. React when someone gives you a compliment?
5. React when someone criticizes you?
6. Tell someone that they hurt your feelings?
7. Tell a teacher that they forgot to give you your accommodations?

Read the following statements. Decide if each statement is aggressive, assertive or passive.
   (teacher copy)

1. A friend asks to copy your homework. Your response is, "I'm sick of you and your laziness. Do your own work for a change." **Aggressive**
2. Someone cuts you in line at lunch. You are starving and angry, but you say, "It's okay, go ahead." **Passive**
3. Someone interrupts you while you are talking. You say, "Excuse me, I was talking and I'd like to finish my thought." **Assertive**
4. You are having a really hard time doing your history homework. You say, "I'm stupid. I'll never learn this, and the teacher gives work that is too hard." **Passive**
5. Your friend invited everyone but you to her house to go swimming. You say, "It really hurt my feelings that you didn't invite me to your house to go swimming." **Assertive**
6. You order a blueberry muffin at the diner, but the waitress brings you a corn muffin. You say, "Oh my god. What is your problem, lady?" **Aggressive**
7. Your teacher forgets to give you extra time on your test. You say nothing even though you know you need the extra time. **Passive**
8. Your teacher forgets to give you extra time on your test. You say, "Hey! My extra time!" **Aggressive**
9. Your teacher forgets to give you extra time on your test. You say, "Excuse me, Mrs. Clark. I'm not sure if you know, but my IEP allows me to have extended time on all my tests." **Assertive**
10. You find out that you failed a test you studied hard for. You say to the teacher, "I'm not certain what happened. I studied so hard. Can we review the test so I can see what I did wrong?" **Assertive**

Copyright material from Mati Sicherer (2020), *College for Students with Learning Disabilities,* Routledge

Sheet 3.c.

Aggressive, Assertive or Passive?

Read the following statements. Decide if each statement is aggressive, assertive or passive.
   (student copy)

1. A friend asks to copy your homework. Your response is, "I'm sick of you and your laziness. Do your own work for a change."
2. Someone cuts you in line at lunch. You are starving and angry, but you say, "It's okay, go ahead."
3. Someone interrupts you while you are talking. You say, "Excuse me, I was talking and I'd like to finish my thought."
4. You are having a really hard time doing your history homework. You say, "I'm stupid. I'll never learn this, and the teacher gives work that is too hard."
5. Your friend invited everyone but you to her house to go swimming. You say, "It really hurt my feelings that you didn't invite me to your house to go swimming."
6. You order a blueberry muffin at the diner, but the waitress brings you a corn muffin. You say, "Oh my god. What is your problem, lady?"
7. Your teacher forgets to give you extra time on your test. You say nothing even though you know you need the extra time.
8. Your teacher forgets to give you extra time on your test. You say, "Hey! My extra time!"
9. Your teacher forgets to give you extra time on your test. You say, "Excuse me, Mrs. Clark. I'm not sure if you know, but my IEP allows me to have extended time on all my tests."
10. You find out that you failed a test you studied hard for. You say to the teacher, "I'm not certain what happened. I studied so hard. Can we review the test so I can see what I did wrong?"

Sheet 3.d.

Emily's Story

Emily is at the beginning of her senior year in high school. She has a diagnosed reading disability and has struggled with reading from as far back as she can remember. She was identified as having a learning disability when she was in third grade, and for the rest of her academic career in elementary and middle school, much of her day was spent in a special education class.

When Emily entered high school, her classes continued to be special education classes, or what her school called "out-of-class resource." These classes were taught by special education teachers and always had fewer than 10 students. Emily always listened in class and did all of her homework in a special study hall taught by a special education teacher. By junior year, her parents and case manager decided that it was time to move her out of most of her small classes. The only small class she remained in was her English class. Her mother had advocated to keep her in the smaller English class because she thought that Emily's struggles with reading had never really gone away. In fact, as time went on, Emily's mother thought that writing and spelling were challenges for her as well. Her placement in the small special education English class gave her teachers continued opportunities to help build her skills in all of those areas.

Emily's math, history and science classes have become a little difficult for her since leaving her small classes. There are so many more students than she had been used to and there is a lot of information to learn, but luckily, the school has made sure that all of those classes are taught by two certified teachers. While one of the teachers teaches the class, the other one is always standing by her side and helping her even before she knows she needs the help. Between them, they give Emily class notes so that she never has to worry about taking notes in class for herself. They even read passages out loud to her if it looks like she is having trouble. They make sure that Emily always gets shorter tests than the rest of the class and even allow her to take her tests over again if she does not do well the first time. She sometimes thinks about asking for the same tests as everyone else in her class, but she is not sure which teacher to ask or if she is even allowed to take the other test, so she never says anything. Her grades are good, but even though she always appreciates the help, she always feels stupid because she is a "special ed" student and likes to imagine what life will be like when she is in college and won't have to be "special" anymore.

Although Emily knows that she has an IEP, she doesn't know much about it. Each year at her IEP meeting, Emily sits at the table with her parents and her case manager and listens to her teachers talk about what a hard worker she is. She likes to hear the teachers say such nice things about her but admits that she stops listening when her case manager starts to read her IEP out loud.

At her last IEP meeting, Emily's case manager encouraged her to get a job, and although Emily has been applying to many local businesses, she has not had any luck. Emily knows that she has a hard time filling out applications. She worries that her prospective employers will see that she is having difficulty, so she makes sure to tell them that she has a learning disability before she even starts filling out the application.

Emily and her family spent the spring of her junior year visiting colleges, and she has already started applying to some of them. She is sure that she will do well in college and is looking forward to saying goodbye to "special education."

The Program **219**

Part 4: Study Skills Grade Level: 9–12

Materials (include activity sheets and/or supporting resources)

- Sheet 4.a. *Time Management Assessment*
- Sheet 4.b. *Time Flies, but Where Does It Go?*
- Board or chart paper
- Markers (different color for each student)
- Sheet 4.c. *Tips and Tricks for Studying and Test Taking*

Engagement

Begin the session by welcoming the group back and reminding the students about the confidential nature of special education and IEPs. Remind the group that it is very important that everyone feel safe and able to speak freely, and the only way for this to happen is to make sure that each member of the group maintains and respects each other's privacy. Remind the group that if there is anyone who does not feel safe or comfortable sharing in the group, they are always free to speak with you individually.

Tell the students that this week, we will be working on study skills. Ask the students to raise their hands if they have ever struggled with studying. Tell the students that for students with learning disabilities, different aspects of studying such as memorizing, organization and time management may be more challenging than it might be for students without learning disabilities. Tell them that this week, we will be looking at effective study skills that can help raise their grades and make them feel more confident.

Procedures (Student Behavior in Bold)

Have each member of the group restate their name, their grade and any career or educational aspirations they may have before starting the session.

Tell the group that today's discussion will focus on different aspects of study skills such as time management and study skills.

Ask the students if they know anyone who seems to use time so much more effectively than other people.

Students will discuss if they know anyone who uses time effectively.

Explain to students that there are only 168 hours in everyone's week.

No matter how well or how poorly people use time, we all have the same amount of time in our week.

Explain that some people are able to use time so effectively that they are able to fit many things into their week, but others have more difficulty.

220 The Comprehensive Program

Explain that people who use time more effectively have learned good time management skills, and explain that developing good time management skills is something everyone is capable of doing.

Tell the students that the activities in this section will help us learn to understand and use time management skills.

Hand out Sheet 4.a. *Time Management Assessment.*

Explain to students that time management is important in order to be able to perform well academically.

Explain that this worksheet will help them assess their time management skills.

Give students 2 to 3 minutes to finish the assessment.

Students will complete sheet 4.a. *Time Management Assessment.*

Ask students to share any thoughts about the assessment.

Students will share their thoughts about the assessment.

Explain that the first step in changing our time management habits is being realistic about how we use our time to begin with.

Hand out Sheet 4.b. *Time Flies, but Where Does It Go?*

Explain that the group will work together on this worksheet to help figure out what actually happens to the time we have and how we can manage it better.

Work with the students on Sheet 4.b. *Time Flies, but Where Does It Go?*

Students will complete (with counselor guidance) sheet 4.b. *Time flies, but where does it go?*

Ask students to share any thoughts they might have about this worksheet.

Students will share their thoughts about the worksheet.

Explain to students that studying and schoolwork always come first, so if there is not enough time left for studying and school work after accounting for all other activities, something will have to be cut out.

Ask students if they have any ideas for good time management.

Students will share ideas about time management.

Write their ideas on the board or chart paper.

Discuss pros and cons of each idea.

Group will discuss pros and cons of time management ideas.

Have students make a list of time management ideas that will work for them.

Students will make a list of time management ideas that will work for them.

Explain to students that good study skills are made up of lots of different components and that time management is just the start of it.

Ask students what they think some of the other components of good study and test-taking habits are.

Students will state what they think some of the other components of good study and test-taking habits are.

Explain that for students with learning disabilities, having solid study strategies is especially important.

Explain that students with learning disabilities who know their strengths and challenges can focus their energy more appropriately for studying and can learn how to study smarter.

Explain that although there are many great study skills tips you can give them, they might also get good study skills ideas from their peers.

Explain that learning how other people with similar challenges manage their studying and test-taking skills can be extremely helpful.

Have eight pieces of chart paper prepared by doing the following:

Draw a line down the middle of the first sheet.

Write "Tips for studying for a multiple-choice test" to the left of the line and "Tips for taking a multiple-choice test" to the right of the line.

Draw a line down the middle of the second sheet.

Write "Tips for studying for an essay test" to the left of the line and "Tips for taking an essay test" to the right of the line.

Draw a line down the middle of the third sheet.

Write "Tips for studying for a math test" to the left of the line and "Tips for taking a math test" to the right of the line.

Draw a line down the middle of the fourth sheet. Write "Tips for general test-taking strategies" to the left of the line and "Tips for general study strategies" to the right of the line.

On the fifth sheet, write, "Tips for taking notes."

On the sixth sheet, write "Tips for organization."

On the seventh sheet, write "Tips for dealing with test anxiety."

On the eighth sheet, write "Tips for remembering things."

Tape the eight pieces of chart paper in different areas around the room.

Have each student take a different colored marker and have them stand in front of the sheet of their choice.

Make sure that each sheet has at least one person in front of it.

Each student will take a different colored marker and stand in front of the sheet of their choice.

Tell the students that they will be writing their most effective study or test-taking tip based on the topic on the chart paper in front of them.

Tell students that after 30 seconds, they will take their marker with them and move to the next piece of chart paper to their right and once again write their most effective study or test-taking tip based on the topic on the chart paper in front of them.

Tell the students that they will continue writing their tips and moving to the next paper until they have returned to the paper they started with.

Students will circle the room and write their best study skills tips on each paper.

222 The Comprehensive Program

Tell students that they will be circling the room again, but this time, rather than adding new ideas, they will be placing stars next to any idea that they believe may be helpful to them or that they might want to know more about.

Students will circle the room and place stars next to any idea that they believe may be helpful to them or that they might want to know more about.

When they have finished reading and marking all eight pieces of chart paper, ask them to sit back down.

Students will go back to their seats.

Hand out Sheet 4.c. *Tips and Tricks for Studying and Test Taking* and explain that this handout may contain many of the ideas from the chart paper.

With the students' input, review the chart paper items with the most marks and have students use Sheet 4.c. to highlight or write notes to use for future reference for studying.

Students will review the chart paper items and use sheet 4.c. to highlight or write notes to use for future reference for studying.

Ask each student to share one idea that they expect to remember and use to help them in the future with test taking and studying.

Each student will share one idea that they expect to remember and use to help them in the future with test taking and studying.

Close the session by reminding students that they have been learning study and test-taking skills.

Ask the group the following review questions:

1. Why is it so important to have good study and test-taking skills?
2. What is one thing that you took away from today's group that you think you will remember?

Students will respond to the review questions.

Sheet 4.a.

Time Management Assessment

Answer the following questions.

1. Do you write down your assignments?
2. Do you meet your deadlines for assignments?
3. Do you complete your hardest assignments first?
4. Do you say no to social activities if they interfere with your schoolwork?
5. Do you write or check a daily to-do list?
6. Do you set specific time aside for studying for tests?
7. Do you have a set time for homework?
8. Do you have a plan for long-term assignments?

Give yourself one point for each "yes" answer. A total of 7 to 8 points means that you have excellent time management skills. A score of 6 or lower means that you can use help with your time management skills.

224 The Comprehensive Program

Sheet 4.b.

Time flies, but where does it go?

This activity will help us figure out exactly where our time goes. There are only 168 hours in a week, and there are a lot of things that we have to do in those hours. This activity will help us see exactly what fills up all of those hours.

Answer each question as honestly as you can.

Table 20.11 Time Flies Part 1

1. What time do you normally go to sleep?	a.
2. What time do you normally come home from school?	b.
Count the number of hours from the time you come home from school to the time you go to bed and insert that number here. This is the number of hours you have left to manage your studying time.	c.

Take the number from box "c" and place it here: ___.

Answer the following questions based on the time in between coming home from school and going to bed from Monday to Friday. Use a daily average.

Table 20.12 Time Flies Part 2

1. How much time do you spend on dinner and snacks?	Daily:
2. How much time do you spend on naps?	Daily:
3. How much time do you spend on grooming activities (shower, etc.)?	Daily:
4. If you work, how many hours do you work during the week?	Daily:
5. How much time do you spend in social activities?	Daily:
6. How much time do you spend on your phone or computer that is not school related?	Daily:
7. How much time do you spend on exercise?	Daily:
8. How much time do you spend on errands?	Daily:
9. How much time do you spend on any activity other than studying that was not listed here?	Daily:
Add up all of your responses and place your answer in the box marked "d."	d.

Table 20.13 Time Flies Part 3

Insert answer "c" here	c.
Insert answer "d" here	d.
Subtract ("c" – "d")	e.

Box "e" is the amount of time you have left to study and do homework.

Copyright material from Mati Sicherer (2020), *College for Students with Learning Disabilities,* Routledge

Sheet 4.c.

Tips and Tricks for Studying and Test Taking

Table 20.14 Studying Tips

Tips for studying for a multiple-choice test • Use flashcards	**Tips for taking a multiple-choice test** • Cross out answers you know are wrong • Answer on your own before reading the choices. • Read all of the choices
Tips for studying for an essay test • Make sure to understand the main points	**Tips for taking an essay test** • Brainstorm on scrap paper • Write neatly • Opening paragraph—restate question, state position • Middle paragraphs—use facts, details and examples to support your position • Final paragraph—restate position, give summary • Answer even if you aren't sure
Tips for studying for a math test • Review homework • Do extra problems • Take practice tests	**Tips for taking a math test** • Turn the problem into a diagram • Show all of your work
Tips for general study strategies • Take planned breaks • Study during your most productive time • Study the most difficult subject first. • Create a specific study space • Review notes every day • Read textbook by scanning and creating an outline • Do your homework • Review, review and review in different ways each time • Take practice tests • Study in a quiet, distraction-free place • Speak aloud while studying • Use note cards	**Tips for general test-taking strategies** • Write quick notes on scrap paper of facts you might forget. Refer to them as needed to answer questions on test • Read directions carefully Find hints or key words in questions • Answer everything (partial credit is still credit) • Keep your first answer • Review your answers before handing in test • Mark questions to come back to them later

(Continued)

Copyright material from Mati Sicherer (2020), *College for Students with Learning Disabilities*, Routledge

Table 20.14 (Continued)

Tips for taking notes	Tips for organization
• Create a shorthand for note taking • Take notes in an outline format • Review notes each day • Leave room for questions in the margins • Take notes while listening actively • Keep writing if you miss something but mark the spot and ask someone about it later • Listen for important points, underline while taking notes • Take notes in outline form from textbook readings • Turn chapter headings into questions that get answered as you write the outline	• Planner (how do you use one?) • Colored folders • Clean things out daily (yes, daily) • Pack things up before bed **Tips for dealing with test anxiety** • Breathing • Visualize test day before test day • Positive thinking **Tips for remembering things** Create relevance Study while moving • Create mental images • Change your mindset • Create rhymes • Create acronyms • Create acronym sentences • Create unusual connections • Connect unusual visualized images

The Program **227**

Part 5: Picking the Right School Grade Level: 9–12

Materials (include activity sheets and/or supporting resources)

- Markers
- Chart paper or board
- Sheet 5.a. *Types of Programs for Students with Learning Disabilities*
- Sheet 5.b. *Questions to ask About Support Services in College*

Engagement

Begin the session by welcoming the group back and reminding the students about the confidential nature of special education and IEPs. Remind the group that it is very important that everyone feel safe and able to speak freely, and the only way for this to happen is to make sure that each member of the group maintains and respects each other's privacy. Remind the group that if there is anyone who does not feel safe or comfortable sharing in the group, they are always free to speak with you individually. Have each member of the group restate their name, their grade and any career or educational aspirations they may have before starting the session.

Procedures (Student Behavior in Bold)

Tell the students that this week, we will be working on the idea of picking the right school.

Ask the students to imagine that they have terrible vision and cannot see without eyeglasses. Ask them to imagine that rather than getting a pair of glasses that are fitted to them individually, they are given a basket filled with glasses and are told to close their eyes and take one.

Students will imagine having to choose a pair of glasses for poor vision out of a basket.

Ask the group what information they might need to make their decision.

Ask the group what the negative consequences of making these choices might be.

Ask the group how different the experience would be if they were fitted for glasses appropriately.

Students will discuss what could inform their decision-making process for choosing the glasses.

Explain that picking the right school without taking their learning disabilities into account is much like picking a random pair of glasses from a basket.

Explain that getting fitted for glasses involves getting appropriate information and making decisions based on that information.

228 The Comprehensive Program

Explain that today's group will explore the idea of what to take into consideration when exploring colleges and universities when students have learning disabilities.

Ask the students to take a minute to think about their learning needs.

Students will think about their learning needs.

Explain that examples could be extra time, seating near the front of the class, reviewing notes nightly, text to speech for reading, speech to text for writing, quiet, music etc.

Ask the students to share some of their needs.

Students will share some of their learning needs with the group.

Write their answers on the board or on the chart paper.

Ask the group to look at the list of needs.

Ask the students if they all share all of the same academic needs or if their needs are different from each other's.

Students will share their academic needs.

Explain that all students' learning needs are different and that colleges and universities offer different levels of programs for this reason.

Explain that since the group has already explored how to assess their needs, it is now time to see how to find schools that will best meet those needs.

Hand out Sheet 5.a. *Types of Programs for Students with Learning Disabilities.*

Review the different levels of service with the group and ask them to take note of which kind of program would best suit their needs.

Students will note which kind of program would best suit their needs.

Tell the students that the college search for students with learning disabilities is essentially the same as it is for students without them.

Explain that, just like for students without learning disabilities, it is important to search for schools that match their location requirements, financial needs, potential occupational training needs, GPAs and (unless they are test-optional schools) standardized test scores.

Tell the students that once they have completed that initial search, they need to determine what kind of level of support they might need. Explain that once they determine what kind of level of support they might need, it is important to become aware of exactly what kinds of services will be available for them at the colleges they are considering.

Explain to the students that every college and university has a central office that works with students with disabilities.

Tell them that many times, this office may be called the office of disability services, and it is where students with learning disabilities go to access the services they require for learning. Explain that it is important for students to make contact with the office of disabilities services during the college search process.

The Program **229**

This initial contact will allow students get a sense of what services might be available to them at the college.

Explain that after they have been accepted, they will need to register with the office in order to get services.

Ask the students to think about questions they might want to ask the office of disability services.

Students will think of questions to ask the office of disability services.

List their answers on chart paper or on the board.

Hand out Sheet 5.b. *Questions to Ask About Support Services in College.*

Ask students to look over the sheet, and ask them why these questions may be important.

Students will look at sheet 5.a. and discuss why these questions are important.

Explain to students that these questions are important ones to ask when meeting with staff from the office of disability services.

Explain that although many of the questions will apply to them, not all of them will.

Explain to the students that it is important for them to look through the questions and figure out which questions might apply to them.

Ask the students to highlight or underline any question that might be relevant to them.

Students will highlight or underline any question that might be relevant to them.

Ask the students if anyone wants to share what they have underlined or highlighted.

Students will share what they have underlined or highlighted.

Ask the students if they have any specific needs that they might want to add to question.

Students will ask any specific questions they might have.

Ask the students how they feel about these questions and how comfortable or uncomfortable they may be asking them.

Students will discuss how they feel about the questions and how comfortable or uncomfortable they may be asking them.

Engage the students in a conversation (as needed) about how to approach the appropriate staff member at a college in order to ask the questions on Sheet 5.b.

Students will practice approaching appropriate staff member at a college in order to ask the questions on sheet 5.b.

Ask each student to share one idea that they expect to remember and use to help them in choosing their college or university.

Students will share one idea that they expect to remember and use to help them in choosing their college or university.

230 The Comprehensive Program

Close the session by reminding students that they have been talking about choosing appropriate schools.

Ask the group the following review questions:

1. Why is it important to understand the different levels of support available at colleges and universities?
2. Why is it important to ask questions of the office of disabilities services at each college during the college search?
3. Why is it important to register with the office of disabilities services after you are accepted at your college or university?
4. What is one thing that you took away from today's group that you think you will remember?

Students will engage in a discussion reviewing this section of the curriculum.

Distribute Posttest (if desired).

Sheet 5.a.

Levels of Programs for Students With Learning Disabilities

Table 20.15 Levels of Programs

Basic Services
Basic services are appropriate for students who require the fewest accommodations. This structure of service might be best for students who might have seen some success in high school with few to no modifications and minimal accommodations.
Basic services:
- May have the most basic level of services
- Offer few services outside of "reasonable accommodations"
- Require documentation in order to receive services
- Differ from college to college
- Are based in the federal mandate to provide "reasonable accommodations"
- May be based on different interpretations of the term "reasonable accommodations"

Basic services may be appropriate for students who:
- Do not require extensive accommodations
- Are self-motivated and independent learners
- Can voluntarily request their accommodations as they are needed

Basic services may provide:
- Limited accommodations based on what is considered "reasonable" and what might be available
- Extended time on tests, separate testing room, alternative testing formats, note takers, text to speech for textbooks

Intensive Services
Intensive services may be more appropriate for students who may require more support and accommodations than most basic services provide. These programs may be helpful for students who may have received some modifications in high school in addition to their accommodations.
Intensive services:
- Provide significant levels of services for students with learning disabilities
- May have at least one certified learning disability specialist on staff
- May require documentation in order to receive services
- May require a separate application
- May have additional fees
- May have admissions criteria that are flexible and separate from the general university

Intensive services may be appropriate for students who:
- Can voluntarily request their accommodations as they are needed
- May have received some modified tests and curricula in high school
- Required some assistance in high school
- Were able to request some services as needed in high school

(Continued)

Copyright material from Mati Sicherer (2020), *College for Students with Learning Disabilities*, Routledge

232 The Comprehensive Program

Table 20.15 (Continued)

Intensive services may provide:
- Extended time on tests, separate testing room, alternative testing formats, note takers, text to speech for textbooks, early registration, enlarged print, reduced course load
- Remedial classes (although most do not)
- Tutors and assistive technology
- Access to a staff member trained in helping students with learning disabilities
- Support programs (study, counseling and self-help skills)
- Assistance with advocacy
- Precollege summer program
- Structured advisement
- Weekly meetings with advisor or mentor
- Precollege summer program

Complete Services

Complete services provide the highest level of support services for students with learning disabilities. Students who require this level of service may have required more intensive services while still in high school. At this level, the school itself is designed for educating students with learning disabilities. At this point in time, there are very few schools in the country that provide complete services for students with learning disabilities.

Complete services:
- Have the highest level of services for students with learning disabilities
- Have significant amounts of support for students
- Staff and director and professor who are trained and/or certified in special education
- May require documentation in order to receive services
- Are embedded in the school itself

Complete services may be appropriate for students who:
- May have received extensive resource services in high school
- May have received modified tests and curricula in high school
- May have had close academic monitoring in high school
- May need high levels of support to maintain academic standing

Examples of what complete services may provide:
- Extended time on tests, separate testing room, alternative testing formats, note takers, text to speech for textbooks, early registration, enlarged print, reduced course load
- Tutors
- Assistive technology
- Access to a staff member trained in helping students with learning disabilities
- Support programs (study, counseling and self-help skills)
- Assistance with advocacy
- Precollege summer program

The Program **233**

- Structured advisement
- Regularly scheduled meetings between support staff and student
- Modified courses
- Study skills and academic improvement classes
- Special orientation programs
- Close academic monitoring
- Counseling

Sheet 5.b.

Questions to Ask About Support Services in College

- Are the provided services basic, intensive or complete?
- Is there a specific program for students with learning disabilities?

If there is a specific program:

- Does it have a separate application?
- Does it have different criteria for admission?
- Does it have an extra fee?
- Is there a special or separate orientation for students who are getting support services?
- What kind of documentation do I need to be eligible for support services?
- How recent does the documentation have to be?
- Is tutoring available?

If tutoring is available:

- Is it done by students or trained staff?
- Is it one on one or in a group?
- Is there an extra fee?
- How far in advance do I need to arrange it?
- Will I be assigned a specific advisor through the office of disabilities?

If there is a specific advisor:

- How frequently do I meet with this advisor?
- Are the meetings mandatory?
- What are the most frequent types of accommodations and services that you provide?
- Is there help with time management skills?
- Is there help with study skills?
- Is there help with navigating social situations?
- Is there any assistive technology available through the office of disabilities?
- Is there a specific place that students take tests if they get extra time or distraction-free environments?
- What is the process to make professors aware of my accommodations?
- Is there mental health counseling on campus?
- Is there a health center on campus?
- Is there a writing center on campus?
- I need _____ in order to learn. Do you provide this?

Copyright material from Mati Sicherer (2020), *College for Students with Learning Disabilities*, Routledge

PostTest

Table 20.16 Posttest

	Strongly disagree	Disagree	Neutral	Agree	Strongly agree
1. I know what the academic expectations of college will be.					
2. I am familiar with the differences between high school and college accommodations.					
3. I have read my IEP.					
4. I know what my challenges and strengths are.					
5. I know what kinds of assistive technology might be useful to me.					
6. I know what self-advocacy is.					
7. I know why it is important to be an effective self-advocate.					
8. I am good at time management.					
9. I know how to study effectively.					
10. I know what mnemonic devices are and how to use them.					
11. I know that there are different levels of support available in college for students with disabilities.					
12. This group has helped me.					
13. The most useful part of this group was _____					

Copyright material from Mati Sicherer (2020), *College for Students with Learning Disabilities*, Routledge

INDEX

Note: Page numbers in **bold** indicate tables on the corresponding pages.

504 plans 89–91, 124–125; versus IEPs 102–104

accommodations 96–97, 112, 189–190; differences between high school and college **188**, 190; recognizing best choices for 98–99
acronyms 138–139
aggressive communication style 127–129, 216
American School Counselor Association (ASCA) 7, 79, 80
Americans with Disabilities Act of 1990 (ADA) 124–125
assertive communication style 127–129, 215–216
assistive technology (AT) 122–123, **123–124**, 201–202, **201–202**
attention deficit/hyperactivity disorder (ADHD) 18, 34, 39, 49–55; definition of 49–50; executive function disorder with 62; interventions for 55; subtypes of 50; symptoms of 54–55; what it's like to have 50–54
auditory processing disorders 33–37

buy-in for program for students with learning disabilities 175–176

child study team 82; documentation by 87–91; IEP meetings and 83–85; understanding different goals for child 85–86; working with counselors 86–87
cognitive skills 148–149; metacognition and 150–152, **153**
college and university selection 156–157; disclosing and accessing services in 167–171; levels of support for 159–162, **160–161**, **231–233**; as part 5 in program for students with learning disabilities 227–234; role of the Office of Disability Services and 162–167, **163–166**; schools with programs for students with learning disabilities and 162; searching for appropriate schools and 157–159
college readiness: being able to self-advocate for 101–102; being organized and self-motivated for 100–101; case study on 104–106; executive functioning skill self-assessment and 187; knowing how to study and 99–100; knowing which accommodations work best and 98–99; program for 180–191; skills for 93–95, 186; student asking for academic help

Index **237**

and 95; understanding learning needs and study styles and 95–96; understanding the difference between accommodations and modifications and 96–97; understanding the difference between IEP and 504 and 102–104; understanding the disability and 97–98

communication: passive/aggressive/ assertive 127–129, 215–216; skills in 126–127; and when to disclose and why 129–130

connecting to time 143–144

counselors: American School Counselor Association (ASCA) and 7, 79, 80; assisting with choosing colleges and universities 156–171; assisting with college readiness 93–106; assisting with self-advocacy by students 101–102, 116–134; attending IEP meetings 83–85; role of 79–81; understanding different goals for children 85–86; understanding IEPs 108–115; understanding study skills 137–155; working with the child study team 82–91

developmental coordination disorder (DCD) 57

Disability Services, Offices of 125–126, 162; disclosure and accessing 167–171; levels of support in college and university selection 159–162, **160–161, 231–233**; role in college and university selection 162–167, **163–166**

disclosure of learning disabilities 167–171

documentation, child study team 87–91

dyscalculia 18, 22–26; definition of 22; interventions for 26; symptoms of 25; what it's like to have 22–25

dysgraphia 18, 27–32; definition of 27–28; interventions for 31–32; symptoms of 31; what it's like to have 28–31

dyslexia 17–21; definition of 17–18; interventions for 20–21; symptoms of 19–20; what it's like to have 18–19

dyspraxia 57–61; definition of 57–58; interventions for 61; symptoms of 60–61; what it's like to have 58–60

Education for All Handicapped Children Act 124

executive function disorder 62–66; definition of 62–63; interventions for 66; symptoms of 65–66; what it's like to have 63–65

goals: planning for 146; understanding different 85–86

imagery 140–142

individual education plans (IEPs) 82, 95, 108–109; versus 504 plans 102–104; accommodations and 98–99; background on 109–110; different goals and 85–86; documentation on 87–91; interpreting test scores and 112–113; meetings on 83–85; models of identification and 110–111; reading 111–112; reading and interpreting the WISC-V and 113, **113, 114**; reading and interpreting the Woodcock-Johnson Test of Achievement and 114–115; understanding strengths and challenges and 192–202; working together on 86–87

Individuals with Disabilities Education Act (IDEA) 109, 111, 124–125

interventions: attention deficit/ hyperactivity disorder (ADHD) 55; dyscalculia 26; dysgraphia 31–32; dyslexia 20–21; dyspraxia 61; executive function disorder 66; nonverbal learning disorder 45–46; processing disorders (visual and auditory) 37; short-term memory issues 74

IQ testing 110, 115; Wechsler Adult Intelligence Scale (WAIS) 88, 113, **113, 114**

learning disabilities: assistive technology for 122–123, **123–124**, 201–202, **201–202**; author's view on, as parent and educator 3–10;

238 Index

building programs for students with (*see* program for students with learning disabilities); case example in recognizing and defining 11–13; disclosing and accessing services for 167–171; dyscalculia 18, 22–26; dysgraphia 18, 27–32; dyslexia 17–21; nonverbal learning disorder 39–46; processing disorders (visual and auditory) 33–37

learning needs and study styles 95–96

least restrictive environment (LRE) 124

material organization 147–148

memory issues 67–74; short-term 73–74; working 67–73

metacognitive skills 150–152, **153**

method of the loci 139–140

mnemonic devices 138–142; acronyms 138–139; imagery 140–142; method of the loci 139–140; rhymes 142

modifications 96–97, 112, 191

nonverbal learning disorder 39–46; definition of 39; interventions for 45–46; symptoms of 45; what it's like to have 40–45

Offices of Disability Services (ODS) *see* Disability Services, Offices of

organizational skills 142–143; connecting to time 143–144; making a schedule 144–145; material organization 147–148; planning for goals 85–86; time management 143; using timers 145–146

organization and self-motivation 100–101

Other Health Impaired (OHI) students 110

passive communication style 127–129, 216

planning for goals 146

processing disorders (visual and auditory) 33–37; definition of 33–34; interventions for 37; symptoms of 36–37; what it's like to have 34–36

program for students with learning disabilities: creating buy-in for 175–176; finding group members for 177; general instructions for group working on 177–178; part 1: college readiness 180–191; part 2: understanding strengths and challenges 192–202; part 3: self-advocacy 203–218; part 4: study skills 219–226; part 5: picking the right school 227–234; posttest in **235**; pretest in **179**

reframing 122, **208**, 208–209, 214, **214**

Rehabilitation Act of 1973 125

rhymes 142

RISE act 91

routine, study 149–150

RTI model 111

schedules, making of 144–145

self-advocacy by students 101–102, 116–117; assistive technology and 122–123, **123**–**124**; case study on 130–134; college and disability services and 125–126; effective communication skills and 126–127; as part 3 in program for students with learning disabilities 203–218; passive/aggressive/assertive communication and 127–129; self-esteem and 120, 121–122; student understanding of disability and learning needs and 117–118; understanding of rights and 124–125; and when to disclose and why 129–130; why students may not understand their disabilities and learning needs and 118–121

self-esteem, student 120, 121–122

self-motivation and organization 100–101

short-term memory issues: definition of 73; interventions for 74; symptoms of 74; what it's like to have 73–74

specific learning disability (SLD) 18, 109–110; identification of 110–111

strengths and challenges, understanding 192–202

Index **239**

study routine 149–150; metacognitive skills 150–152, **153**

study skills 99–100, 137–138; acronyms 138–139; case study 154–155; cognitive skills 148–149; connecting to time 143–144; imagery 140–142; making a schedule 144–145; material organization 147–148; method of the loci 139–140; mnemonic devices 138–142; organizational skills and 142–148; as part 4 in program for students with learning disabilities 219–226; planning for goals 85–86; rhymes 142; study routine 149–150; time management 143, 223–224, **225**; tips and tricks for studying and test taking 225, **225–226**; using timers 145–146

study tips 225, **225–226**

symptoms: attention deficit/hyperactivity disorder (ADHD) 54–55; dyscalculia 25; dysgraphia 31; dyslexia 19–20; dyspraxia 60–61; executive function disorder 65–66; nonverbal learning disorder 45; processing disorders (visual and auditory) 36–37; short-term memory issues 74

test scores, interpretation of 112–113

test taking tips 225, **225–226**

time management 143, 223–224, **225**

timers 145–146

visual processing disorders 33–37

Wechsler Adult Intelligence Scale (WAIS) 88; reading and interpreting 113, **113**, **114**

Wechsler Individual Achievement Test (WIAT) 88

Woodcock–Johnson—Tests of Achievement 88, 110; reading and interpreting 114–115

Woodcock–Johnson—Tests of Cognitive Ability 88

working memory issues: definition of 67–68; interventions for 72–73; symptoms of 72; what it's like to have 68–72

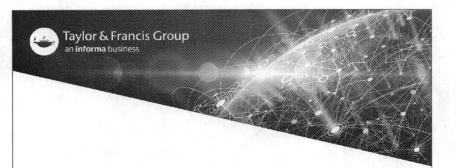

Printed in the United States
by Baker & Taylor Publisher Services